'Gerri Chanel's account of how Fran... ...art from both
the destruction of war and the pillaging of the German occupiers
reads like a thriller'  Caroline Moorehead, *TLS*

'Fantastic ... At its best this is a story of the inhabitants of a humiliated country doing all in their power to preserve their nation's
cultural heritage ... The black-and-white photographs in this book
are worthy of an art exhibition in themselves.'  *Daily Mail*

'Chanel's history is a work of substance and scholarship that should
be part of every art history collection and required reading for anyone who cares about Western civilization.'  *Booklist* (starred review)

'A brilliant piece of storytelling explaining how the masterpieces of
the Louvre escaped Göring's mantelpiece and Himmler's walls ...
This is a grippingly written and meticulously researched contribu-
tion to the history of the Second World War.'  *The Tablet*

'A compelling true account of the men and women who fought to
save France's heritage and a fascinating story of art and intrigue.'
*France Magazine*

'This book tells a fascinating story.'  *Choice*

'*Saving Mona Lisa* is a detailed, inspiring account of the wartime courage, daring and ingenuity shown by the men and women of the
Louvre who risked their lives to save France's art treasures from
the voracious Nazi plunderers. Gerri Chanel's comprehensive, careful survey fills an important gap in the literature dealing with this
chapter of history and gives long overdue recognition to the bravery
of those who were prepared to fight to the death for beauty, art and
the achievements of civilization.'  Catherine Hickley, author of
*The Munich Art Hoard*

# SAVING
# MONA LISA

THE BATTLE TO PROTECT THE LOUVRE
AND ITS TREASURES FROM THE NAZIS

GERRI CHANEL

ICON

Previously published in the USA in 2014 by Heliopa Press, LLC,
P.O. Box 8, FDR Station, New York, NY 10150
and in the UK and USA in 2018 by Icon Books Ltd,
Omnibus Business Centre,
39–41 North Road, London N7 9DP
email: info@iconbooks.com
www.iconbooks.com

This edition first published in 2019 by Icon Books Ltd

Sold in the UK, Europe and Asia
by Faber & Faber Ltd, Bloomsbury House,
74–77 Great Russell Street,
London WC1B 3DA or their agents

Distributed in the UK, Europe and Asia
by Grantham Book Services,
Trent Road, Grantham NG31 7XQ

Distributed in the USA
by Publishers Group West,
1700 Fourth Street, Berkeley, CA 94710

Distributed in Australia and New Zealand
by Allen & Unwin Pty Ltd,
PO Box 8500, 83 Alexander Street,
Crows Nest, NSW 2065

Distributed in South Africa
by Jonathan Ball, Office B4, The District,
41 Sir Lowry Road, Woodstock 7925

Distributed in India by Penguin Books India,
7th Floor, Infinity Tower – C, DLF Cyber City,
Gurgaon 122002, Haryana

Distributed in Canada by Publishers Group Canada,
76 Stafford Street, Unit 300
Toronto, Ontario M6J 2S1

ISBN: 978-178578-549-8

Book design by Jordan Wannemacher

Printed and bound in Great Britain
by Clays Ltd, Elcograf S.p.A.

Above all, France was obliged to save the spiritual values it held as an integral part of its soul and its culture. To put its artworks, its archives and its libraries out of harm's way was indeed one of our country's first reflexes of defense.

— ROSE VALLAND, *Le Front de l'Art*

There are fights that you may lose without losing your honor; what makes you lose your honor is not to fight.

— JACQUES JAUJARD, *Feuilles*

# CONTENTS

# MUSÉE DU LOUVRE

COLONNADE COUR          GRANDE     TUILERIES
WING        CARRÉE         GALERIE     GARDENS

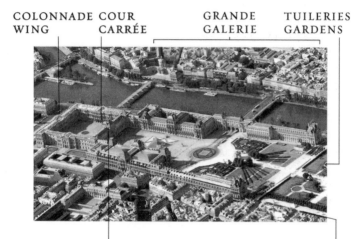

PAVILLON DE              RUE DE
L'HORLOGE             RIVOLI

# PRIMARY LOUVRE STORAGE DEPOTS
## DURING WORLD WAR II

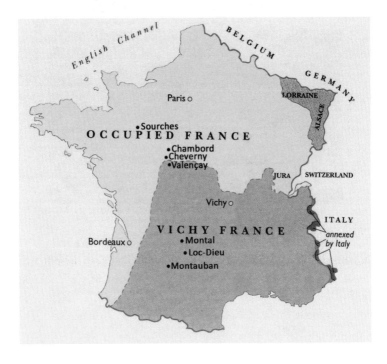

PRINCIPAL LOUVRE STORAGE SITES DURING WORLD WAR II,
AND THE PARTITION OF FRANCE JUNE 1940 TO NOVEMBER 1942

# ITINERARY OF
# THE *MONA LISA*

*September 1938* Paris to Chambord

*September 1938* Chambord to Paris

*August 1939* Paris to Chambord

*November 1939* Chambord to Louvigny

*June 1940* Louvigny to Loc-Dieu Abbey (Martiel)

*October 1940* Loc-Dieu to Montauban

*March 1943* Montauban to Château de Montal (Saint-Jean-Lespinasse)

*June 1945* Montal to Paris

# SELECTED
# INDIVIDUALS *&*
# ORGANIZATIONS

## INDIVIDUALS –
## EARLY ROLES DURING WORLD WAR II

### *FRENCH*

*Marcel Aubert*  Curator of the Louvre's Department of Sculptures.

*Germain Bazin*  Assistant curator of the Louvre's Department of Paintings, reporting to René Huyghe; head of art depot at the château de Sourches.

*Joseph Billiet*  Assistant director of the Musées Nationaux (French National Museums), reporting to Jacques Jaujard, director.

*Jacqueline Bouchot-Saupique*  Art historian and professor at the École du Louvre; also served as Jacques Jaujard's assistant during the war.

*Abel Bonnard*  Appointed Minister of National Education in April 1942, replacing Jérôme Carcopino. The French Fine Arts Administration fell under his purview.

*Jérôme Carcopino*  Minister of National Education 1941 to 1942, replaced by Abel Bonnard.

*André Chamson*  Until the war, assistant curator at Versailles; also a writer. Resided at the Louvre evacuation depots with his wife, Louvre archivist Lucie Mazauric.

*Christiane Desroches Noblecourt*  Louvre staff member specializing in Egyptology.

*Carle Dreyfus* Curator of the Louvre's Département des Objets d'art and first depot director at Valençay.

*Hans Haug* Depot director at Cheverny as of 1940.

*Louis Hautecœur* Secretary General of Fine Arts from summer 1940. The French national museum system—including the Louvre—was under his control. He reported to the Minister of National Education. Replaced spring 1944 by Georges Hilaire.

*Magdeleine Hours* Louvre staff member specializing in painting restoration.

*René Huyghe* Head curator of the Louvre's Department of Paintings, reporting to Jacques Jaujard. Head of various Louvre evacuation depots.

*Jacques Jaujard* Appointed acting director of the Musées Nationaux in December 1939 and director in September 1940. Responsible for the Louvre. Reported to the Secretary General of Fine Arts, Louis Hautecœur.

*Suzanne Kahn* Jaujard's assistant when the war began.

*Lucie Mazauric* In charge of the Louvre archives. Resided at the Louvre evacuation depots during the war; married to André Chamson.

*Pierre Laval* Vichy Prime Minister June to December 1940 and April 1942 to August 1944, reporting to Head of State Philippe Pétain.

*Philippe Pétain* Head of Vichy government.

*Pierre Schommer* One of the senior administrators of the French national museum system; head of the Chambord evacuation depot.

*Charles Sterling* A curator in the Louvre's Department of Paintings; assigned to the evacuation depots.

*Rose Valland* Volunteer staff member at the Jeu de Paume Museum.

*Gérald Van der Kemp* Louvre staff member; appointed head of the Valençay evacuation depot in autumn 1940.

*Henri Verne* Director of the Musées Nationaux from 1926 to 1939; succeeded by Jacques Jaujard in 1940.

## GERMAN

*Otto Abetz* Appointed German ambassador to France in 1940. Ally of Joachim von Ribbentrop.

*Hermann Bunjes*  Art historian assigned in 1940 to Kunstschutz art protection agency, reporting to Franz von Wolff Metternich. Ally of Hermann Göring.

*Karl Epting*  Worked for Otto Abetz as a cultural advisor.

*Joseph Goebbels*  Hitler's Reich Minister of Propaganda.

*Hermann Göring*  Hitler's second-in-command and head of the Luftwaffe, the German Air Force.

*Heinrich Himmler*  Overseer of the Gestapo, the SS and the Ahnenerbe cultural research group

*Felix Kuetgens*  A senior member of the Kunstschutz.

*Otto Kümmel*  Director of the Berlin State Museums and head of the project to identify certain art of German "origin" located in other countries.

*Joachim von Ribbentrop*  Hitler's Minister of Foreign Affairs.

*Alfred Rosenberg*  Official philosopher and racial theorist of the Nazi party; in summer 1940, also appointed head of the Einsatzstab Reichsleiter Rosenberg (ERR).

*Bernhard von Tieschowitz*  Second-in-command at the Kunstschutz.

*Count Franz von Wolff Metternich*  Head of the Kunstschutz, effective spring 1940.

# ORGANIZATIONS

## FRENCH

*Forces Françaises Libres (FFL—Free French Forces)*.  Resistance group led by Charles de Gaulle from his base in London.

*Forces Françaises de l'Intérieur (FFI—French Forces of the Interior)*.  Formed upon the unification of a number of Resistance groups in February 1944.

*Milice*  Vichy-sponsored secret paramilitary force.

*Musées Nationaux (French National Museums system)*.  Umbrella organization for all French state-owned museums, including the Louvre and other museums such as Cluny, Jeu de Paume, Guimet, Musée d'Art Moderne and Versailles. Later in the war, provincial museums also came within its purview. Jacques Jaujard was director of the system during the war. The Musées Nationaux was under the auspices of the Fine Arts Administration, which, in turn, was under the control of the Ministry of National Education.

*Vichy regíme*   The pro-Nazi French government created in the summer of 1940 under the leadership of Philippe Pétain. Named for the central France town in which the regime had its headquarters.

## GERMAN

*Ahnenerbe*   Research group dedicated to substantiating Hitler's belief in the existence of a lost Aryan master race from which, according to Hitler, modern Germans were descended. Headed by Heinrich Himmler.

*Einsatzstab Reichsleiter Rosenberg (ERR—Reich Leader Rosenberg Taskforce)*.   Nazi Party organization dedicated to appropriating cultural property; led by Alfred Rosenberg.

*Kunstschutz*   Unit of the German armed forces (Wehrmacht) responsible for the protection of monuments, works of art and other items in occupied territories.

# PROLOGUE

THE LOUVRE IS the most visited museum in the world. When the vast majority of its almost 10 million annual visitors come to pay homage to the *Mona Lisa*, Venus de Milo, the Winged Victory of Samothrace and the breathtaking array of other masterpieces, they take for granted that the collections have always been calmly and majestically on view, but nothing could be further from the truth, for the Louvre lies in a city that has known much war.

At 5 p.m. on August 25, 1939, nine days before France declared war against Germany, the Louvre closed its doors to visitors. Moments later, a small army of museum staff and volunteers began toiling around the clock to unmount, wrap and crate some of the world's most precious art and antiquities as they launched the largest museum evacuation in history. At 6 a.m. three days later, convoys of trucks began spiriting away the Louvre's treasures to châteaux in the Loire Valley. Items were marked with a system of dots: two red dots for those with the highest evacuation priority, green for the most significant among the rest and yellow for lower priority works. Of the many thousands of treasures, only a single one had three red dots, the painting about which a biographer of Leonardo da Vinci once said, "If it were decreed that all the paintings in Europe save one must be destroyed, we know which one would have to be saved."

The *Mona Lisa* left in the first convoy, set first into a custom-made poplar case cushioned inside with red velvet, then packed carefully into her crate. During the six years of her exile, she would be moved six times, each time with baited breath. At the countryside depots, she would often sleep at the bedside of curators who were painfully aware of the heavy responsibility they held for one of the world's most famous and valuable pieces of art.

Over 3,600 paintings would be evacuated from the Louvre, along with many thousands of drawings, engravings, sculptures, antiquities and objets d'art, plus the museum's archives and much of its library. The initial steps of the operation would unfold in large part like a well-rehearsed ballet due to almost a decade of intensive planning.

But an evacuation can be planned, a war far less so. The administrators of the Louvre could not know what plans the Germans would have for France's art during the Second World War or that they would also have to battle the leaders of France's Vichy government. For six years, the Louvre's directors and its staff would risk their jobs and, in many cases, their lives, to protect the artworks and the Louvre palace not only from the personal appetites of the German leaders but also from bombing, fire, flood, theft and the viciousness of German military reprisals. This is their story.

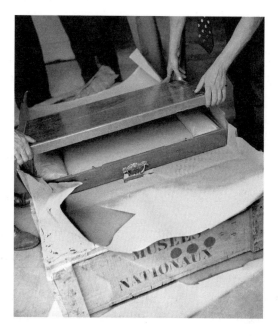

THE *MONA LISA* IN HER CASE

# PART
# I

# FROM WAR
# TO WAR

*Fall 1187 to Summer 1938*

# ONE

# PROTECTING PARIS, PROTECTING ART

THE LOUVRE OWES its existence to the military prowess of a twelfth-century Egyptian sultan who never set foot in France: Salah ad-Din Yusuf ibn Ayyub, also known as Saladin. In October 1187 he captured Jerusalem; within weeks, the Pope called the kings of Europe and lesser nobles to embark on the Third Crusade to reconquer Jerusalem from Saladin. Both monarchs knew the fight could mean an absence of years from their territories, a particularly sensitive point for King Philippe Auguste of France, who had long been fighting with England over territory not far from Paris. During the long preparations for the Crusade, Philippe considered how he might gain an advantage over the English when the Crusade was over and they would inevitably begin battle again.

A week before he departed for war in June 1190, Philippe commanded the bourgeois of Paris to build, in his absence, a strong, high wall to encircle the city's developed area north of the river Seine. Philippe realized, however, that there would be a weak point in the

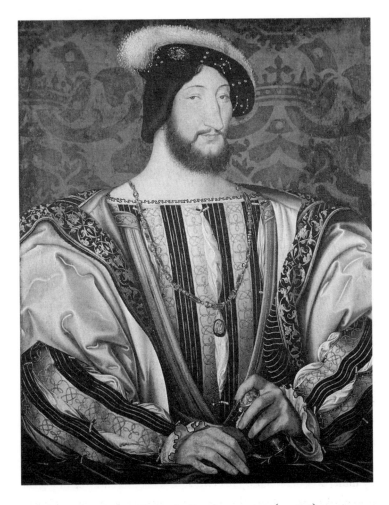

PORTRAIT OF *FRANÇOIS I*, JEAN CLOUET (C. 1513)

LOUVRE, RICHELIEU WING, SECOND FLOOR

defense where the western edge of the wall met the river, which runs through the city horizontally and then on towards Normandy, the direction from which the English were likely to attack. His solution? Build a fortress where the wall met the river and surround it with a moat. He named his fortress the Louvre.

By the late 1300s, the Louvre's defensive function was made obsolete by Charles V's new wall around a growing Paris. The king transformed the dark fortress into a larger, brighter royal residence with elaborately carved windows and ornately decorated rooftops. After Charles, the castle fell into a long period of neglect that made an abrupt about-face during the reign of François I, who took the throne in 1515. François set plans in motion for a sumptuous Renaissance palace. He began by demolishing Philippe Auguste's massive keep to make way for a central courtyard to host Renaissance feasts. The courtyard and the buildings around it would later be enlarged and renamed the Cour Carrée; they would later bear witness to some of the most dramatic events at the museum during World War II.

François was also an art patron who sponsored an Italian named Leonardo da Vinci. When da Vinci's previous patron died in March 1516, François invited the artist to France, offering him the title of First Painter and Engineer and Architect of the King. The 64-year-old da Vinci made the three-month journey from Italy by mule, accompanied by his two assistants and carrying along his notebooks and at least three of his paintings: *Virgin and Child with Saint Anne*, *Saint John the Baptist* and *Mona Lisa*. All three works legally came into François' hands shortly after da Vinci's death three years later. The king's collection of paintings was small—perhaps less than 100 paintings—but it had a large stature. The château of Fontainebleau, which then housed most of the works, became a noted cultural center to which distinguished visitors streamed from

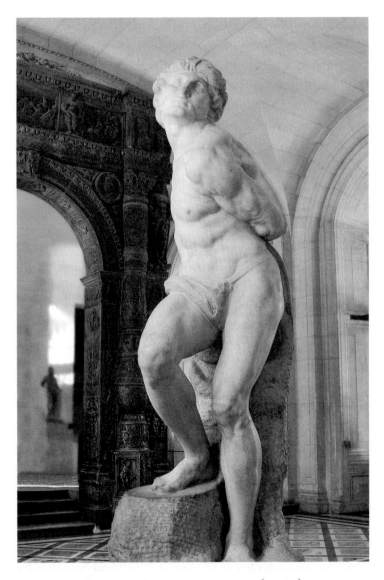

*REBELLIOUS SLAVE*, MICHELANGELO (C. 1513)

LOUVRE, DENON WING, GROUND FLOOR

across Europe. This small but prestigious collection formed the seed that would grow into the Louvre Museum.

I n the 250 years after François's reign, the Louvre palace grew exponentially. In the early 1600s its footprint stretched west when Henri IV built a one-third-mile-long gallery along the Seine—eventually called the Grande Galerie—to connect the Louvre with the nearby Palais des Tuileries (Tuileries Palace). At a cost of half the annual budget of the kingdom, the gallery had been conceived by the former queen, Catherine de Medici—who died long before it was finished—simply so that she could move between the two palaces without enduring bad weather or curious eyes. Henri's successor Louis XIII built, among other construction, the Pavillon de l'Horloge (Clock Pavilion), which extended the Cour Carrée. In late August 1944, the French museum administration would gather in the Cour Carrée in front of the Pavillon de l'Horloge to raise the French flag atop its roof when they believed—erroneously—that danger to the museum and its staff was over.

Under Louis XIV, the palace spread east; Louis was also responsible for an exponential growth in the royal art collections. However, many pieces, like the *Mona Lisa*, were stored or displayed at Versailles, having been moved from Fontainebleau by Louis long before. It would take a revolution to create the Musée du Louvre and to bring the *Mona Lisa* to Paris.

The museum, which opened to the public in November 1793, displayed only a fraction of the items from the former royal collections; *Mona Lisa* remained at Versailles. A few of the items on display at the new museum came from François I's original collection, but most items on view and many of the additional items that would soon join them came from later royal acquisitions and from items seized during the Revolution from aristocratic families who had fled France.

Two such pieces were Michelangelo's 7-foot-high *Slave* sculptures. In 1794, additional art and antiquities began to arrive, looted from Belgium by France's Revolutionary troops.

But the plunder of the former French aristocracy and Belgium would pale in comparison to the pillaging across Europe by Napoleon Bonaparte beginning in 1796, much of which was hauled to the Louvre. A great deal of the loot came from Germany and Austria. Although later treaties legally allowed France to retain some of these items, Adolf Hitler and his art experts would begin plotting in the 1930s to get them back.

Napoleon's river of plunder flowed to Paris for more than a decade. One of his greatest acquisitions arrived at the Louvre in 1797: Veronese's *Wedding Feast at Cana*, a sixteenth-century portrayal of the New Testament story of the wedding feast in Galilee at which Jesus turned water into wine. The massive 32-foot-long by 22-foot-high work, which had been displayed in the rectory of Venice's San Giorgio Maggiore monastery for 235 years, was sliced in half by Napoleon's troops to make it easier to haul back to France.

Later the same year, the *Mona Lisa* finally left Versailles for the Louvre. Several years later, the painting was moved to the apartments of Empress Josephine in the Palais des Tuileries, then returned once again to the Louvre when Napoleon had himself crowned emperor of France in 1804. Napoleon also installed a new museum of antiquities in the palace, furnished in part with additional items from Versailles, such as the 2,000-year-old marble sculpture of the goddess of hunting, Artemis with a Doe (also known as the Diana of Versailles), which had been a gift from Pope Paul IV to Henri II.

During his glory years, Napoleon undertook major renovations both inside and outside the palace. He also had a grand vision for

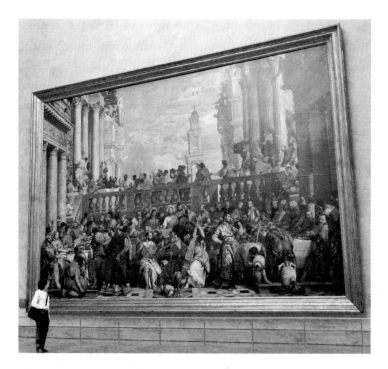

*WEDDING FEAST AT CANA*, PAOLO CALIARI,
KNOWN AS VERONESE (1562–1563)

LOUVRE, DENON WING, FIRST FLOOR

its development that included, among other features, long new
wings running along the new rue de Rivoli to finally connect the
Palais des Tuileries to the Louvre. But the plan remained dormant
because by 1815, defeated at Waterloo, Napoleon's glory days were
over. When Napoleon fell from power, more than four thousand pillaged paintings, sculptures, objets d'art and antiquities in the Louvre
went back to their rightful owners. The works that remained did so
legally under the terms of treaties negotiated at the end of hostilities. Of all the paintings Napoleon had taken, only one hundred or

so would remain in France, among them Veronese's *Wedding Feast at Cana*, which ultimately was considered too fragile to travel. Instead, the monastery from which it had come accepted a large painting by Le Brun in exchange. In 1939, Veronese's masterpiece would be spirited away from the Louvre with more care than Napoleon's troops had taken; curators would roll it carefully—and intact—onto a giant oak column.

When Napoleon fell, so did the Louvre's first museum director, Vivant Denon. Denon's successor set out to replenish the museum. One of the major acquisitions of the 1820s was an ancient Greek statue of Aphrodite, the Greek goddess of love and beauty, called Venus by the Romans. The almost 7-foot-high Venus de Milo was discovered in 1820, buried in a field among other ancient ruins on the Greek island of Melos. Other works acquired in the same era included the 3,100-year-old pink granite sarcophagus of Ramses III and Géricault's giant *Raft of the Medusa*, depicting the wreck of a French frigate off the coast of Senegal in 1816 with over 150 men on board. During the great evacuation of 1939, the painting itself would almost be destroyed.

In July 1830, the Louvre was stormed during a revolution in which King Charles X was overthrown and replaced by Louis Philippe, Duke of Orleans. As agitation stirred, insurgents headed towards the symbols of power: City Hall, the Palais des Tuileries— the king's residence—and the Louvre. By evening, angry crowds lined the long stretch of the Grande Galerie and the eastern, Colonnade end of the Cour Carrée. It was the first time the Louvre's artwork was at significant risk, and, astoundingly, nobody had ever considered how to protect it.

After assessing the volatile scene along the quai from a window of the Grande Galerie, the museum's secretary general, 93-year-old

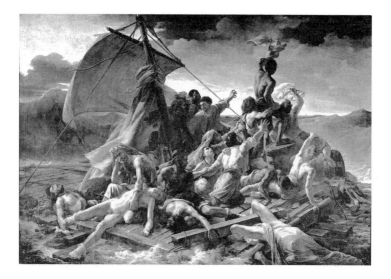

*RAFT OF THE MEDUSA*, THÉODORE GÉRICAULT (SALON OF 1819)

LOUVRE, DENON WING, FIRST FLOOR

Vicomte de Cailleux, instructed the museum guards to start taking down the paintings immediately. Museum practice at that time favored paintings hung from floor to ceiling, requiring the guards to work through the night and into the morning, climbing up and down ladders to empty the packed walls. Shortly thereafter, crowds forced their way into the palace in search of royal troops. Once inside, they surged through the museum, shooting out door locks to get into closed rooms. In the midst of the agitation, the Vicomte de Cailleux placed some small signs at the entrance to the Louvre with a short, simple request for the insurgents: "Respect the national property."

And with minor exceptions, they did. Only several items were mutilated, simply because they represented the monarchy. Likewise, there was minimal looting, given the size of the crowd, the magnitude of the treasures and fact that most of them had been left virtually unguarded after Swiss Guards assigned to the palace left to protect other Parisian buildings.

July 1830 had been a violent month for the Louvre; the year finished violently as well. On the night of December 21, thousands of insurgents again pressed towards the doors of the palace after learning that Charles X's ministers, after being put on trial, had avoided a death sentence. A large number of guards had been readied in the Cour Carrée. When angry crowds arrived, this time the doors remained shut tight.

In February 1848, the Duke of Orléans was ousted in yet another revolution. Around the Louvre, the scene was eerily reminiscent of July 1830 as crowds surged through the Tuileries.Some of the insurgents again made their way into the adjacent Louvre, where artworks had been stacked along the walls of the Grande Galerie in preparation for an upcoming exhibition. Along the parquet floor in front of the piles of paintings, the curators had quickly written a message in chalk: "*Respect à la propriété nationale et au bien des Artistes*" (Respect the national property and the interests of artists). Of all the unguarded works of art, some of them great masterpieces, amazingly not a single one was touched or damaged except for one small German work.

Late that year, Napoleon Bonaparte's nephew, Louis-Napoleon Bonaparte, became France's first elected leader. By 1852, after a coup d'état, he was Emperor Napoleon III. Under his rule, the Louvre again exploded in size, including new long wings finally linking the Louvre and Tuileries as Napoleon Bonaparte had envisioned. A number of galleries received elaborate décor, including a massive painting, *Apollo Slays Python*, designed and executed by Delacroix for the central ceiling area of the luxurious Apollo Gallery.

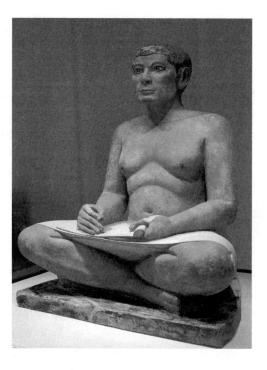

THE SEATED SCRIBE (C. 2620–2500 BC)

LOUVRE, SULLY WING, FIRST FLOOR

The Louvre also made some spectacular acquisitions during that era, including, in 1852, Boucher's *Diana Leaving her Bath*, a painting of the Roman goddess of the hunt and one which Joachim von Ribbentrop, Hitler's minister of foreign affairs, would later covet. Two years later came the almost 2-foot-high, ancient painted limestone sculpture, the Seated Scribe, a gift from the Egyptian government.

In 1863, the museum acquired the 9-foot-high marble Winged Victory of Samothrace, portraying Nike, the Greek goddess of victory at the prow of a 9-foot-high ship. The work had been named

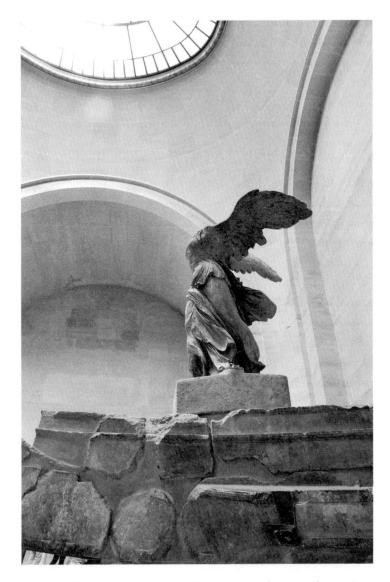

WINGED VICTORY OF SAMOTHRACE (c. 190 BC)

LOUVRE, DENON WING, ESCALIER DARU, GROUND–FIRST FLOOR

after the island on which the 2,000-year-old sculpture was discovered in 1863. After reassembling the statue's 118 pieces, not including the ship's prow, which was excavated and acquired over a decade later, the Louvre put the Winged Victory on display in the Cour Carrée's Salle des Caryatides in 1866. Workers would later move it to the top of the monumental Daru staircase from which it would descend in 1939.

Until 1870, the Louvre peacefully grew its collections, then came war once again, after tensions between Prussia and France escalated. On July 18, 1870, Napoleon III declared war on Prussia, after which various German states quickly joined Prussia. It was reasonable to conclude that if the Germanic armies captured the city, they would loot the Louvre just as Napoleon's armies had done in Prussia. On August 30 the government quickly decided to evacuate the most precious items to military buildings in the far northwest port city of Brest on the Channel coast. From there, they could be quickly evacuated to England if necessary. The 1870 evacuation of the Louvre was the first time such a measure had ever been taken.

The Grande Galerie became a frenzied packing workshop where curators and assistants had what they felt was the impossible task of unframing, packing, crating and shipping several hundred fragile items in four days; in 1939, curators would evacuate thousands of items in a similar amount of time. Readied crates were loaded onto horse-drawn carriages that headed to the train station, accompanied by museum guards in civilian dress rather than their uniforms in order to draw less attention. The first pieces of art left for Brest on September 1. Among the items aboard were the huge—and rolled—*Wedding Feast at Cana* and the *Mona Lisa*. Over the next several days, additional crates headed towards Brest.

In mid-September, by which time 123 crates had safely reached Brest, authorities called off further evacuation amid concerns that crates in transit to the train station would be hijacked by insurgents for use as barricades. Attention then turned to protecting the palace itself and the art and antiquities still within. Ground-floor windows deemed to be vulnerable to enemy fire were sheathed with sandbags, as were some of the exterior architectural sculptures. The most valuable remaining works of art and antiquity were either moved to hallways or brought down to ground-floor rooms and to basement areas judged by palace architects to offer the most strength against enemy projectiles. In the Egyptian gallery, jewels and papyrus were tucked inside the same sarcophagi that would hide something far more volatile during World War II.

By mid-September 1870, Prussian troops had completely encircled Paris with the intent of starving the city into surrender. The siege went on for months. By the start of 1871, the enemy began pounding the outskirts of the city with cannon fire and launching shells into the city itself. At midnight on January 6, Louvre officials spirited Venus de Milo out of the museum and arranged for a hiding place in the basements of a nearby police building. At the end of January, the French finally surrendered and a three-week armistice was declared, during which a new government, the Third Republic, was formed, headed by Adolphe Thiers. The new government agreed to a humiliating preliminary peace treaty with Prussia, signed at Versailles in February 1871, but peace in the city was short-lived.

Many Parisians suspected that the new government was planning to restore the monarchy and there was widespread discontent with the terms of the treaty. In mid-March, just as the Louvre was preparing to return the evacuated items from Brittany, civil war erupted after Thiers moved his government to Versailles and tried to disarm Paris. A loose confederation of socialist and reformist groups

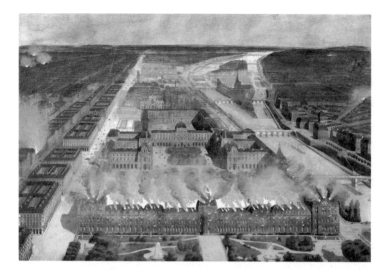

*Panorama de Paris. Incendie des Tuileries, 24 mai 1871*, anonymous,
Louvre's cour carrée at rear, Grand Galerie at right,
parallel to the Seine, engulfed in smoke

Musée Carnavalet

took control of the city and formed their own government: the
Paris Commune. Through April and into May, violence escalated
as Thiers's forces tried to take back the city. After a bloody massacre
of Communards ensued on May 21, their compatriots began to torch
public buildings across the city.

In the early evening of May 23, insurgents rolled carts full of
gunpowder, turpentine and paraffin oil into the Palais des Tuileries,
spread it onto floors, stairways, wood paneling and draperies across
the palace and set it all ablaze. The fire quickly spread out of control
into a spectacular inferno that destroyed the palace's floors, roofs
and contents. The blaze also threatened to swallow up the adjacent
Louvre. It spread partway along the wings bordering rue de Rivoli

before it was extinguished there, reducing 80,000 volumes of the library to ashes. The fire also spread across the rooftops and roof joists to the wings along the Seine, licking at the roofs of the Grande Galerie. The curators and firefighters knew that if the fire propagated further it would quickly reduce the museum's art to ashes.

The collections were at particular risk due to shockingly inadequate fire protection measures. Minor protective measures had been taken following a 1661 fire in the Petite Galerie, but a hundred years later, in spite of years of pleas by curators, the Louvre still did not have an adequate system of fire protection. The museum would likely have been lost but for the courage of curators willing to enter the burning building to identify a point where firefighters might isolate the blaze from the Grand Galerie. A battalion of 100 men then formed a relay—while surrounded by Communards threatening to shoot—and delivered enough water to extinguish the flames.

In September 1871, the 123 crates of artwork that had been evacuated to Brest the previous year were returned to Paris; the *Mona Lisa* was placed in the Salon Carré, the room off the eastern end of the Grande Galerie where she had made her very first appearance at the Louvre at the end of the 1700s. Venus de Milo was returned from the police building under which she had safely survived both war and revolution. The Louvre turned to repairing damage from the fire (demolition of the last vestiges of the Tuileries was authorized in 1882) and to the work of running and growing a museum.

Earlier in 1871, Thiers's government had signed a final peace treaty with Germany. One of its provisions required France to pay the staggering sum of 5 billion gold francs as war reparations; it also stipulated that German troops would remain in France until the obligation was discharged. By September 1873, the debt had been paid in full and the last German soldiers left France. In 1914 they would be back.

# TWO

# WORLD WAR I

I N THE VERY early years of the twentieth century, the Louvre was not under immediate threat of war, but it faced other risks. Theft, for one. Fewer than 150 guards protected collections spread across almost eight acres of exhibition space. Other security measures were also shockingly weak. *Mona Lisa* had been covered with glass in 1907 for protection against vandalism but like the other paintings in the museum it was attached to the wall only by several hooks. The artworks were not more strongly secured, a director of the museum had said, because the Louvre was not built to be a picture gallery: it was not fireproof and there was an even higher risk of fire since there were other users of the building. In case of fire, he said, the paintings could be quickly pulled off the walls and taken to safety.

There were other security problems as well. Any official photographer could carry off a painting to the building's photo studios without permission or an escort and a notice of explanation was not required to be posted if a work had been removed. Moreover, there was no alarm system and numerous passkeys opened every door in the museum. In early 1911, a reporter successfully hid overnight in a sarcophagus to expose the lax security. No precautionary measures were taken in response.

Just before closing time at the Louvre on Sunday August 21, 1911, a man slipped into a supply closet. Early the following morning, he slipped out of the museum with the *Mona Lisa*. The theft went unnoticed for more than twenty-four hours and, once it was discovered, all leads soon went cold. In December 1913, the painting was finally found in Florence, Italy, where the thief had recently taken it. The culprit, Vincenzo Peruggia, was a handyman with a minor arrest record who had briefly worked at the Louvre in 1908, helping to protect the artworks with glass. For more than two years, police had speculated that the *Mona Lisa* had been spirited away to a foreign buyer by a sophisticated ring of international art thieves. But all that time, the *Mona Lisa* had been just over a mile away from the Louvre, tucked away in a false-bottomed wooden box in Peruggia's room in a rundown Paris rooming house. In late 1913, after Peruggia took her to Italy in hopes of arranging a sale, authorities apprehended him and retrieved the painting.

*Mona Lisa* enjoyed brief but wildly popular viewings in Florence, Rome and Milan before being prepared for her return to her adopted home. She had first crossed the border from Italy to France in late 1516. At 3 a.m. on New Year's Day, 1914 she crossed the border again, this time by train instead of mule. On January 4, after great celebration, she was back on display at the Louvre, surrounded by record crowds—and better security measures.

Six months later, France was no longer celebrating. Instead, the country was facing imminent war with Germany, following a spiral of events after the June assassination of the Austrian Archduke Ferdinand. On July 31, only one day before Germany declared war on Russia and three days before Germany and France declared war on each other, Henri Marcel, the director of the Musées Nationaux, wrote a confidential report indicating the need to secure the art of the national museums and, above all, of the Louvre. He pointed out that the risks were even more serious than in 1870 due to advances in explosive devices and aeronautics, including the projectile-laden German Zeppelin.

The next day, action was taken to protect the most precious pieces of the museum. As in 1870, workers moved some items under vaulted arches, others to recesses in particularly thick walls and yet others to the floors below. Certain works were sheltered in place by timber-framed sandbag fortresses and workers once again piled sandbags against sculptures and windows to protect against explosions.

The German army advanced into France on August 24. At noon the following day, Marcel urgently gathered the museum curators to assign new instructions, this time to prepare as many paintings and other works of art as possible for shipment to Toulouse in southwest France. By August 28, the staff were told to do it faster and at any cost. One curator said that the crating process felt like filling and nailing coffins.

On August 30, two hours were needed just to remove David's immense (20 by 32 feet) *Coronation of Napoleon* from its frame and supports and roll it onto a large wooden cylinder. That evening, in spite of frenzied, non-stop activity, a government minister told them to work even faster. Venus de Milo was brought down from her base and readied to leave the palace as in 1871, though this time she left in broad daylight rather than under cover of darkness. And instead of heading towards a secret tomb in Paris, she was loaded into a wagon and put on a train for Toulouse along with other works. The following day, crate number 6 was prepared. Into it went, among other works, Clouet's *François I* and finally—under heavy watch—the *Mona*

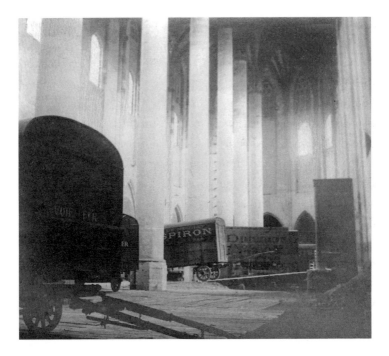

LOUVRE ARTWORKS IN JACOBINS CHURCH, TOULOUSE, WORLD WAR I

*Lisa.* The *Wedding Feast at Cana*, considered too large to move, would remain in place for the duration of the war.

On September 1, vehicles arrived and the loading process began. After they ran out of crates, artwork was loaded bare into trailers. Loading continued the following day. Curator Paul Leprieur wanted to hold back a fragile drawing; he said he had faith in the hiding places of the Louvre and that he would lie to the enemy to have them believe that the artwork had been removed. "But if this was discovered," other staff members asked him, "do you know what you risk?" "Oh well, yes," Leprieur replied, "maybe they'll shoot me, that's all." He would die in service to the Louvre, though not as he speculated, ultimately suffering a fatal fall on one of the museum's staircases in May 1918.

Towards 6:30 p.m., as the staff were loading the last vehicle, they saw a German plane flying over the Louvre. The containers holding Venus de Milo, 770 evacuated paintings and drawings and two crates of objets d'art were loaded onto four train cars at the gare d'Austerlitz. Venus de Milo, packed carefully in a wooden crate, traveled in her own wagon. As the train prepared to leave for Toulouse, the staff at the Louvre could hear the distant, heavy sounds of the large artillery of the Germans through the open windows of the galleries.

The evacuated items—a tiny proportion of the Louvre's holdings compared to what would be evacuated on the eve of World War II— safely reached Toulouse, where they were stored under the soaring vaulted arches of the medieval Jacobins Church, most of the artwork remaining in the wagons in which they had traveled from Paris.

B ack in Paris, some areas of the museum were used to store items evacuated from other museums. Behind the scenes, waiting for the war to end, the museum updated some of the galleries and continued to acquire new pieces. Twice during the war, the museum opened a few galleries to the public, mainly exhibiting sculptures that had remained behind. However, it closed at the end of January 1918 after German bombers conducted their first raid on Paris. The Louvre was hit, although the administration was relieved to find that the projectiles had not penetrated to the lower levels where the art was stored.

In March 1918, as the Germans began to fire upon the city with new, huge long-range cannons, additional evacuations brought artworks to the château de Blois. In June, as the cannons drew perilously close to Paris, the museum's administration decided to try to evacuate as much as possible of what had remained. This was not an easy task since much had stayed behind, including almost all the antiquities. On June 6, Georges Bénédite, curator of the Department of Egyptian antiquities, issued a bold appeal to the director of the Louvre that his department's items finally be evacuated. He noted that his department had a number of items far more valuable than the paintings that had gone to Blois, "a value not only artistic, but monetary," citing, among others, the ancient Egyptian Seated Scribe. He ended his request with a final personal plea: "I have not left my post since the declaration of war, I have not taken any kind of time off, nor left Paris for a single night, I believe that I have the right to ask for assistance at such an urgent and difficult moment."

The evacuated items in Toulouse were joined in August 1918 by one final shipment of artworks that had been sent from Paris amid ongoing fears of air raids. There and in Blois, the collections waited out the final months of the war. On November 11, 1918, as cannons and church bells announced the signing of an armistice, preparations began to return the artworks. Less than five weeks later, crates began heading back to Paris. The Louvre progressively reopened during January and February 1919 as the public enthusiastically returned to galleries that had been cleaned, reorganized and enriched.

The Louvre and its artwork had escaped another war without destruction or significant damage and life at the museum was soon back to normal. However, by the early 1930s French fine arts authorities were worrying once again about war with Germany and the accompanying risks to French museums and collections. This time, however, they would not wait until three weeks before a declaration of war to develop protection plans; this time they would begin almost a decade ahead.

# THREE

# DRUMS OF ANOTHER WAR

T HE TREATY OF Versailles, signed on June 28, 1919, officially ended the war between Germany and France and
the Allied powers. Among its other provisions, the treaty
required Germany to make substantial concessions of territory, to
pay reparations to various countries and to disarm. As the Germans
signed the treaty, they were outraged about its terms but did not have
the military strength to object. As the Allies signed, they knew that
peace might be precarious. Ferdinand Foch, Supreme Commander
of the Allied Armies, prophetically said of the treaty, "This is not
peace; it is an armistice for twenty years."

As early as May 1920, the French considered creating a fortified
zone along the border between Germany and France; by 1930, in a
project championed by André Maginot, France's minister of war,
construction of massive fortifications began along the border. The
French put their hopes for protection from Germans in a future
war into the Maginot Line. It would prove to be a false hope: when
war finally would come, the Germans would simply swing north
and bypass it.

After the onset of the world economic depression in 1929, France and the rest of Europe watched the continuing rise of Adolf Hitler and the Nazi party. The French fine arts administration was watching as well—and unlike in previous wars, they were not about to wait to develop a plan to protect the country's art until an enemy was only miles away. In February 1932, the fine arts administration agreed to work with Paris civil authorities on a plan for protecting the city's museums. France was not alone in its preparations; as early as 1929, the Dutch had requested a study of ways to protect its national collections and in 1933 the British were discussing air raid precautions.

Concern and planning escalated apace with developments in Germany. In the July 1932 German elections, the Nazi party—with Hitler at its helm—became the largest party, though not yet a majority, in the German parliament. Shortly thereafter, Henri Verne, director of the Louvre and the other museums in the Musées Nationaux system, sent confidential letters to curators asking them to make priority lists of the works to be evacuated in case of "an eventuality that must be expected, even while hoping it will not happen."

On January 30, 1933, tens of thousands of Nazi troops marched in a torch-lit parade through the streets of Berlin to celebrate Adolf Hitler's appointment as Chancellor of Germany. Within six months, French authorities forecast the most likely areas of military action and museum authorities used the information to begin identifying safe locations for art evacuation depots. Verne established an evacuation plan for the French national museums' treasures and a plan for items to be protected in place. Before the end of the year, he was also considering the effects of German incendiary bombs and by spring 1934, the fine arts administration was considering specifications for bomb shelters to protect its employees. They were right to be concerned: In November 1936, during the Spanish Civil War, the Prado Museum would be hit by nine German-built bombs within a single hour.

E arly in the planning process, it became clear that it would simply not be realistic to evacuate all the art and antiquities from the Louvre, much less from Versailles and the other museums under the auspices of the Musées Nationaux. There would be neither enough money, people, materials or vehicles in the event of war to move them all, nor enough appropriate places to store them. Thus the first challenge was deciding what to evacuate and what to leave in place. For curators, with a deep devotion to their art, making priority lists of such treasures was a bit like asking a parent to choose their favorite child. The most valuable objects in monetary or artistic terms were obvious preferences but selections also had to take into account the size, weight and condition of individual pieces. A number of the Louvre's pastels were considered too fragile to travel any distance and even as war was declared in September 1939, the 8,800-pound Winged Victory of Samothrace was considered too heavy to evacuate at all.

The next challenge was determining where to store the evacuated treasures. Fine arts administrators concluded that storage depots should be far from anticipated front lines of combat as well as from potential Paris-area bombing targets; to identify such areas they would consult with military authorities. Based on the military's assumption that the Germans would enter France from the east, depot locations in the center and west of France were considered ideal. On the other hand, it was also important that depots not be inordinately far from Paris or from each other, to facilitate transportation of the works and the movement of curators and staff for restoration and other purposes. Another criterion was that depots should be as isolated as possible, not only far from cities but also from main roads, bridges, industrial sites or any other feature that might be a target for bombing or other military activity.

Specific storage depots then had to be identified; the country's many châteaux quickly became a clear preference. Often they were in isolated locations and many were perfect strongholds, with vaulted basements and thick stone walls that had stood the test of time. Châteaux were evaluated, in part, on how well curators could control temperature and humidity, not an easy task in old stone castles. Floors had to be strong enough to hold tons of crates; later in the war curators would learn the consequences if this step was overlooked. Potential depots also needed large ground floor rooms and entryways wide enough to easily bring in large items and to remove them just as easily in case of fire, which, after bombing, was by far the most significant concern. And each depot needed a substantial nearby water source in case of a fire. Moreover, any depot or its vicinity had to provide adequate accommodations and food sources for curators and numerous guards, many of whom had families.

By 1933, the Loire Valley, roughly 100 miles south of Paris, had been identified as one of the potentially safest areas for the collections of the Louvre and the other Paris-area museums. The region was both fairly close to Paris and far from the German border and it was also reasonably close to England in the event further evacuation was needed. There were also a great many châteaux that might serve as depots.

Authorities debated whether to use a single large shelter or multiple ones. A single depot would allow concentration of transport, personnel and supplies. On the other hand, multiple depots would be more complicated but would spread the risks of enemy attack and fire. Very early in the planning process, the château of

Chambord was chosen as a key location. As one of the largest châ-teaux in France, it was vast enough to contain everything and, in the midst of miles of surrounding forests, it was isolated enough. It could not be bombed in error because it was easily recognizable from the air and it could be camouflaged easily by smoke if necessary. By February 1934, Chambord had been identified as the primary depot, with collections also to be dispersed among other châteaux. It would also serve as a way station where items would be checked in as they arrived from Paris and then sent onward to their final destinations.

The fine arts administration then had to arrange for the use of specific châteaux. This was not a problem with Chambord, since the French government already owned it, but permission to use others had to be arranged. Subsidies were given to those who granted use of their property, but the amounts were too small to provide much motivation. In some cases, owners were inspired by patriotism or love of art, but more often than not their motivation was to reduce the likelihood that an owner's castle or manor house would be com-mandeered or ransacked by the Germans.

Initially, fewer than two dozen châteaux were requisitioned for possible shelter of collections of the Louvre and the other French national museums. Later, provincial collections would fall under the auspices of the Musées Nationaux as well, requiring additional depots. By the end of World War II, more than eighty châteaux—many of them far beyond the Loire Valley—would have served their country for some period of time.

Another issue was transportation. Authorities considered rail transport, which had been used for the World War I evacuation to Toulouse, but there was little enthusiasm for this option. Planners felt that railroads would be encumbered by military transport and supply, as they had been during World War I, and that citizens should have priority access to trains in case of impending war.

Moreover, with Chambord as the staging depot, evacuated works would require a secondary transfer from the nearest rail station.

Using barges was also an option, given the multitude of France's rivers and canals. Proponents argued that barges offered advantages not only over rail transport but also over trucks, which, they said, would face roads clogged by military vehicles and could also break down and catch fire. Barges could also be loaded quickly since the Seine ran right alongside the Louvre. Moreover, it was argued, barges would not be a high-profile enemy target: The enemy would not immediately be looking for them and it was also unlikely that Germans would waste time following their meanderings or attack a random isolated barge. Opposing arguments included the time required for barge transport. Water transport to Chambord would take five or six days while trucks, so it was thought, could get to almost any destination in twenty-four hours. Moreover, as with rail transport, barge transport would still require a secondary transport by truck from canalside to Chambord since studies indicated that the canals were not navigable all the way.

However, evacuation by truck was not an ideal option either. Bridges could be blown, truck convoys could be aerial bombing targets, and roads could be blocked by military vehicles and fleeing civilians, which would later prove to be the case. And in the case of war, there could be (and would be) shortages of both vehicles and fuel. On the other hand, trucks offered the simplicity and speed of a single mode of transport to Chambord and the other depots and assistance could be obtained from companies that specialized in moving works of art.

Ultimately, even up to the weeks just before war was declared in 1939, the museum administration readied trucks for most of the works but still considered barge transport an option for items such as sculptures and certain objets d'art that would not suffer from either humidity or even immersion. In the end, trucks would bring the artworks into exile.

As the 1930s went on, Europe inched closer to war. The Treaty of Versailles had set a strict limit on the size of the German military and had forbidden the country to re-arm itself, but Hitler eventually simply ignored most of the treaty. After two years of re-arming in secret, Hitler announced in March 1935 that the Luftwaffe had 2,500 warplanes and that he had built up a 300,000-man army and planned to almost double that number. The Treaty of Versailles also banned German troops from certain territory along the Rhine River. In 1936, Hitler again disregarded the treaty as his troops marched into the Rhineland and by year's end he announced plans to take over Austria and Czechoslovakia. By March 1938, he had annexed Austria and set his sights on the Sudetenland, a former German territory that had become part of Czechoslovakia under the Treaty of Versailles.

By mid-August 1938, the Musées Nationaux were actively mobilizing. They sought trucks for evacuation and made arrangements to lease two large vaults at the Banque de France in Paris for certain fragile items. Huge quantities of crates and packing materials arrived.

After Hitler indicated on September 22 that he would take the Sudetenland, by force if necessary, Europe seemed on the brink of war. The same day, the Musées Nationaux set into motion the measures it had been painstakingly refining since almost the dawn of the decade to protect the art and antiquities from anticipated bombing of Paris. In early evening on Monday, September 26, the Louvre received the long-anticipated evacuation order.

It took the Department of Paintings only an hour and a half to carefully remove from gallery walls every item designated most urgent—including the *Mona Lisa*—and bring them to packing and crating areas. Some crates had been purposely left temporarily in a hallway with shipping labels noted "New York" in a futile attempt to keep the entire project secret but the extent of the packing and the number of cases and temporary workers were clear evidence of what was actually going on.

At 6 a.m. on September 27, 1938, several trucks loaded with some of the Louvre's most precious art and antiquities rolled away from the capital towards the château de Chambord. Because military vehicles and road traffic jammed the road as had been feared in the years of planning, it took more than fourteen hours for the convoy to reach Chambord, a distance of only 100 miles.

Aboard the convoy were the crown jewels and other objets d'art from the galerie d'Apollon, plus the essential pieces from the Grande Galerie and the paintings by Rubens that had been commissioned in the 1600s by Marie de Medici, Henry IV's wife, to depict important events in her life. Also aboard was the *Mona Lisa*. On her original voyage to France in the sixteenth century, she had traveled in da Vinci's leather bag. This time she traveled in a special double-walled poplar case, cushioned inside with red velvet, which had been custom made for the evacuation.

As Pierre Schommer, a senior administrator in the Musées Nationaux, unpacked crates at Chambord on September 28, he learned that one of them contained the crown jewels. In light of numerous security concerns, he discreetly took them the following day to nearby Blois and secured them in a Banque de France safe deposit box.

A second convoy of art arrived at Chambord that day and a third came on September 29, as Edouard Daladier from France, Neville Chamberlain from England, and Benito Mussolini from Italy met with Hitler in Munich in a last-ditch effort to avoid war in Europe.

On the morning of September 30, as the Chambord staff were unloading crates from the third convoy, they learned of the previous night's signing of the Munich Agreement, allowing Germany to annex the Sudetenland, thus avoiding immediate war. The furious ongoing packing at the Louvre ceased and within a week, the *Mona Lisa*, the other artwork at Chambord and the jewels stored in Blois were back in Paris. The Louvre would have eleven months' grace before war would finally come.

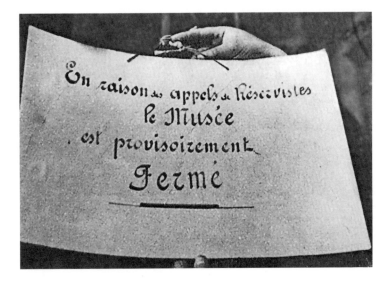

SIGN POSTED AT THE LOUVRE, SEPTEMBER 1938
(DUE TO CALL UP OF RESERVISTS, THE
MUSEUM IS TEMPORARILY CLOSED)

# PART II

---

# INTO EXILE

*Fall 1938 to Spring 1940*

# FOUR

# FINAL
# PREPARATIONS

FTER THE SIGNING of the Munich Agreement, the Louvre's art had returned to its galleries along with museumgoers and seeming normality, but behind the scenes, the museum administration intensified efforts to prepare for war. The Louvre's head architect had envisioned several huge bomb shelters under the building to protect not only museum personnel but also the administrative staff of the Musées Nationaux headquartered in the palace and the staff and students of the École du Louvre, a training ground for curators and those in related disciplines. Underground rooms were dug, walls erected and the whole of it strengthened by a forest of metal reinforcing bars.

In the basements and storerooms stood wagons and baskets ready to move items and huge wooden cylinders on which to roll the largest paintings. Storerooms were also filled with huge quantities of packing material—special paper, cotton batting and other padding—plus ladders, tools and nails for securing the crates, and other supplies. Two thousand crates had been ordered for the 1938 evacuation, though only a small number of them had been used for the quickly aborted operation. In anticipation of a much larger evacuation, the museum administration ordered thousands more crates and additional packing materials. When there was no more room in storage areas, crates sat openly in the exhibition galleries, a reminder that all was not business as usual.

For works that could not be evacuated, specialists examined ways to reduce humidity levels in basement rooms and determined the resistance of walls to potential direct bomb strikes and the permeability of rooms to gas attacks. The museum purchased almost a million sandbags to protect windows and artworks that were to remain on site and assessed the quantity and location of sandbags and sand supplies to battle fires from a bomb hit; especially vulnerable were the museum's ancient wooden roof beams.

The curators devised ways to pack and transport the large paintings and redesigned the baskets and wagons to speed the movement of paintings from gallery to staging areas. The staff codified a labeling system for crates to identify their contents. Each crate would have the initials "MN" for Musées Nationaux, plus several letters indicating the department of the museum, among them LP for the Louvre's Paintings Department, LR for the Greek and Roman Antiquities and LB for the contents of the library and archives. Each crate was also assigned a unique number.

Curators refined priority lists and evacuation routes within the museum and assigned teams of people to specific sectors. Workers carefully measured the dimensions of each item as well as the elevators and stairways, in order to match items to evacuation routes. They also held practice drills to be sure that, in the case of a bomb alert, the major works could be immediately rushed to the basements.

The museum administration hired specialized workers, including professional packers, movers and woodworkers and searched for volunteers, knowing that staffing would be difficult as men went to war. The museum's administrators were also painfully aware that it would be difficult to obtain enough vehicles because the best ones would be requisitioned for military duty. Planners searched for large capacity trucks designed to expedite smooth loading and unloading, ideally enclosed ones that would hide contents from curious eyes and protect the works in case of rain. But such vehicles would be hard to come by; the museum would have to settle, in part, for open-back trucks and tarps to cover the crates. For months, they searched for vehicles and negotiated contracts for their use. Meanwhile, they continued to evaluate the possibility of water transport.

Successfully developing and coordinating all these arrangements under difficult circumstances and inspiring commitment and solidarity from the entire staff, from guards to curators, would require the multi-faceted talents of an extraordinary person. Though nobody could know it yet, protecting the collections in the years to come would also require unfathomable energy, nerves of steel and an unwavering will to do the right thing. In fact, the Musées Nationaux had such a person in Jacques Jaujard, its deputy director, a man who, unlike virtually every other senior person in the Musées Nationaux administration, had no art or art history training or experience before he came aboard in 1926. Instead, he had been an insurance salesman and then a journalist who dreamed of being a man of letters. Yet by 1933, the finely dressed, usually quite serious and always quite private Jaujard was made deputy director of the Musées Nationaux and by 1939 he had been handed the lead role in preparing the museums for war. Jaujard would be appointed acting director in December 1939 and director in September 1940 at age 44. By early 1939, he was already known for his diplomacy. In the years to come, the unlikely hero would become known for far more.

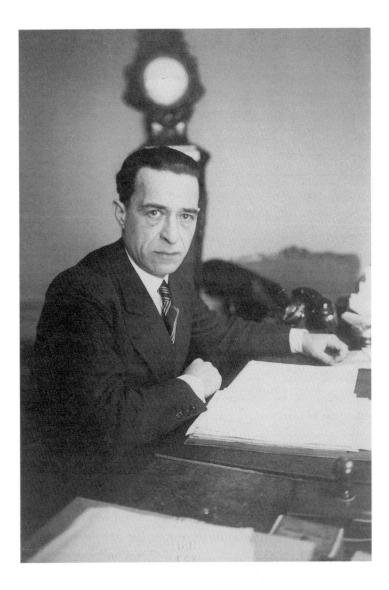

JACQUES JAUJARD

In March 1939, Hitler seized the remainder of Czechoslovakia and by early summer it was clear that Poland was next. By mid-July, France's ambassador to Germany had repeatedly warned the French Foreign Minister of "Germany's obvious preparations for the possibility of an impending war . . . and to be prepared for any eventually from August onwards." By the first days of August, with tension in the air throughout Europe, the Louvre had begun final preparations for war.

Horse-drawn wagons pulled up alongside the museum to unload piles of wood fiber for packing. In the Tuileries Garden adjacent to the museum, workers dug trenches for some of the outdoor sculptures. Other workers yet again piled sandbags in front of many of the Louvre's windows. They also laid thousands more sandbags across the floors of the attics, placed stocks of sand everywhere and tested fire extinguishers. By August 5, every department had portable electric lamps, gas masks and pharmacy supplies in case of an enemy attack while the staff were preparing the collections. A watchtower was in place atop the roof of the Salon Carré—the room next to the Grande Galerie's eastern end where the *Mona Lisa* was displayed until World War I; from the roof, firemen could keep a lookout for falling projectiles.

By early August, Jaujard faced a serious shortage of vehicles for the evacuation. Though he had estimated that thirty vehicles were critical, to be used in multiple waves of convoys, military authorities informed him that they could only cede seventeen. Then he learned that five of the seventeen had been requisitioned, leaving him with only twelve. Though he quickly signed contracts with the owners of the twelve trucks—and soon with some others—he knew the measures could be for naught if the owners themselves were called up for military duty. By the time of the evacuation, he would successfully beg and borrow additional trucks.

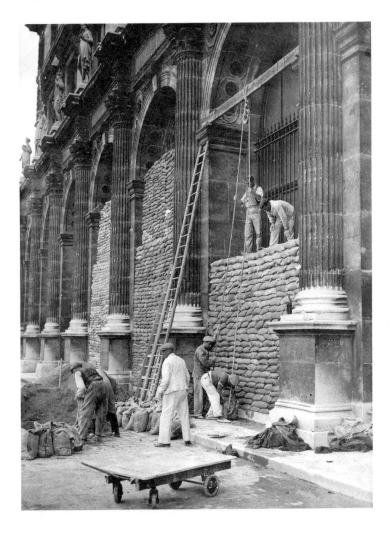

WORKERS PROTECTING LOUVRE WINDOWS AS WAR APPROACHES

After the many years of preparing, revising and prioritizing lists of the items to be evacuated, final lists were made, reflecting almost 4,000 paintings and many thousands of sculptures, antiquities and objets d'art. Each item was quickly tagged with a colored sticker, part of the plan arranged years before: red for top priority, green for the most significant among the rest and yellow for lower priority works. The fifty or so most prestigious works received two red stickers. *Mona Lisa* alone received three stickers. Staff were trained in meticulous procedures for removing artwork from walls. Instructions indicated when two or more workers were needed for removal and provided that paintings should face the wall as they were set down and, above all, never to lay a painting flat on the ground. Not only could they be damaged by nearby tools, nails and other evacuation supplies but in the rush, anyone might lose their balance and step right into the middle of a masterpiece.

Final security plans for the transport were also in place. Each convoy would be accompanied by two senior staff members of the Musées Nationaux, one preceding the convoy and the other following, both in passenger vehicles. Armed guards would be aboard the vehicles and police on motorcycles would escort each convoy.

Late on August 23, Germany and the USSR signed a non-aggression pact. At day's end on August 24, London's museums closed and began their evacuation preparations. On Friday August 25, Great Britain and Poland concluded a pact of mutual assistance; it meant that war was imminent. At 5 p.m. that day, the Louvre received the long-awaited order: Start packing.

# FIVE

# HOW TO MOVE A MASTERPIECE

Within minutes of the Louvre closing its doors to visitors in the early evening of Friday, August 25, packing began. From all corners of the museum, workers removed the top-priority movable paintings, antiquities, and objets d'art—from religious relics to furniture to the crown jewels—from walls, pedestals and cases. As paintings were removed, first from the walls and then from their frames, workers marked the empty spaces with chalk to note their location to facilitate rehanging upon their return.

Workers took items along the carefully planned routes to designated triage areas where others wrapped and crated them, then nailed the crates shut, sealed them and applied more colored priority stickers. The tasks were all the more difficult after dark since workers had only the dim light of small portable lamps, a precaution in case of a bombing raid.

By 1 a.m., all fifty or so of the most prestigious paintings considered readily movable had been moved to the triage areas. Workers

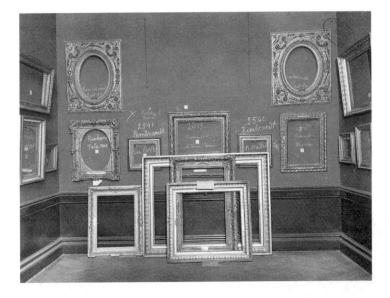

THE LOUVRE'S RUBENS GALLERY EMPTIED OF PAINTINGS

then rushed back to the galleries to begin the next round. The atmosphere was frenzied, but the packing went smoothly; every part of the endeavor had been analyzed again and again over multiple years and then rehearsed.

With the military draft underway, it had been a mad scramble for Jaujard to assemble the small army of people needed for the massive operation. Museum staff members were called back by telegram from their August holidays. Museum guards—most of whom were men injured in World War I—helped out alongside curators, technicians, professional packers and movers. Jaujard had obtained approval from military leaders and other authorities to use civilian volunteers. Among those helping out were dozens of men on loan from several of the big Parisian department stores, including the Samaritaine, whose owner, Gabriel Cognacq, was vice president of

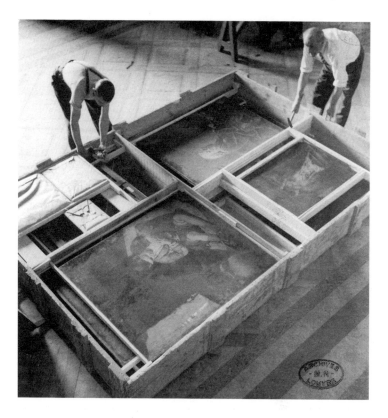

WORKERS PACKING UP PAINTINGS, AUGUST 1939

the National Museum Council. At one point, young staff member Magdeleine Hours walked into a gallery to find men from one of the department stores packing up fourteenth- and fifteenth-century paintings. Like the other workers, they were dressed in long work smocks, but they also wore mauve tights and striped caps. Hours was stupefied; they looked to her just like characters in the medieval works they were packing.

In the triage areas, antiquities were packed in protective material. Smaller paintings were wrapped first in fire-resistant paper, then in leatherette to resist humidity; fiber spacers separated multiple paintings packed in a single crate. Dust swirled in the air and hammers clattered as typists furiously tapped out quintuplicate lists of the contents of each crate. To disguise the contents of crates, they bore only three markings: the initials "MN," the department initials and a crate number; the anonymity was intended to discourage theft and to frustrate searches by Germans. Moreover, to keep unauthorized individuals from knowing where the items were going, all shipping labels said Chambord, even though many items had already been assigned to other final destinations in the Loire Valley.

The official evacuation order came on Sunday, August 27, after two days of around-the-clock packing. The Cour Carrée was closed to the public and empty trucks began rolling into the courtyard; Jacques Jaujard presided over the loading and verification operation. By evening, the first trucks were ready and waiting for departure early the following morning. The *Mona Lisa*, carefully wrapped in layers of special paper, set into her special velvet-lined case and packed in her own crate, was aboard a truck with thirty-one other crates. These other crates, according to procedure, bore the initials "MN," the department initials and a crate number. Not so for *Mona Lisa*'s crate, which for additional security during the trip had been vaguely marked simply "MN." Jaujard handed the convoy leader a handwritten note to be handed to Pierre Schommer at Chambord. "Truck Chenue 2162RM2," Jaujard wrote, "contains a crate marked MN in black without letters or numbers. This crate contains the Mona Lisa. Mark it LP0 in red."

At 6 a.m. on August 28, 1939, the first convoy of eight trucks, loaded with the *Mona Lisa*, the Seated Scribe, the crown jewels and 225 other crates of some of the world's most precious art and antiquities rolled slowly away from Paris towards the French countryside.

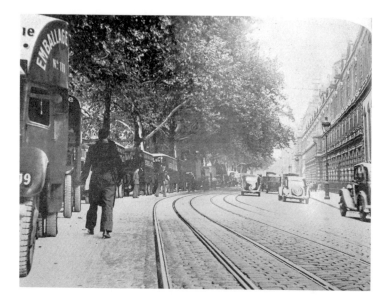

TRUCKS LINED UP ALONG THE SEINE, MUSEUM AT RIGHT

Six additional trucks were loaded that morning; they left in a second convoy at 2 p.m. By the following day, the pace had picked up, with twenty-three trucks leaving Paris. As soon as trucks returned empty from the Loire, they were quickly loaded again. Two convoys left each day until September 2, when only one convoy of nine trucks headed south. Not all evacuated items went to the Loire; between August 28 and 30, several dozen of the museum's best pastels deemed too fragile for a long journey, among them Boucher's *Madame de Pompadour* and seven works by Degas, were moved to the two climate-controlled underground vaults at the Banque de France that had been leased the previous year. Many works did not leave the museum at all. Those items deemed too fragile or heavy to move—like the ancient sarcophagi, Venus de Milo, Artemis with a Doe and Michelango's *Slaves*—either remained in place or were moved to areas

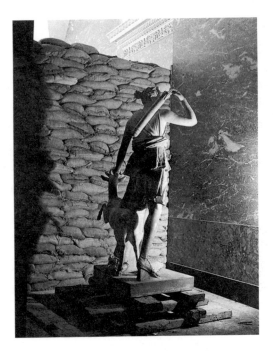

ARTEMIS WITH A DOE DURING THE WAR (1ST–2ND CENTURY AD)

LOUVRE, SULLY WING, GROUND FLOOR, SALLE DES CARYATIDES

deemed strong enough to withstand the force of a bomb; sandbags added additional protection.

In the pre-dawn hours of September 1, as 1.5 million German troops began pouring into Poland, workers in the museum picked up the pace even more. On September 1 and 2, they worked through the night as war became more inevitable by the minute. By then, they had turned towards the challenging task of evacuating the very large paintings. The Louvre's largest painting of all, the *Wedding Feast at Cana*, was removed from its chassis and rolled onto a giant oak column; David's giant *Coronation of Napoleon* was also rolled. Too long to fit in a truck, these and other rolled paintings were loaded onto huge scenery trailers loaned by the Comédie-Française.

M oving the giant *Raft of the Medusa*—22 feet wide by 16 feet tall—caused unique problems. Géricault had used bitumen, used in making asphalt, in large areas of the painting to achieve a saturated black. Because the sticky material never completely dries, the painting could not be rolled and its massive height made it a challenge to transport since the convoy would have to pass under bridges and utility wires.

The route was carefully studied. Arrangements were made for agents of the French post office and telecommunications agency to precede the convoy with insulated poles that could temporarily disconnect telephone and telegraph wires to allow the convoy to safely pass. Even the weather report was consulted to be sure the depiction of sailors and their sails would not itself be cast adrift by heavy winds.

Reassured—or so they thought—of the painting's safety en route, the convoy, which included other large nineteenth-century paintings, set out in the early evening of September 1. Daytime travel would have been easier, but the scenery trailers could crawl along at only eleven miles per hour and evening travel would cause less disruption to traffic.

Except for a detour around the viaduct at Passy, which did not provide sufficient clearance for the combined height of the *Raft* and the scenery trailer, the convoy passed uneventfully under the other bridges from Paris towards Versailles, one of the towns along the route to the Loire Valley. But as the convoy passed the Versailles town hall, the museum staff suddenly heard loud crackling, giant sparks flew everywhere and the *Raft's* trailer was thrown sideways. The route planners had not taken into account overhead trolley wires, into which the giant painting had crashed. As sparks lit up

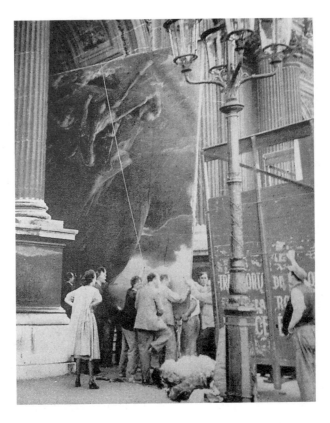

RAFT OF THE MEDUSA LEAVING THE LOUVRE, SEPTEMBER 1939

the night, electricity to the entire town had to be shut off, plunging the town into darkness and setting off panic among residents, who thought surely it was a German attack. Curators feared not only a fire, but also rioting by the angry mob that gathered around the convoy. To the curators' surprise, the painting was not damaged. René Huyghe, curator of the Louvre's Department of Paintings, later commented that it was "unthinkable that after having escaped the furious sea, the *Raft* would fall victim to flames."

As the scene calmed, the convoy leader realized that the continued presence of the *Raft* could cause similar problems along the rest of the route. He sent Louvre curator Magdeleine Hours to ask the curator at the nearby château de Versailles if he would shelter it and the other paintings on the trailer until other arrangements could be made. Hours spent more than a quarter hour in the pitch-black darkness feeling her way bar by bar along the château's closed gates before she finally found the bell. Her repeated ringing received no response. Finally, the curator appeared in his nightclothes; he had gone to bed early to be ready for an evacuation at dawn of some of the château's own artworks. He opened the gates wide for the large scenery trailer loaded with its even larger artwork.

After hearing about the day's debacle, Jaujard changed the route for the next shipment of large paintings scheduled to head to Chambord. He was concerned not only about more potential wire problems, but also whether the other large unrolled works, and even the rolled *Wedding Feast at Cana*, would fit through the low entry to the Chambord courtyard. He decided that the newest shipment of large works would join the others at Versailles for several weeks as a temporary measure until the administration could find safe routes directly to the châteaux that would host the paintings, bypassing the Chambord way station altogether. When they were finally moved to the Loire Valley, the 100-mile journey would take sixteen hours.

By the morning of September 2, the Louvre had already removed every item on the three top-priority lists. While workers packed yet more items and protected those that would remain, Jaujard faced another unexpected challenge: bringing the 9-foot-high, 3.5-ton Winged Victory of Samothrace down from the top of the soaring Daru staircase. Curators had originally considered the

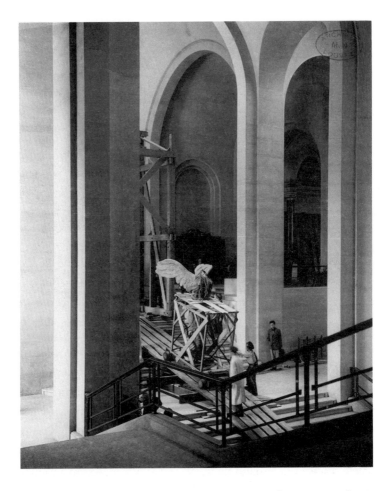

MOVING WINGED VICTORY OF SAMOTHRACE (1945 RETURN)

statue impractical to move, but believed sandbags and the vaulted ceiling above could adequately protect it. However, a subsequent examination indicated the ceiling was, in fact, not strong enough to withstand a bomb impact. On September 2, using a thick pulley, chains and ropes mounted to a huge wooden frame constructed

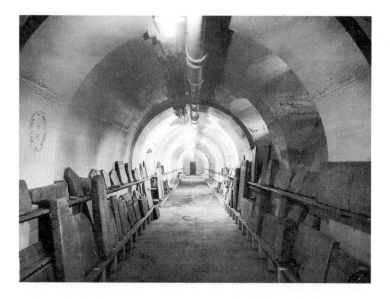

ANCIENT STONE SLABS IN LOUVRE UNDERGROUND SERVICE CORRIDOR

around the statue, the Winged Victory—made of 118 pieces, some just fragile plaster replacements—rose slowly from its base and onto a specially built wooden ramp, along which it was slowly inched down the fifty-three steps of the staircase while a small group of staff members watched, holding their collective breath. Once it had safely reached the ground floor, the statue was moved to a vaulted wall recess supported by giant pillars and covered with a thick barrier of sandbags.

A last pre-war convoy left on the evening of September 2. By then, dust-covered workers had toiled around the clock for days, catching brief naps in the museum. By that point, ninety-five truckloads had carried away more than 1,200 crates of the Louvre's treasures. As in previous wars, items deemed too fragile or heavy to evacuate had been brought down to the ground floor and the

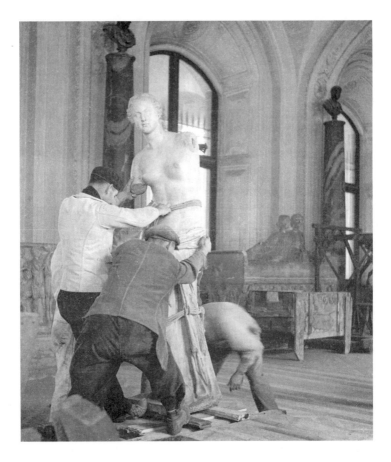

WORKERS MOVING VENUS DE MILO (1945 RETURN)

basements, many protected with sandbags. Some were tucked into vaulted recesses or other safe areas, while others were stacked along the endless underground service corridors.

The only items remaining in the largely deserted museum were items of lesser value, including 600 paintings, plus works deemed too fragile or large to move, including the Venus de Milo and the

Winged Victory of Samothrace. These two items would not remain for long.

On September 3 at 9 a.m., England issued an ultimatum to Hitler that it would declare war if it did not hear within two hours that Germany was prepared to withdraw its troops from Poland. At noon, France issued a similar ultimatum expiring at 5 p.m. At 5 p.m., France declared war on Germany. No trucks left the Louvre that day. Almost ninety percent of the museum's paintings were already gone; the only trace of them was white chalk marks on gallery walls and empty frames on the floors. The majority of the transportable antiquities and objets d'art were also gone, tucked away safely—or so it was hoped—at Chambord and other châteaux of the Loire.

Paris waited in dread that night for German bombers, but none came. The following night, the city's residents heard the sirens of an air raid alert, but again there was no sign of German planes. Nor did they come in the days that followed. By September 6, the Louvre administration felt it safe to begin evacuating—on a far smaller scale—still more items of lesser importance. However, on September 20, Jaujard and the Commission of Historic Monuments and Buildings concluded that the important large sculptures still in the Louvre were not safe enough. In the first days of October, a twenty-ninth convoy left from the Louvre, this one heading to the Loire Valley château de Valençay. It carried the Venus de Milo, the Winged Victory of Samothrace and Michelangelo's *Slaves*, along with 2,400-year-old frieze fragments from the Greek Parthenon and Houdon's eighteenth-century bronze sculpture, *Diana*.

Just over a week later, restoration specialists balanced on shaky scaffolding that reached almost to the top of the 45-foot-high galerie d'Apollon while they removed Delacroix's *Apollo Slays Python* from the room's ceiling. The large work was then rolled onto a long custom-made wooden cylinder. René Huyghe was not happy about the rolling since it could cause the paint to crack, but he knew there was no choice.

Smaller convoys continued to remove items to châteaux in the countryside. By the end of October, more than 2,000 crates filled with treasures had been removed from the Louvre in more than 200 truckloads. The museum had been emptied of 3,691 paintings plus many thousands more antiquities, engravings, drawings, sculptures, and objets d'art. Sixty percent of the herculean task had been accomplished in the six days between August 28 and September 2, and ninety-two percent of it all by the end of September. Virtually all the rest had been removed before the end of October.

In addition to orchestrating the massive evacuation at the Louvre, Jaujard also supervised the evacuation of 465 crates from the Cluny, Luxembourg, Jeu de Paume and other Paris museums under the jurisdiction of the Musées Nationaux, 599 crates from Versailles and the other non-Paris national museums under its control, more than 1,400 crates from the Musée des Arts Décoratifs and other public institutions, and almost 600 crates from private collections, most belonging to prominent Jewish collectors.

With most of the Louvre's treasures spread across the French countryside, nobody knew how long they would stay away. In fact, they would not start heading home for almost six years.

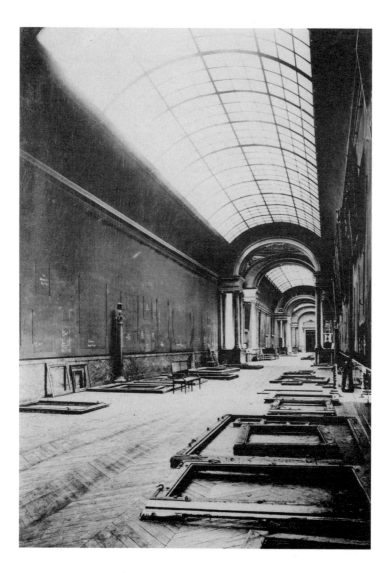

THE LOUVRE'S GRANDE GALERIE, EMPTIED OF ITS ART

# SIX

# CHAMBORD

C HAMBORD'S MASSIVE WHITE château rises unexpectedly from a clearing in the largest enclosed forest park in
Europe. Construction of the 440 rooms, 365 chimneys
and myriad minaret-like towers began in 1519 under the direction
of the then 25-year-old King François I, who wanted yet another
occasional hunting lodge, but one that would also be a symbol of his
power. When he died almost thirty years later, he had spent a total of
only ten weeks at Chambord, hunting and supervising the ongoing
construction, which would continue for almost 200 years.

According to rumor, François I kept the *Mona Lisa* in his bath-
room at Chambord. While there is no evidence that the king
brought the painting to Chambord to adorn any room, *Mona Lisa*
would indeed arrive at the château in August 1939. Another long-
held belief, this one more likely, is that the château's double-helix
central staircase was either designed or influenced by da Vinci,
who lived in nearby Blois during his stay in France under Francois'
patronage.

In the 250 years following François' death, the château fell out of
royal favor and into such a condition of neglect that, in 1679, Colbert

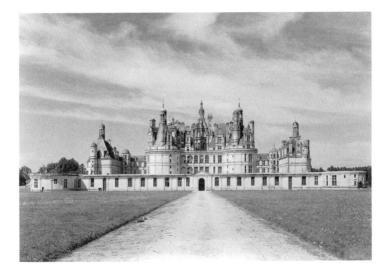

CHÂTEAU DE CHAMBORD

wrote that it was "in a pitiful state, without doors, without windows, without windowpanes... it rained everywhere." Louis XIV brought Chambord up to standard and spent more time there than any other French king; an invitation by the Sun King to be part of a royal trip from Versailles to Chambord was a sign of high social standing.

In 1743, Louis XV gave soldier Maurice de Saxe the title of Maréchal (Marshal) as a reward for his military prowess. Two years later the grateful king gave him Chambord. The château—minus some of its furnishings—subsequently survived the French Revolution as well as a battle with the Prussians in December 1870, though the castle's southwestern wall would forever after bear the scars of the scuffle. The château moved from one owner to another until it came under the control of the French government in 1915; ownership followed in 1930. By then, it was one of the top tourist attractions in France.

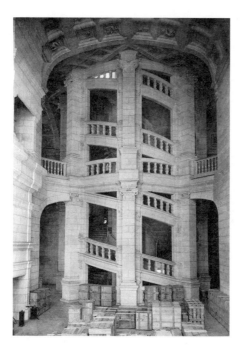

"DA VINCI" STAIRCASE AT CHAMBORD WITH EVACUATED CRATES

Just a few years later, Chambord was identified as the primary storage depot for the French national museums' art in the event of war. Only several hours from Paris, it was close enough for coordination and movement of staff, yet far enough from high-profile military targets, including not only Paris but also industrial sites, urban centers and major transportation hubs. And with its many rooms, it seemed at first glance to offer almost unlimited storage capacity. By the mid-1930s, it had been decided that Chambord would serve not only as a main depot and administrative center but also as a stopping point for all works evacuated from Paris. They would stop here to be checked in, then those destined for other châteaux would be sent on their way.

But a majestic Renaissance palace does not necessarily lend itself easily to serving as a working museum storage depot. During the years of preparation for war, planners raised repeated concerns about both the structure and condition of the château in terms of its adequacy for art storage. In March 1937, art historian Philippe Stern told Jaujard that its dangers far exceeded any advantages: not only was it highly visible from the air due to its isolation, but its low doors, many steps and narrow passages would cause significant problems of access and movement.

In August 1938, in anticipation of war, Pierre Schommer visited Chambord with the Musées Nationaux's chief architect. Upon his return to Paris, Schommer filed a five-page report detailing the château's shortcomings. Among them: the gateway leading to the château's main entrance was too narrow for large trucks. Trucks would need to be unloaded outside the entrance, an operation that would be time-consuming and even more difficult in the event of rain. The turns of the spiral da Vinci staircase were impractical for bringing artworks upstairs, he said, and would risk damage to the historical staircase itself, while some floors would have to be braced to support heavy loads. Fire protection and security arrangements were inadequate.

But those concerns paled in comparison to the sixteen-page report Schommer wrote shortly after the 1938 evacuation, in which he reiterated his previous concerns about the old castle and its staircase in stronger terms and voiced a litany of new ones. The spiral staircase, he said, was difficult and time-consuming to use during the day and even more so at night. Moreover, he noted, in terms not unsimilar to Colbert's words of 1689:

Chambord is a building in poor condition: where there are shutters, there are no windows; where there are windowpanes, there are no locks. When there is a door, there is no lock, and if there is one, one push of the door is enough to open it. An exterior door is open, but if you ask for the key, you are given a cartful of four hundred rusty keys to choose from. If you think a door has been well secured, you will discover [otherwise].

Not only were there structural concerns, Schommer indicated, there were also numerous security concerns, among them:

Indeed, a greater danger at Chambord is the multiplicity of rooms at varying levels, its secret cupboards and hidden staircases (74 of them). They form veritable labyrinths, susceptible of hiding intruders in spite of the most rigorous surveillance, and to reach [these places], there are two principal points of entry: the ground floor of the north façade and the wall of the southeast courtine.... Moonless nights would be particularly useful for such activities.

Schommer went on to warn of the heightened risk of theft since it was no longer a secret that Chambord was the main depot. In addition, he said, the town of Saint-Pierre-des-Corps, fifty miles away, could draw German planes. Chambord was only five miles from the easily identifiable Loire and the castle itself was also an easy-to-spot target given its immense whiteness against the surrounding open lawns and forests. In addition, he said, it would be difficult to heat "this glacier" with electric radiators. It was too visible in every way, he said, too apparent to the public. And, he noted, there were significant fire risks that could not be eliminated. Lastly, he added that one of the guards was an alcoholic whose friends considered him dangerous. Nevertheless, at the very end of the report, he stated that if the museum administration divided the artworks among several depots, Chambord could, in his opinion, serve as a way station from which artworks could be directed to their final destinations.

I n the end, for the great evacuation of 1939, the museum admin-istration used Chambord both as a way station and as a storage depot. The château was closed to the public as of August 27 and the following day, convoys began the hundred-mile trip southwest from Paris. During the course of the war, Chambord would shelter more than 2,500 crates of art, antiquities, archives, books and other items, by 1944 comprising over 141,000 cubic feet, the most of any depot. The depot would hold items not only from the Louvre but also from other national and provincial museums and libraries.

But only a tenth of the Louvre items that arrived would stay; the rest were rerouted to other destinations after being veri-fied by Schommer. Chambord retained only a small percentage of the Louvre's paintings, including the Delacroix ceiling, but it stored almost the entire collection of drawings plus a collection of prints donated to the museum by Edmond de Rothschild in 1935. Chambord also sheltered the Louvre's archives and its library as well as a collection of three-dimensional models of fortified cities that had been created, for the most part under Louis XIV, for military purposes. Everything else from the Louvre was sent on to other châteaux, three of them nearby (Cheverny, Fougères-sur-Bièvre and Valençay) and five others (Louvigny, Courtalain, Chèreperrine, La Pelice and Aillières) clustered one hundred miles to the north-west. Trucks made their way through one small village after another, drawing curious onlookers. Was an army coming through, perhaps, or a theater company? "It's a circus!" exclaimed someone within earshot of one of the convoy's guards. The guard, sworn to secrecy like all the others, responded, "It's true, it is a circus, and under the largest tarp, we're hiding a giraffe."

The antiquities went primarily to Fougères, Courtalain and Cheverny, except for the larger Greek and Roman items, which went to Valençay, along with the Louvre's engravings, items from the

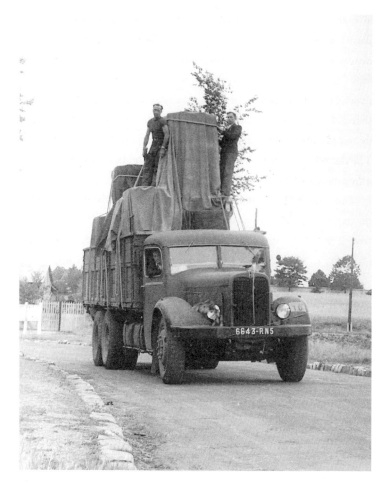

ARTWORK ON THE MOVE

Department of Asiatic Arts and about half the objets d'art, including the crown jewels.

The museum's paintings were spread among La Pelice, Louvigny, Chèreperrine, Aillières and Chambord. La Pelice and Louvigny initially held the largest share, with the very large unrolled works at Louvigny; the large, rolled paintings went to Chèreperrine. The paintings were distributed among multiple châteaux to spread the risk; however, they were clustered relatively near each other to allow staff to move among the depots, to allow easy movement of the paintings for restoration and, in many cases, to open them for conservation purposes, since certain paintings needed to be exposed to light periodically so that the colors would not darken.

Many of the items that arrived at Chambord stayed less than a day, just enough time to be verified; others stayed a bit longer. Some of the Egyptian antiquities would stay a month before moving on to Courtalain and some of the paintings—including the *Mona Lisa*—remained while improvements were being made at Louvigny.

After the scenery trailer with the *Raft of the Medusa* was waylaid in Versailles, the rest of the convoy had continued toward Chambord, inching through the night without lights in case of German bombing. When it reached the banks of the Loire, where a thick fog had set in, the convoy leader stopped to count the trucks and realized that the one carrying the works by Antoine Watteau was missing. He sent staff member Magdeleine Hours in search of the missing truck and driver. She found them near the riverbank; in the darkness and the fog, the driver had followed the tail light of a bicycle that had inserted itself between two trucks in the convoy.

When the convoy finally reached Chambord in the pre-dawn hours of the following day, everyone there was sleeping except the exhausted Schommer, who had been awake since the previous dawn. Since every one of the few beds in the castle was occupied, Hours was directed to a cot in a vast gallery lit only by a flashlight. As soon as she turned it off, a terrible racket echoed through the room as dozens of bats began to swarm. When she got up to drag the bed into a nearby hallway, she spotted a ray of light under a door. Under normal circumstances, she never would have disturbed whoever was in the room, but this was war, she reasoned. It turned out to be Lucie Mazauric, the Louvre's archivist. When Hours began to explain what happened, Mazauric interrupted, saying simply, "Let's share my bed and get some sleep," adding an expression born of a country that had already known much war: *"A la guerre comme à la guerre"*—effectively, we'll make do with what we have.

And making do was necessary for the museum staff at Chambord, as they settled into unfamiliar and often uncomfortable quarters after being pulled away from home by the commitment to serve their art and, in a number of cases, pulled away from loved ones who had marched off to war. In Mazauric's case, her husband André Chamson, assistant curator at Versailles, had just been called to active military duty and they had put their young daughter in the care of Mazauric's mother in southern France. Mazauric chose to help out at Chambord, joining Pierre Schommer and his wife as well as Jacqueline Bouchot-Saupique, an art historian and professor at the École du Louvre who also served as Jaujard's assistant during the war. Several other staff members were also at the depot along with more than thirty guards.

In the first weeks of their stay, the staff slept on makeshift bedding in the château. But the largely unfurnished, unheated, damp and partly dilapidated castle offered no hope of providing adequate winter lodging for the personnel, and, in many cases, their families. The women were sent to scour nearby villages for possible lodging. Arduous searches and the help of parish priests, local mayors and policemen managed to locate simple quarters—for the most part small, sparse and uncomfortable—in hotels and rooms in the village of Chambord, plus some in Bracieux, almost four miles away, to and from which most workers had to walk or bicycle each day. A canteen for single guards was set up in the rectory of the local church.

While Mazauric got to work unpacking and organizing the contents of the displaced Louvre archives and library, Pierre Schommer continued to welcome and process the waves of incoming convoys, painstakingly verifying each load and then reconfiguring drivers and trucks arriving from diverse locations into new convoys that would bring items to their final locations. For the items that were to stay at Chambord, the staff had to open crates to take inventory and, in many cases, to unpack them. The men had to heave full crates from one place to another to create a semblance of organization, and negotiate the difficulties—as Schommer had predicted—of the da Vinci staircase to haul items upstairs.

Schommer had allowed the staff to choose their workspaces; in a castle of 400-plus rooms, they had no shortage of choices. Lucie Mazauric chose the former dining room of the Maréchal de Saxe. The first day, she happily set herself up at the room's huge marble table that provided a workspace far larger than she could ever have hoped for at the Louvre. That night she decided to read about the château, only to learn that, upon the maréchal's death in 1750, his diseased body had been autopsied on that very table. Early the next day, she quickly gathered up her belongings and moved to another room.

Once the rerouting to other depots was complete and the staff had organized the depot, they turned their attention to ongoing safety measures, such as testing the fire protection equipment, and to art preservation, including measures such as verifying humidity levels, removing items from crates that needed aeration and opening crates containing still-packed paintings, drawings and engravings to be sure the works were not being damaged by insects, dampness or other problems. This was no easy task since many crates contained numerous pieces, often in separate compartments, and there were multiple layers of packing material. For these inspections, a specialist traveled from one depot to another to oversee the unpacking and repacking.

On October 15, Schommer wrote to Jaujard with concern about the cryptically described contents of a "non-numbered case from the Louvre's painting collections to which you called my attention upon its arrival at Chambord and which was labeled LP0 according to your instructions." Schommer had been observing the unnamed case for four or five days, he said, and was certain that the temperature and dampness were damaging it. A safer place was needed to store the item, he said; either a vault in the Banque de France in the town of Blois, where the crown jewels had been sent during the 1938 evacuation, or perhaps the depot at either Louvigny or Chèreperrine. Four days later, he wrote urgently to René Huyghe, the head curator of the Louvre's Department of Paintings: "I have no doubt; the wood is moving . . . . If you cannot respond immediately, I will deposit the precious package in the vault of the Banque de France, where the climatological conditions are much . . . better than in the middle of my forest. She awaits your decision."

Jaujard decided it was time to move Chambord's most honored guest to the depot in Louvigny, a tiny village of less than 200 people; the *Mona Lisa* and certain other works were to have gone there sooner, but the château had been undergoing upgrades to provide better protection. Considerably more care was taken for the *Mona Lisa*'s new transfer than in the fall of 1516, when Leonardo first brought her to France. As for her 1938 trip to the Loire and for her transfer to Chambord in August 1939, she would travel to Louvigny in her special case. On November 14, 1939 she traveled again in a convoy, this time consisting of an escort vehicle, a specially equipped truck for the painting, and a back-up vehicle. The truck had been fitted with an ambulance stretcher attached to the vehicle by an elastic suspension as an improvised shock absorber. As the depot staff circled around the truck, *Mona Lisa* was carefully secured to the stretcher and Schommer climbed aboard next to her, feeling that for safety's sake, he should ride alongside. The back of the truck was then hermetically sealed to prevent humidity along the way and the convoy set off on its 125-mile journey. When it arrived at Louvigny, Schommer was almost unconscious from lack of air.

The *Mona Lisa* was set into her new home, an armoire in the château's *petit salon*, and Pierre Schommer returned to Chambord, turning his attention to caring for the items there and overseeing the depots at Cheverny and Fougères-sur-Bièvre. Schommer had to travel to these depots by bicycle. With Cheverny a seven-mile ride and Fougères-sur-Bièvre seventeen miles away, this was brisk exercise even in pleasant weather; winter was another story. During the winter of 1943–1944, he would write: "The other day, riding towards Fougères [from Cheverny], I was so drenched by melting snow and so frozen by the headwind that it was certainly due to the charity and cup of boiling tea provided by the Haugs [Cheverny curator and his wife] that I avoided bronchitis." No amount of tea could have fortified him, however, as he made his rounds during the frigid, almost record-setting winter of 1939–1940, during which temperatures plummeted to −4 degrees Fahrenheit.

Though France and England had declared war against Germany on September 3, 1939, neither nation went on the offensive; instead they waited to see what the Germans would do. On September 27, Hitler convened his military leaders and informed them he had decided to attack as soon as possible. But then he reconsidered, issuing fourteen postponements throughout the fall and winter, during which no significant land-based military activity was conducted in Europe by either side, leading the U.S. and England to call it the "phony war" and the French, the *drôle de guerre*. The unnaturally calm situation would stretch into the spring of 1940. Then life would turn upside down.

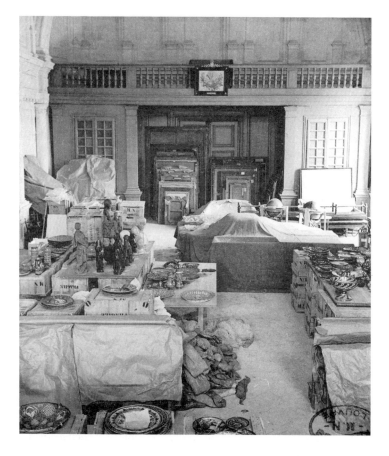

CHAMBORD CHAPEL WITH STORED ART

# SEVEN

# CHEVERNY

A FIFTEEN-MINUTE DRIVE from the entrance to the Chambord forest, the regal château de Cheverny was built in the 1600s by the Hurault family to replace a sixteenth-century half-medieval fortress, half-pleasure palace that had in turn replaced buildings going back to the year 1315. In 1528, the owner of the earlier château, also a member of the Hurault family, had to give it up for financial reasons. It was eventually acquired in 1551 by Diane de Poitiers, the mistress of Henri II, who had given her possession of the beautiful Loire Valley Chenonceau château four years earlier. Diane had several good reasons to want a home such as Cheverny. There was ongoing litigation about her right to use Chenonceau and she wanted another residence in the area until the matter was resolved in order to better keep an eye on her rival, Henri's wife Catherine de Medici. After the litigation was resolved in her favor in 1555, Cheverny remained her home base while she oversaw reconstruction at Chenonceau. In 1565, five years after losing Chenonceau to her rival upon Henri's death, Diane sold Cheverny back to descendants of the Huraults, the original owners. In the early 1600s, they razed the structure to construct a new,

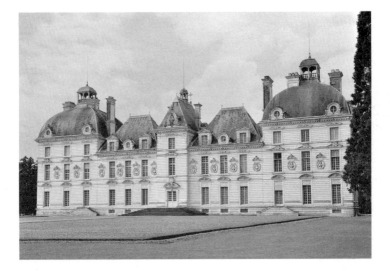

CHÂTEAU DE CHEVERNY

elegant château of local white stone, flanked with two large, square-domed pavilions.

Eventually, heirs once again sold the château to outsiders; then in 1825, it was once again repurchased by a member of the family and luxuriously furnished with antiques to match the elegant fireplaces, painted paneling and ceiling beams.

In 1922, the owners opened the château's grounds and certain rooms to the public, one of the first private châteaux in France to do so. In 1939, the family put part of the château and several outbuildings at the disposition of the Musées Nationaux, a decision the owner, the marquis de Vibraye, may have begun to rue when depot workers damaged stone steps of the château's main staircase and tiles of the vestibule's classic black and white floor while moving crates.

Ninety-one crates arrived at Cheverny from the Louvre's Department of Near Eastern Antiquities, plus 352 crates from the Department of Greek and Roman Antiquities. One item was too

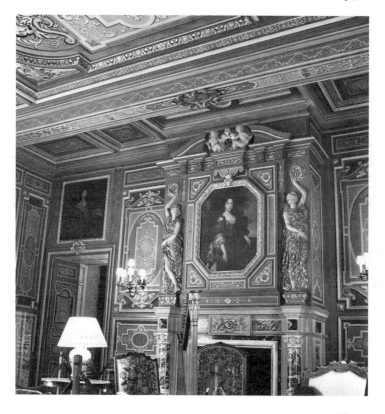

GRAND SALON AT CHEVERNY, USED FOR MUSÉES NATIONAUX STORAGE

big to bring into the château: a 13-foot-high crate containing the almost 3,000-year-old Babylonian law code engraved on a stone stele. When workers could not fit the crate though the château's small doors, it was taken to Valençay.

More than 400 additional crates arrived from the Cluny and Camondo museums, the Musée des Arts Décoratifs and from other public institutions. Some items were brought down to the château's basements, while others were dispersed among four ground-floor rooms, including the sumptuous formal drawing room, the *grand salon*.

The items least vulnerable to dampness went to outbuildings, including a former orangerie that the marquis had only recently turned into a small hunting museum whose walls sported the antlers of two thousand stags in commemoration of Cheverny's long hunting tradition.

The marquis also ceded rooms in the château for the lodging of the two curators and the head guard plus their families. Eighteen additional guards were lodged in outbuildings. Outside work hours, the guards filled their time growing vegetables and raising chickens and rabbits as well as painting and wallpapering their simple quarters and decorating them with posters and etchings. But work hours were a more serious matter, and there were strict security procedures, as at all the depots. At each depot, sentinels were to stand guard day and night, with attention to nighttime security, when potential intruders trying to approach from the surrounding woods of the countryside châteaux could not easily be seen. To address this concern, instructions indicated that guards were to be stationed close by each château and accompanied by dogs, the instructions noting that "[a] dog that barks is worth at least three sentinels. This does not mean a police dog, any noisy dog will do just fine." And if a nighttime intruder were to be spotted, the instructions were quite clear: "Shoot on sight."

Although Cheverny was a popular tourist destination on the Loire château circuit, the marquis de Vibraye had agreed to suspend public visits when the artwork and antiquities arrived in 1939. But by spring 1940, as the *drôle de guerre* stretched on, he reconsidered, writing to Jaujard on April 18 that he had invested considerable sums of money in Cheverny and more than five years of construction and publicity to attract the public. The château should be partially reopened to them, said the marquis, because life was returning to normal. He spoke a bit too soon. Just over two months later, German soldiers would be at the front door.

# EIGHT

# COURTALAIN

B Y THE THIRTEENTH century, there was already a small, fortified castle in the tiny village of Courtalain, with a tower to shelter the lord of the domain in case of attack, quarters for his men and a tribunal for doling out justice to his vassals. In 1483 the medieval château, ruined by the Hundred Years War and other battles, was replaced with a newer one that was ravaged in 1586 during the French religious wars. The castle was again rebuilt, then expanded and renovated over the subsequent centuries, including the ironic nineteenth-century addition of a new medieval-style tower.

In the sixteenth century, the château and its five hundred acres of land came into the hands of the noble Montmorency family, and in 1862 to Louis de Gontaut-Biron, when he married the niece of the last duke of Montmorency. In 1939, Louis's descendant Marquis Arnaud de Gontaut-Biron offered the use of part of his château to the Musées Nationaux. Trucks of art and antiquities began arriving on September 6. More than half of the 400-plus crates that arrived that fall contained items from the Louvre's Department of Egyptian Antiquities, among them the Seated Scribe, the Stele of the Serpent King and the bas-relief Goddess Hathor Welcomes Sethos I. Crates came also from

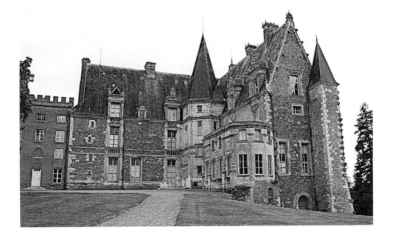

CHÂTEAU DE COURTALAIN

the Musée Malmaison, the École des Beaux-Arts and from several private collections. The treasures were lodged in the *grand salon* and in several basement rooms. Charles Boreux, depot head and curator of the Louvre's Department of Egyptian antiquities, was lodged in the château, as was his assistant, while eight guards and their families were provided furnished rooms in other buildings on the property.

As at other depots, once the items had arrived, the staff settled in to watch over them and, above all, take precautions against the primary risk: fire. The depot head at Courtalain had obtained fire extinguishers and hand pumps and made arrangements with the local fire department to use its motorized pump and men, if needed. In case of fire, they could draw water from the nearby viaduct. While the water from the viaduct was almost limitless, they worried that it was also a potential target for enemy aircraft—and lay only one-half mile from the château. They also worried about the fact that, as the closest depot to Paris, Courtalain would be at early risk from approaching Germans. The following spring, both fears would be well justified.

# NINE

---

# VALENÇAY

THE SMALL LOIRE Valley town of Valençay is well-known for its cheese—a chèvre pyramid with its tip removed, the shape created, it is said, to avoid insulting Napoleon when he dined at the château of Valençay on his return trip from Egypt, defeated. But the town is also known for the Renaissance château itself, a majestic stone structure of domes, towers, arches and 100 rooms, surrounded by expansive lawns and miles of forest. During World War II, the château would host not only some of the Louvre's greatest masterpieces, but also Resistance fighters, thousands of fleeing French and, late in the war, Nazis with machine guns who wanted to burn the château to the ground and who left death in their wake.

A Gallo-Roman villa sat on the site in ancient times, then a medieval fortress at the turn of the first millennium which was later replaced in the 1540s with a Renaissance pleasure palace, as were many other French medieval castles. By the seventeenth century, it had gained a reputation as one of France's most splendid noble residences.

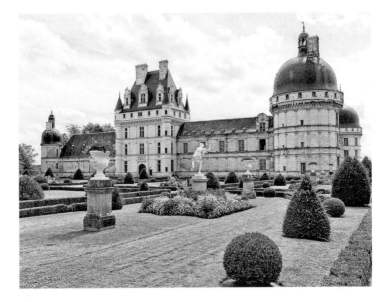

CHÂTEAU DE VALENÇAY

Napoleon's foreign minister at the turn of the nineteenth century was Duke Charles-Maurice de Talleyrand. The writer Stendhal noted that "the supreme happiness of M. de Talleyrand was to reunite a million [francs] and to spend it." The duke made his most spectacular purchase—the château de Valençay—in 1803, just after he negotiated the sale of the territory of Louisiana to the United States on Napoleon's behalf and purportedly received a large bonus. For the then-staggering sum of 1.6 million francs, Talleyrand purchased the château and its more than forty square miles of property spread across twenty-three villages and towns—one of the largest private properties in all of France. Talleyrand entertained there on a grand scale. Legislators, dignitaries and other guests arrived by a plane tree lined approach lit with candles and torches, and feasted on delicacies prepared by renowned chef Marie-Antoine Carême. After a visit in March 1834, the writer George Sand described the château and its grounds as one of the most beautiful places on earth. She also described it as an oasis, which it had been for 400 years—and would continue to be until the fall of France in the spring of 1940, after which it would be anything but.

By the 1930s, the château had come into the hands of Talleyrand's great-great-great nephew Duke Boson de Talleyrand-Périgord, also called the duc de Valençay. As the German threat loomed in the late 1930s, the duke offered to shelter some of the Louvre's artworks. Like other châtelains, the duke may have hoped to better protect his château by offering its use to the Musées Nationaux, but he also had another reason to believe it might be safe. He also held the Germanic title of Prince de Sagan by virtue of land holdings in Polish Silesia and, since the time of Louis XV, Sagan-owned property had been considered neutral territory by the Germans. If the museum administration felt reassured by the connection, it was a false sense of security; later in the war, the duke would consider a sale of his title and his "principality" to Hermann Göring, Hitler's second in command.

Valençay offered many strong points as a depot. Surrounded by countryside and at the edge of a vast forest—and thus away from main roads or industrial areas that might draw military activity—the château also had many spacious, high-ceilinged rooms perfect for depot use, including a *grand salon* stretching almost half the width of the château. It even had a hidden vault, which would later prove to be an important stroke of luck. Carle Dreyfus, curator of the Louvre's Département des Objets d'art, was appointed head of the depot, assisted by Jean Cassou. The two men could not have been more different. Dreyfus, age 64 at the start of the war, was born

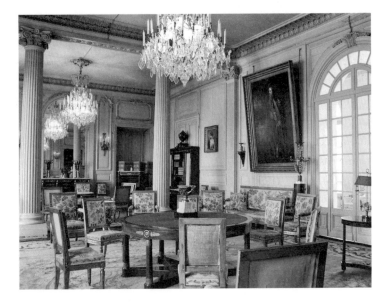

*GRAND SALON* AT VALENÇAY, USED FOR ART
STORAGE DURING THE WAR

into a family of art collectors with one of the most famous Parisian collections. He was a stately gentleman, an "old-time Parisian, extremely elegant." Cassou, age 42, was born in Spain to a French father and a Spanish mother. His father died when Cassou was 16, after which his family fell upon hard times. While doing odd jobs to support his family, he earned a degree from a Paris school. A writer, translator and art critic with outspoken political views that would be his undoing during World War II, he became part of the French civil service in 1923 and eventually went into the fine arts section of the French museum administration.

Throughout the *drôle de guerre*, Dreyfus and Cassou enjoyed a calm château life watching over the works at Valençay. When not working, they enjoyed the Loire Valley as did the other depot curators, visiting the grand châteaux as tourists had done before the war, only now they had the privilege of having friends and colleagues living there. And with the war's severe food shortages still to come, they also enjoyed the gastronomic specialties of the area.

Everything changed quickly in the spring of 1940 when German troops closed in on the French border. Life for those at the château at Valençay—and for those at all the other depots—was about to change as well.

# PART
# III

# EXODUS, ART AND OCCUPIERS

*Spring 1940 to Fall 1942*

## TEN

────────────────

# EXODUS

I N THEIR LONG years of preparation for another war with Germany, the French had focused on a single strategic object-ive: deflecting a ground attack from the German border by constructing the Maginot Line, a series of massive concrete fortifica-tions, tunnels and other defenses along the French-German border from which the enemy had surged in World War I. The line was not extended northwest along the French-Belgian border, however, since Belgium was neutral, friendly territory and because France's military strategists believed the dense Ardennes forests and moun-tains along the border between the two countries—and the Meuse River just beyond—formed a natural barrier to an effective attack.

In May 1940, the massive investment in the Maginot Line quickly became worthless as the Germans simply swung north of it into Belgium, then pushed unexpectedly through the dense forests and rough terrain of the Ardennes forest into France. The French then destroyed the bridges across the nearby Meuse River in the belief that the river's deep valleys and steep banks would halt the Germans. They were mistaken there as well. In mid-May, in the midst of heavy combat around the town of Sedan, the Germans successfully crossed the river in rubber boats, erected pontoon bridges and began to roll endless numbers of Panzer tanks across the river. It was the beginning of the end for the defense of France. The battle in and around Sedan was particularly ironic since it was the same location where Napoleon III had been captured in 1870 in the battle that had essentially decided the war in favor of Prussia.

During the night of May 14–15, the battle of the Meuse was lost and a breach fifty miles wide opened in the French line; the road to Paris was unprotected. The next day, the military governor of Paris called Prime Minister Paul Reynaud to say that he could not guarantee the security of the French government after May 16 at midnight and suggested that the government evacuate, with the exception of ministers responsible for national defense. On May 16, political leaders decided against an immediate evacuation, but the Ministry of Foreign Affairs on the quai d'Orsay frantically began hurling archives out the windows into a giant bonfire in the court-yard. The column of smoke was visible from the nearby Louvre.

The French museum administration was closely monitoring developments. Nobody knew how fierce a battle for Paris might be, how far it would extend, and what risks an air war might entail for the Loire châteaux, only minutes from Paris by air. They also could not predict what damage the Germans might inflict through either intentional attack or collateral damage when they reached the Loire itself. It was evident the treasures of the Louvre in the storage depots were at serious, imminent risk and that they had to be moved yet again—and fast.

In some ways, the new evacuation plan that was quickly developed was similar to that of the previous summer. Items would leave based on the same priority lists, their sorting facilitated by the colored markings already attached to each crate. For security, the vehicles would again travel in convoys, each with multiple escort vehicles. And, like the previous summer, once a convoy emptied its contents at a new depot, the empty trucks would return to load the next run.

But there were also crucial differences from the previous evacuation. The last plan had been honed over almost a decade; there had been plenty of time to evaluate potential depots, select which artworks would go where, pack them all carefully and at least try to arrange enough staff, supplies, vehicles and fuel. However, this new plan had to be created and executed within just days, given the unexpected breach of the French border and the speed with which the Germans were driving towards Paris. Moreover, during the first evacuation, the roads had been relatively calm. This time they were clogged with millions of refugees in flight from Belgium and northern France.

The hard reality for the Louvre administration was that there was simply not enough manpower or transport available to move the many thousands of items in the Loire storage depots and some items were considered too fragile or cumbersome to move again under current road conditions. They had to make tough and fast choices as to what was most important of what had already been determined to be the most precious. It was decided that the Louvre items at Louvigny, Aillières, Chèreperrine and La Pelice and as many as possible of those at Courtalain would be moved to the isolated Loc-Dieu Abbey in France's southwest, eighty miles northeast of Toulouse.

However, the very large paintings still on their frames could not be moved across the long and partially mountainous route to Loc-Dieu. Road conditions were deteriorating by the hour, the same utility wire issue that had plagued the trips to the Loire was problematic, and the scenery trailers that had been used before were designed only for traveling short distances around Paris, not for traversing the steep hills of southwest France. The museum administration decided that, under the circumstances, these large paintings would be centralized at the château de Sources, deep in the countryside 125 miles southwest of Paris, not far from Le Mans. Four notable exceptions, however, would be brought south to Loc-Dieu in spite of their size: *Wedding Feast at Cana*, David's *Coronation of Napoleon*, plus Gros's *Napoleon Visiting the Plague Stricken at Jaffa* and his *Battle of Eylau*. Museum officials felt that these works, either taken by Napoleon (*Cana*) or depicting Napoleon's battles, might be of particular interest to the Germans.

Delicate pastels and drawings would stay at Chambord; Venus de Milo and the other large ancient sculptures would remain at Valençay. The antiquities at Cheverny would remain in place and the most precious Egyptian antiquities would be moved from Courtalain to the château of Saint-Blancard in the deep southwest, fifty miles west of Toulouse.

On Wednesday May 29, Jaujard met with Germain Bazin, assistant curator of the Louvre's Department of Paintings (René Huyghe, the chief curator, was away on military duty), and Albert Henraux, president of the art acquisition organization, Société des Amis du Louvre, and an escort of multiple convoys during the 1939 evacuation. They crafted a painfully tight timetable and gave the order to the Loire depot heads: Start packing the most important masterpieces immediately so that they would be on the road by Sunday or Monday at the latest. Preparation began within hours.

There was a serious shortage of personnel to properly wrap, pack, check and load it all in such a short period of time, particularly with so many men having been called off to war. Many Louvre guards who had returned to Paris during the *drôle de guerre* returned once again to the Loire and soldiers were begged and borrowed from nearby barracks.

There was also a severe shortage of fuel and trucks due to military requisitions. To help compensate for the shortage, some museum staff drove their personal vehicles, including Jacqueline Bouchot-Saupique, École du Louvre professor and Jaujard's acting assistant. She shuttled between Paris and Chambord so many times to evacuate additional items that her car tires became thin as paper, causing the Chambord staff to watch in anguish each time she left for yet another return trip.

Drivers were also hard to come by, partly due to the number of men who had been mobilized and partly because, in an era when many people got around by bicycle or motorbike, not a single guard knew how to drive a car. On June 1, Louvre Egyptologist Christine Desroches Noblecourt headed a two-truck convoy from the Loire to Saint-Blancard with a first load of the most precious Egyptian antiquities that had been stored at Courtalain, including the Seated Scribe, the Stele of the Serpent King and the frieze Goddess Hathor Welcomes King Sethos I. Jaujard had told her: "I'm giving you two partially tarp-covered trucks and two drivers. Make do with that; it's all I can do." But two trucks were not nearly enough and they were both too small; Desroches Noblecourt had to shuttle between the Loire and Saint-Blancard three times, each one-way trip covering over 400 miles and crossing almost half the country. As the trucks returned from the second drop off, they were almost hit by a bomb attack along the way. By the third trip, the convoy was moving between enemy lines. In the end, many of the antiquities would have to stay at Courtalain.

Germain Bazin, who was on military leave recuperating from knee surgery, cancelled his treatments so he could travel to the Loire to help out. He ended up driving, ignoring his still-unhealed injury.

Lucie Mazauric bravely drove an escort vehicle in the difficult road conditions, having just passed her driving exam days before.

There were rare instances of less courageous Louvre staff. At one point, Jaujard asked a curator to retrieve some artworks from a museum not far from a combat area. When the curator refused to go, Jaujard replied, "Since the noise from the cannons frightens you so much, I'll go myself." Jean Cassou offered to go instead in order to allow Jaujard to continue supervising the evacuation. Elsewhere, the head of the La Pelice depot fled with his family, leaving behind some of the Louvre's masterpieces in the sole care of a young Louvre staff member. But when trucks arrived to take some items to Louvigny in preparation for the move south, even she had left, leaving nobody at all to protect the paintings.

In the early afternoon of Monday, June 3, 1940, German bombs fell on the outer arrondissements of Paris, killing 254 people, injuring 652 and terrifying the remaining Parisians who watched several hundred enemy warplanes roar across the city's skies. As the bombs fell, an armed convoy carrying the *Mona Lisa* and other highest-priority artwork was already heading south, having left Louvigny at 7 o'clock that morning.

The first scheduled stop for the convoy was at La Ferté Bernard, only twenty-seven miles from Louvigny. But between a truck breakdown and the crowds on the road, the trip took almost four hours, a worrisome delay for an invaluable cargo on roads that might be bombed at any moment. The convoy finally reached its next scheduled stop, at Chambord, later in the day.

The convoy left Chambord at 6 p.m., heading to its next stop via a shortcut known to one of the convoy's escorts. But two-thirds of the way along, the head driver became confused and they went the wrong way. When they realized the error, the entire convoy had to turn around, truck by truck, adding another half-hour delay. The head of the convoy, holding his temper, took over the lead and they set off once more.

The trucks arrived at Châteauroux, still 200 miles north of Loc-Dieu, at 10:30 p.m., having taken 4½ hours to cover the sixty miles from Chambord. The delay had not just been due to the traffic and the missed turn; the convoy had also needed to stop periodically to check the ropes and strapping holding the crates in place, since the convoy had been less than meticulously loaded in the urgency to get it on the road. In Châteauroux, the trucks were parked on the grounds of a château and a convoy member camouflaged them and assigned sentinels. The crew headed off in search of food, only to find that every café and restaurant was closed for the night. They finally found a military canteen that gave them some canned food, and the crew managed to eat, after a fashion, shortly after midnight.

The following morning, the men were still quite tired and unhappy from the previous evening. It did not improve matters when their departure was delayed for an hour due to a bomb alert. Then, as they finally began to assemble the convoy, a truck became hooked onto the gate of the property, delaying their departure yet again.

The *Mona Lisa* and the rest of the convoy spent all that day and the next lumbering southward. The gentle hills of the Loire were behind them and more difficult terrain lay ahead. The steep slopes of high plateaux and tight curves of mountainous roads taxed the heavily loaded vehicles and required numerous stops to allow the overheated vehicles to cool down and to check the strapping that was holding the priceless loads in place. At one point, they noticed that the crates atop one truck were almost toppling at every bend in the road and that some of the hastily fastened strapping had become almost completely frayed due to friction from all the bouncing around—a particular worry since this was the truck containing the *Mona Lisa*. There was no extra material with which to resecure the load; all the convoy leader could do was to have the drivers slow down and down-gear more on each descent. When they reached that night's stop he managed to arrange extra strapping for the next morning.

In total, the trip took three long, exhausting days. The convoy with *Mona Lisa* finally arrived at Loc-Dieu at 5 p.m. on June 6. The following day, the staff unloaded the nine trucks, and on June 8 at 4 a.m., the empty vehicles headed back to the Loire for the next round of artworks.

The carefully orchestrated timetable had begun to fall apart from its inception. The first convoy had almost missed its critical departure date after a worker was seriously injured loading a forklift onto a truck to bring it to another depot, resulting in a dozen men being diverted from other tasks to load trucks manually. Once the convoy got underway, it had been plagued by road conditions, mechanical problems and the consequences of the hasty packing. The delays were particularly worrisome since pressure to complete the evacuations became more urgent by the day as the Germans came ever closer. On June 5, the evacuation of La Pelice was accelerated after it was concluded that its location was particularly at risk, a decision justified soon afterwards when bombs landed on the château's grounds. On June 8 came news that the Germans had crossed the Seine, further accelerating the operation's urgency. The situation became even more complicated on June 10, when Italy declared war on France. For security reasons, several Italian truck drivers had to be replaced in spite of the dire shortage of drivers, and increased fears were raised for the safety of paintings of Italian origin and the works depicting Napoleon.

The pace of the evacuation was also hindered by the ragtag array of old trucks, half of which were gas-powered, the other half slow, diesel-fueled ones. The disparity made it impossible to keep a convoy moving at a constant speed, which caused large gaps between vehicles, allowing other fleeing vehicles to slip into the middle of a convoy. Putting the slower diesel vehicles in front only served to overheat the gas-powered vehicles bringing up the rear, causing their brakes to slip and necessitating frequent stops for repairs.

On June 11, a strange, thick cloud of black soot hung low over the city of Paris, cloaking a brilliant blue sky. Some thought it was an enemy tactic to mask their entrance into the city; others thought city authorities had set off a smoke screen to assist residents in fleeing unseen. Still others thought the French government had arranged it so that they could flee unseen themselves. In fact, it was smoke from fires French authorities had ignited the previous day to eliminate suburban petroleum depots so they would not fall into enemy hands. Agnès Humbert, an art historian at the Musée National des Arts et Traditions Populaires, made her way through the soot that day to the Louvre, where Jaujard had convened staff from the Paris-area museums under his command to accompany a last convoy heading to the Loire with additional books from museum libraries, archival material and other items, plus the personal effects of the staff. In spite of the soot, Humbert said, Paris had never looked more beautiful. She wrote of the morning in her journal:

The Cour du Carrousel looks as if it is ready for a flower show. I gaze at it from the office of the Director of the Musées Nationaux, where we have all gathered, suitcases in hand. We talk in low voices, as though in the presence of death. M. Jaujard moves from one group to another, so calm and controlled. I hear him say: 'I would like my Jewish colleagues to leave first.' The trucks are in the courtyard. We take our places in them, invited to do so by our director with the same unruffled cordiality, the same attentiveness to every detail, the same encouraging smile for each of us as he hands us our evacuation orders . . . . With our spirits lifted and our minds almost at peace, we leave Paris for the château de Chambord.

The vehicles headed off towards the Loire as the soot was carried away by a strong wind, leaving a brilliantly sunny day behind. The same day, the second convoy of artworks left the Loire for Loc-Dieu with five trucks jammed with art, plus two escort vehicles and a truck with extra gas.

In the early morning of June 14, a third convoy left the Loire. The museum administration thought it would likely be the last one they could get out, since they had just received word that the Loire bridges would soon be blown in order to slow down the Germans. The convoy included five trucks, one with extra fuel and the others loaded with artwork, including a scenery trailer carrying the *Wedding Feast at Cana* and the three large rolled paintings depicting Napoleon. *Cana* had been quickly and clumsily rolled and, in the desperate rush to get the convoy on the road with the enemy only thirty miles away, some of the artworks had been loaded with no wrapping at all. Also among the treasures aboard was da Vinci's fragile chalk-on-paper sketch of Isabella d'Este, which like the *Mona Lisa* traveled in its own private case. Custody of the work was assigned to the best driver of the convoy, Madame Eugny, with instructions not to leave Isabella alone day or night.

The convoy took almost twelve hours just to cover the 125 miles to its overnight stop at Chambord since the roads had become so crammed with refugees that they were practically impassable. Perhaps 6 to 10 million people from Belgium, the Netherlands and northern France had fled their homes, including almost half the population of Paris and its surrounding suburbs. And they were jamming the same routes as the trucks. The worst of the crowds were on the roads leading south from the Loire, jammed with "slow moving cars, vans, lorries and horse-drawn carts piled up with furniture, mattresses, agricultural tools, pets, birdcages . . . . The roadsides were strewn with the corpses of horses or with cars abandoned for lack of petrol." The writer and pilot Saint Exupéry wrote that from the air the roads were so thick with the slow-motion crowds they looked like syrup, and that it looked as if a "great boot had smashed into an anthill in the north and the ants were on the move." At times, low-flying Italian planes and German Stuka dive-bombers emptied machine guns into the fleeing populace.

Progress was further slowed due to chains that police had stretched across certain roads to impede the enemy. The smaller trucks of the convoy could fit below the chains, but not the scenery trailer. Then a tire on the heavily loaded trailer fell into a roadside ditch; it was simply a matter of luck that two powerful trucks soon came along and got the 40-foot-long vehicle and its priceless cargo back on the road.

On Friday June 15, the convoy headed toward Valençay, crawling along the almost impassible roads while German planes flew overhead. At one point, the bumper of Mazauric's car got caught on another vehicle in the convoy. They might have been crushed in the melee if someone had not come quickly to their rescue. By evening, the convoy was settled at Valençay, whose equestrian center had been transformed into a huge temporary shelter for more than 2,000 refugees on their way south. The château itself was also packed, not only with artworks, but also with depot personnel and refugees. It was a scene of apparent insanity—and a moment of literal insanity—when a refugee group of patients from a nearby asylum arrived with their white-jacketed driver. A Louvre curator expressed concern to the driver about allowing them in the middle of the treasures of the Louvre. "Nothing to fear," responded the driver, "the dangerous lunatics have already escaped."

The convoy members improvised sleeping arrangements that night, their fitful slumber interrupted by the loud explosion of a nearby bomb. The following morning, they continued south from Valençay. The roads became steeper but also calmer. Enemy planes became scarce and instead of the terrified mobs further north, they occasionally passed only picnickers along the embankments, enjoying the summer day as if nothing were amiss. They passed the next night on cots in a classroom of an elementary school, with da Vinci's *Isabella d'Este* resting between Mazauric and Madame Eugny. In the early evening of June 16, the heaving trucks giving clear signs of fatigue, the convoy safely reached the isolated abbey of Loc-Dieu.

At dusk the previous day, Bazin had left Louvigny with a Louvre staff member and two guards in a race for time to bring one last load of thirty-seven unwrapped paintings and five crates across the Loire before the French destroyed the bridges. The escort driver had refused to go, so Bazin got behind the wheel in spite of his still-unhealed knee. He had assumed the roads would be clear since night was falling, but a column of French tanks blocked the road and the commander barked at him to get out of the way. After looking at Bazin's papers and listening to his explanation, he told Bazin and the others to squeeze between two tanks and take the first road at the right. But the designated road was a dirt one and they found themselves in the middle of a field in the darkness. They finally made their way back to the road, guided by a fire burning on the horizon.

The group finally got across the river at Saumur at 6 a.m. the following morning, just before traffic was halted to prepare the bridge for explosion. They continued on until shortly before noon, when the clutch on the truck blew, immobilizing the small convoy in place for two full days. Further along, another clutch problem immobilized them again. They arrived at Loc-Dieu at 3 p.m. on Thursday June 20, having required almost five days to cover the three hundred miles from Chambord.

By that point, bombs had fallen in Louvigny and on the grounds of the just-abandoned depot at La Pelice. They had also fallen several hundred meters from the still-operating depot at Courtalain, where German troops were now camped on the grounds. The troops also demanded entry to the château, where they forced open some cases, including one enticingly labeled "various old paintings." Inside, they found only some porcelain plates.

I n just over two weeks, under constantly deteriorating conditions, the Louvre staff and French soldiers had accomplished the extraordinary task of wrapping, packing, loading and moving 3,120 of the Louvre's 3,691 paintings and untold thousands of other items of artwork and antiquities, and had also moved the staff and their belongings plus huge quantities of supplies. They had miraculously escaped theft, road accidents, enemy machine guns and bombs along the way. The treasures were safe from potential Paris or Loire Valley bombing. Now it remained to be seen if they would be safe from the Germans.

# ELEVEN

# DEBACLE

O N JUNE 13, 1940, as the Louvre's evacuated collections were heading south and the Germans were only miles from Paris, French generals Pierre Héring and Henri Dentz informed the city's residents that Paris had been declared an open city, not to be defended. That evening, just hours before the German troops arrived, Jacques Jaujard left the Louvre for Chambord; he wanted to formally represent the Musées Nationaux to the Germans upon their inevitable arrival and to try to obtain guarantees of protection for the national museums and the depots.

The same day, French writer and theater critic Paul Léautaud noted in his journal that he had taken a long walk across Paris through the empty streets. "Not a single guard on duty at the Louvre," he wrote. "You could set it on fire without any problem." Léautaud did not know that Jaujard had considered what might befall the deserted palace if there were no French official on hand when the Germans arrived. In anticipation, Jaujard had already arranged for someone to be inside the building: Gabriel Rouchès, the curator of the Louvre's collection of drawings and a fluent speaker of German. During the night of June 13, alone in the vast deserted museum except for a

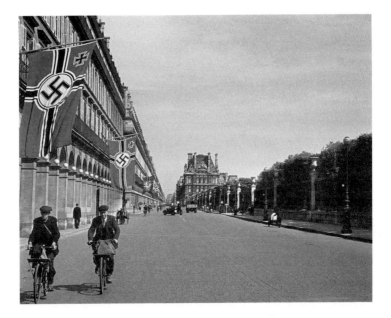

RUE DE RIVOLI, LOUVRE IN BACKGROUND

single guard who had accompanied him to Paris, Rouchès called Chambord to calmly reassure them that all was still well.

But Paris would only be well for a matter of hours. Shortly after 3 a.m., the first German was spotted on a motorcycle in the 11th arrondissement at place Voltaire (later renamed place Léon Blum). By dawn, German soldiers in trucks and tanks were rolling into a silent, largely empty city, quickly executing the detailed plan they had developed long before. Vehicle-mounted loudspeakers announced that the population was to stay indoors for forty-eight hours and that any act of hostility, aggression or sabotage would be punished by death. By noon, Nazi flags were flying along the portion of rue de Rivoli stretching west from the Louvre to place de la Concorde, as troops commandeered the French navy headquarters and all the luxury hotels along rue de Rivoli and neighboring streets. This several-block stretch would harbor the largest concentration of Nazi command buildings in all of Paris and would house in great luxury many of the thousands of German military and civilian personnel that would soon flood into the city. By evening, the first members of the Gestapo had settled into the Hôtel du Louvre just off rue de Rivoli, a block from the museum.

There was no danger to the Louvre's art that day; by the time the footsteps of German boots echoed on the sidewalks outside the museum, its treasures were tucked far away and at least momentarily safe.

The French government had left town several days earlier, first staying in the Loire Valley, then in temporary quarters in Bordeaux. For days, they debated whether to capitulate or continue to fight. Among those present were Prime Minister Paul Reynaud and 84-year-old Henri-Philippe Pétain, the recently appointed deputy prime minister who had been honored with the title maréchal in 1918 to recognize his exceptional achievements as general during World War I. Reynaud favored an ongoing defense while Pétain wanted an armistice with Germany. Also present for part of the deliberations was Brigadier General Charles de Gaulle, who just a week earlier had been appointed Under Secretary of State for National Defense and put in charge of coordination with England.

On June 16, while de Gaulle—who sided with Reynaud—was on a brief emergency trip to London, Reynaud resigned after realizing that he was outnumbered by leaders in favor of an armistice; Pétain quickly took his place. When de Gaulle returned and heard the news he was appalled. He left the next morning for London and would not return to France until 1944. The day of de Gaulle's departure, Pétain gave a radio broadcast to the country saying it was necessary to stop the fighting and that night he ordered French troops to stop fighting in any community with more than 20,000 people. The following day, de Gaulle sat in a London BBC studio empty but for a British announcer. Dressed in full military uniform and shining boots, de Gaulle took to the airwaves with his famous "appel du 18 juin," calling for the French people to resist. Few people initially heeded the call of the largely unknown soldier. By the time he would next set foot on French soil in June 1944, he would be a household name and the active Resistance would number in the hundreds of thousands.

On June 22, 1940, Pétain's government signed an armistice with Germany that took effect two days later; an armistice with Italy soon followed. No one could believe France had fallen so quickly and at such a cost. In the less than seven weeks between the German entry into France and the signing of the armistice, 84,000 soldiers had died, 120,000 had been wounded and 1.5 million taken prisoner. Pétain declared June 25 a day of mourning. The fall of France would be aptly named *le débâcle*.

Under the terms of the armistice, France was split into two zones, one governed by the Germans and the other controlled by Pétain's government, nicknamed "Vichy" after the town in which the government was based. It was called the "free zone" although many of the measures Vichy would take were harsher than those of the Nazis. The German occupied zone included roughly the northern half of the country plus a western area tapering to a point as it went south toward the Spanish border. The shape was not an accident: it gave the Germans control of the Channel and Atlantic coasts, most of the largest cities in France and some of the richest agricultural lands. The "free" zone included many of the poorest, most rugged and least populated parts of the country. Under the armistice, Germany also annexed Alsace and Lorraine, both of which shared borders with

Germany and had long been a subject of dispute between the two countries. The Franco-Italian armistice signed several days later annexed several small areas in far southeast France to Italy.

Some of the Louvre's depots resided within the free zone, including Saint-Blancard, Loc-Dieu—the Louvre's new primary depot for paintings other than the very large ones—and, just barely, Valençay, which lay only nine miles south of the demarcation line. But because the June evacuations could not move everything south, some of the Louvre depots fell within the occupied zone, including Courtalain, Sourches, Cheverny and several others that held items from other museums and private collections. Chambord, the largest depot of all, was also in the occupied zone.

The Musées Nationaux had tucked away their artistic treasures in châteaux to protect them from bombing, not to hide them from Germans, though they had tried to keep as low a profile as possible regarding depot locations. But even if museum officials had wished to keep the locations hidden, it would have been a vain effort; within days of the Germans occupying Paris, the German military had already assembled numerous reports noting the depots they had discovered and plans for their "protection."

Where did the information about the depot locations come from? The Germans could have learned about Chambord simply from reading newspaper reports from 1939. Additionally, immediately upon their arrival in Paris, the Germans had combed through French government archives, which held copies of detailed reports of many of the evacuation plans and actions. Moreover, when the Germans arrived in the city, one of their first stops was the Louvre itself. They roamed the cavernous building with their boots echoing off the ancient stone steps, stupefied that the museum had been emptied. There, too, they obtained information. Neither Gabriel Rouchès nor the guard on duty, the two men sent from Chambord

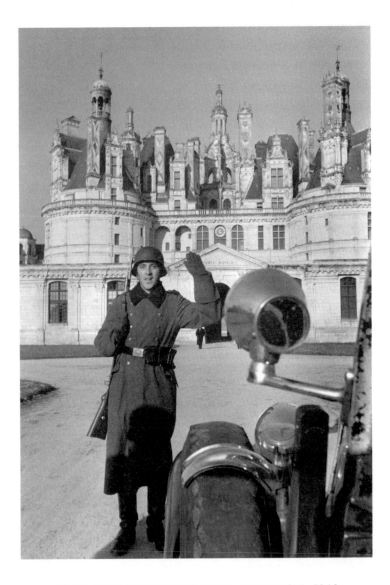

ARMED GERMAN SOLDIER ON DUTY AT CHAMBORD, 1940

to guard the museum, would have been in a position to withhold information while facing German machine guns.

On June 19—five days before the armistice went into effect—Nazi troops arrived at Chambord. Jacques Jaujard was there to greet them. "You are, *monsieur le Directeur*," they said, "the first senior French public official we have found on duty."

The German military immediately stationed soldiers at Chambord and the other depots in the occupied zone. Was it to protect the collections from damage, as required by the Hague Convention—or to keep a close eye on them for their own purposes? The answer seemed to lie in a June 30 communiqué to the German commander of Paris from Wilhelm Keitel, German Field Marshal and head of the Supreme Command arm of the German military. Issued a mere eight days after the armistice, it contained an order from Hitler to take into custody privately held, "primarily Jewish-owned" valuable art and antiquities—plus the "French state-owned art treasures." It seemed the Germans were about to grab the entire artistic heritage of France.

SECRET      30.6.1940

TO THE COMMANDER OF PARIS, GENERAL

VON BOCKELBERG, PARIS


THE FÜHRER, FOLLOWING THE PRESENTATION OF THE
REICH FOREIGN MINISTER, HAS ORDERED THE SAFEGUARDING
BY THE OCCUPYING POWER OF—IN ADDITION TO THE FRENCH
STATE-OWNED ART TREASURES—PRIVATELY HELD, PRIMARILY
JEWISH-OWNED, VALUABLE ART OBJECTS AND ANTIQUITIES,
SO THAT THEY WILL NOT BE STOLEN OR HIDDEN. THE
FORMER FRENCH OWNER WILL BE PUT ON RECORD. THIS IS
NOT INTENDED TO BE AN EXPROPRIATION, BUT RATHER A
TRANSFER TO OUR CUSTODY AS COLLATERAL FOR THE PEACE
NEGOTIATIONS.

AMBASSADOR ABETZ HAS BEEN INFORMED BY THE
REICH MINISTER OF FOREIGN AFFAIRS.


THE COMMANDER IN CHIEF OF THE WEHRMACHT.

SIGNED: KEITEL


COMMUNICATION FROM KEITEL
TO VON BOCKELBERG, JUNE 30, 1940

# TWELVE

## OCCUPIERS WITH AN EYE FOR ART

**A**DOLF HITLER'S DELUSIONS were numerous and extreme. Among them, he believed himself to be a prophet, a man ordained for greatness by "divine Providence," and the creator of a glorious empire that would rule for a thousand years. His megalomania also extended to his feelings about art. "All my life I have wanted to be a great painter in oils," he said in a 1939 interview. "[A]s soon as I have carried out my program for Germany I shall take up my painting.... I feel that I have it in my soul to become one of the great artists of the age and that future historians will remember me, not for what I have done for Germany, but for my art." In reality, he had twice been refused admission by the Vienna Academy of Fine Arts and though he fancied himself an art connoisseur, he considered the work of artists from Chagall to Cézanne and from Gauguin to van Gogh to be "degenerate" trash. Part of his vision for the Thousand Year Reich was a massive cultural center he planned for his childhood hometown of Linz, Austria. The center's crowning glory would be the colossal Führermuseum, the most spectacular art museum of all time. To stock his planned dream museum, he would buy certain pieces; other items he expected to receive as tribute as part of a Nazi party culture in which gift giving was an important ritual for establishing status and currying favor. He was also quite content to enhance his collections through plunder and the masterpieces of the Louvre were high on his wish list.

While Hitler had no qualms about violating many of the provisions of the Hague Convention—which prohibited seizure—he knew that an outright theft of the Louvre's collections would create a major international outcry. If need be, he planned to demand whatever he wanted as war reparations upon his final victory. But that would require him to wait for a peace treaty rather than an armistice so instead, as soon his armies occupied France, he tested the waters with another strategy. His June 30, 1940 order for the transfer of the French national collections to "safeguard" them had carefully avoided the word "seizure."

The Führer had based his order on a report of his foreign minister, Joachim von Ribbentrop. Hitler's propaganda minister and Ribbentrop rival Joseph Goebbels later said that Ribbentrop had bought the "von" in his name, married his money and swindled his way into office. The icy-eyed, arrogant Ribbentrop did in fact buy the "von," his wife was wealthy and whether or not he swindled his way into power, he would use that power to enrich both the Führer's art collections and his own—including, at least temporarily, one of the Louvre's eighteenth-century masterpieces.

Field Marshal Keitel's June 30 order on Hitler's behalf was relayed to Otto Abetz, Ribbentrop's right-hand man and soon-to-be ambassador to France. The tall, charming, blue-eyed Abetz, a former art teacher at a girl's school, had lived in France with his French wife before the war. By the end of 1934 he was in charge of Ribbentrop's new French bureau for foreign affairs and part of the social elite of pre-war Paris, sharing salon evenings with Coco Chanel and other glitterati acquaintances. In July 1939 the French government had expelled him for subversive activity. Less than twenty-four hours after the Germans marched into Paris the following June, a delighted Abetz was back and calling himself the ambassador to France, though he would not receive the appointment until August. Anointed by Ribbentrop as the liaison to the new Vichy government, Abetz settled into the sumptuous German embassy on the Left Bank's rue de Lille, steps from the Seine and the Tuileries Garden. Almost immediately, he began testing his wings as an art pillager.

A day after the military's June 30 order for the "safeguarding" of Jewish and state-owned art objects, Abetz himself issued a new order, this one calling explicitly for their "seizure," in blatant disregard of the Hague Convention. The order also extended the previous "safeguarding" order to artworks owned by any city museum. Then he took action. On July 6, Abetz launched a massive three-day raid on the homes and galleries of prominent Jewish art collectors, hauling a fortune of paintings, sculptures and other items to an annex of the German embassy.

French museum officials could only hold their collective breath and wonder if public collections were next, especially since on June 28, the German military had already instructed Jaujard to return the artworks and antiquities in the state collections to Paris. However, if they were to believed, the purpose was to reopen the Louvre as part of a German effort to give the impression that the cultural life of Paris was returning to normal. From June 29 to July 3, Abetz's representatives combed through the depots in the occupied zone and specified the number of crates at each depot to be returned to Paris. They said the depots in the free zone would not be addressed "for the moment," thus making it clear that the art and antiquities in the free zone were not off limits. They belonged to the state—and the

French state was now in the hands of Maréchal Pétain, who quickly revealed his intent to collaborate with the Germans.

Jaujard could not flatly refuse the German demand. Instead, he turned to a strategy he would employ endlessly throughout the war: delay. While issuing instructions to his staff in respectful compliance with the order to return all the evacuated items, he also kept pointing out to authorities that the evacuations had protected the artworks from bombing and that the threat still existed. Germany was fighting with England, he said, and low-flying planes flew over the Louvre daily. Moreover, machine guns were still poised on the roof of the Hôtel de Crillon, just a short way up rue de Rivoli, and in any case, he argued, there were simply not enough trucks available at the moment to bring it all back. Could we not simply wait? he asked. By July 10, the Germans tentatively agreed to a delay, although less than two weeks later they would again start pressing for the works to return.

Meanwhile, a worrisome silence reigned with regard to Abetz's seizure order. In spite of the German military's demand to reopen the Louvre, museum officials knew that Abetz meant business, as witnessed by the raids on the Jewish-owned galleries. But after three days, the raids had inexplicably stopped. The French had no way of knowing that the German secret police had, for the moment, refused to continue the raids after learning that Abetz had not obtained appropriate military approval.

On July 15, the German military commander of Paris, General Alfred von Vollard-Bockelberg, issued an order in direct contradiction to Abetz's seizure order. Effective immediately, he strictly forbid, "in order to prevent any theft or damage," the movement of any movable art from its current location without written authorization of a senior commander of the German military administration in France. The new order was not a pure-hearted attempt to prevent the seizure of French art; rather, Bockelberg wanted more guidance as to what to seize. He also wanted to send a message to Abetz that the military would control the disposition of French art, not the German embassy. This was an early example of the pervasive internal Nazi battle over turf, a practice actively encouraged by Hitler. Putting individuals in competition with each other would spur them on, he believed. The paranoid Führer's divide-and-rule strategy was also intended to create animosity among the various factions of his administration, discouraging them from joining forces and seizing too much power. The early months of the German occupation, with roles not clearly defined, provided a ripe environment for multiple, conflicting attempts to seize French collections.

The July 15 prohibition against moving artworks without permission quickly proved problematic for the Louvre administration, since it applied even to transportation for conservation purposes. Jaujard inspected the vaults at the Banque de France holding the fragile pastels, among them Boucher's *Madame de Pompadour* and seven works by Degas. Though he found them damaged from humidity due to a breakdown in the bank's air-conditioning system, it took almost three weeks to obtain German permission to remove some of them, and then only subject to Jaujard's guarantee that they would remain at the Louvre and "always available." German permission to remove the last of them would not be received until November.

While the specter of imminent seizure hung in the air and the Germans again indicated that they wanted the Louvre's artworks returned to Paris, the French had to grapple with another provision of the July 15 prohibition order: owners of any item of movable art with a value exceeding 100,000 francs were required to declare it to the German authorities by August 15, including the name and address of the owner, an exact description of each item and its exact location. Museum officials did not know whether the national museums were subject to the order or whether another contradictory order would be forthcoming. And what was the purpose of such a list?, they wondered. It was reasonable to fear that such an inventory might be used simply as a road map for the Germans to more efficiently seize them.

Their fears were justified. Hitler wanted the best pieces of the Louvre and he had additional wish lists. In 1939, he had sent several researchers on a secret mission to scour French libraries and museums to identify works looted by Napoleon since 1794. In the summer of 1940, he commissioned yet another aspiring Nazi plunderer, the Reich Minister of Propaganda Joseph Goebbels, with the task of building on the earlier mission by identifying all artwork and historically important objects of "Germanic origin" that had been removed at any time since the year 1500 "without German consent or on the basis of dubious legal acts." To Hitler's mind, "Germanic origin" included not only items created or owned within the greater German empire but even those created in a so-called German style. And to his mind, illegal or dubious removal included transfers under the terms of the legal treaties ending the Napoleonic wars and World War I.

To develop the list, Goebbels in turn commissioned a team led by Otto Kümmel, the director of the Berlin State Museums and a committed Nazi, who led a secret mission to France to identify any such "Germanic" items located there. He and his men worked primarily at the Bibliothèque Nationale, investigating catalogues of sales and museums and the weekly gazettes of the Hôtel Drouot, the most prestigious Paris auction house. The Kümmel report's most strongly worded narrative was against France and it listed some

1,800 French-owned works, of which 350 were in museums or public places. In the report's first draft, seventy-five of these items were listed as being at the Louvre, including two works by Rembrandt, two by Rubens and nine by Dürer.

As July turned to August, the Louvre depots were preparing inventories for administrative purposes while they wondered what the Germans would do next. In fact, the various German factions were separately scheming how they might obtain French art. As Kümmel and his staff compiled their lists and reported to Goebbels, Ribbentrop and Abetz plotted to circumvent the military's prohibition against moving art. To help their cause, Ribbentrop provided Abetz with the help of an aide, Eberhard von Künsberg, a veteran of large-scale German raids on archives and museums in Poland and a major in the military's secret police. By the beginning of August, Abetz had targeted 1,500 items at Chambord to be hauled away to Germany and gave an order to Künsberg to seize them, telling him not to involve the military. However, the seizure would not be as easy as they hoped since another, quite different, German had just joined the arena: Count Franz von Wolff Metternich.

Responsible for the conservation of German monuments, a noted scholar of Renaissance art and architecture and a conservation professor at the University of Bonn, Wolff Metternich had been designated in May 1940 as the head of the Kunstschutz, a German military program intended to protect art and monuments in certain occupied territories, though its ultimate raison d'être was to preserve such works for the benefit of Hitler's envisioned empire. Ironically, Wolff Metternich was a descendant of the nineteenth-century Austrian diplomat who had played a part in negotiating the return of Napoleon's plundered art. The earlier Wolff Metternich had been a slippery master politician and notorious philanderer, but his twentieth-century descendant, a lifelong Francophile, was a man of strong principles.

Wolff Metternich was transferred to France at the beginning of August. One of his first meetings was with Kümmel, who informed him of the project to repatriate German artworks. Wolff Metternich later said that he, too, would have liked to see "the works of art which once adorned German churches and museums returned to Germany." However, he believed it was his responsibility to respect the Hague Convention to the letter and he hoped repatriation could eventually be achieved legally.

Jaujard and Wolff Metternich met for the first time during the first week of August, two men with similar morals and similar goals. Wolff Metternich agreed to a definitive postponement of the demands to return all the artworks to Paris. He also said the July 15 order to provide detailed inventories did not apply to the Musées Nationaux, although that reprieve would not last long: Ribbentrop and Abetz wanted art from the French collections, and they were not ready to give up.

The day after Abetz gave Künsberg the order to seize the 1,500 items at Chambord, Wolff Metternich learned of the plan and told the military high command, which responded with a new order forbidding any confiscations without Hitler's consent. Still Abetz would not be stopped. At a secret meeting on August 12, he and Otto Kümmel invented a new ploy, claiming that a large number of the objects evacuated to Chambord—not just items "stolen" from Germany—should be returned to Paris because they had been inadequately packed and stored. In reality, Abetz simply wanted to force them back to Paris, where he felt it would be easier to select items for shipment to Germany. When Wolff Metternich learned of the "need" to return the items to Paris, he tried to delay the plan by saying he would request an inventory from the Louvre director.

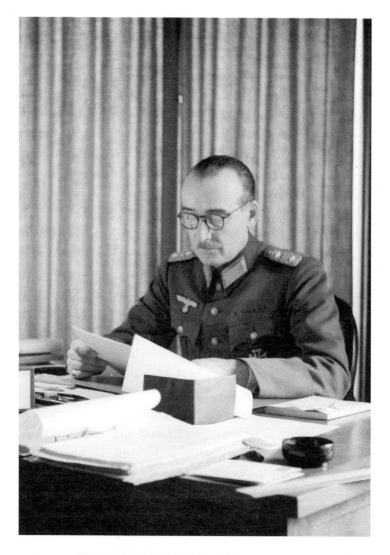

COUNT FRANZ VON WOLFF METTERNICH IN HIS
PARIS OFFICE AT THE HÔTEL MAJESTIC

He also said he would go along with Künsberg's plan, but only if presented with a written order from the commander in chief of the German army and if in fact the items were actually at risk. He had called their bluff; only an inspection would resolve the stalemate.

The August 15 inspection at Chambord was well attended. Wolff Metternich was there with several assistants; Künsberg and his men were there as well. Also on hand were several experts sent by Ribbentrop from the state museums of Berlin. Pierre Schommer, head of the depot, watched as they conducted a careful examination, only to find that every item they checked had been meticulously packed and irreproachably stored. Ironically, the items stored at the German embassy were later found to have been stored improperly.

Still Abetz was not prepared to give up. He said that once he received the French inventory lists, he would choose between twenty and twenty-five artworks with exceptional value to be moved to Paris, with or without military permission. When the military learned of his plan, they issued yet another order forbidding any such transport. All Abetz could do was demand the inventories. And demand he did. Wolff Metternich had relayed the inventory request to Jaujard but when days passed and the lists did not show up, Abetz sent his staff in search of them. At the depot at the château de Sources, an agent confiscated incomplete lists. At Chambord, an agent ripped unfinished lists from the hands of the staff and threatened to open the crates by force. This only delayed preparation of the lists, which were at long last provided to the German embassy by the end of August.

When Abetz finally realized that Hitler was unlikely to hand him the military support needed to get his hands on any part of the French state collections, he turned his attention back to looting the assets of Jews, orchestrating a new, massive four-day round of confiscations from leading Jewish collectors at the end of August.

He sent off some choice items to Ribbentrop and hauled the rest to the German embassy, where he continued to entertain Paris high society and top Nazis in salons now decorated with paintings stolen from the Rothschild family apartments. During the gala events, champagne flowed like water, live orchestras played and the windows of the embassy glowed brightly against the Parisians' nightly blackout.

A betz may have been high on the social scale, but his star as an art looter had fallen; Alfred Rosenberg's, on the other hand, was on the rise. In January 1940, Hitler authorized Rosenberg, the virulently anti-Semitic, anti-Communist and anti-Masonic racial theorist of the Nazi party, to set up a research institute to examine opponents of Nazi ideology. In July, when Hitler empowered him to confiscate French manuscripts and books in support of his mission, Rosenberg did it under the auspices of a newly operational agency, the Einsatzstab Reichsleiter Rosenberg (Reich Leader Rosenberg Task Force, or ERR). In early September Hitler also gave Rosenberg the authorization—and the military support he had not given Abetz—to confiscate all "ownerless" Jewish art, representing items left behind by Jewish individuals who had fled the country between May 20 and June 30 without official permission and, in doing so, abandoned their French citizenship by virtue of a July law promulgated by the collaborationist French government.

Within days of his appointment, Rosenberg sought the collaboration of Hermann Göring, Hitler's second in command and head of the German Air Force, who offered the use of Luftwaffe trains and guard staff, plus other assistance for seizure, sorting and transport. Even though Hitler had already authorized military support for Rosenberg's operation, the arrangement with Göring gave Rosenberg even more assurance that he would get the help that

Abetz had not. In turn, the arrangement gave Göring a way not only to enter the looting operation for Hitler but also to obtain first-hand access to the booty for his own collections. His strategy would be breathtakingly successful: after Hitler, Göring would be by far the biggest Nazi looter of all.

When Rosenberg was tapped to take control of looting operations, the fruit of Abetz's earlier seizures, stacked to overflowing in the German embassy, came under his control. Where could he move it all, and where could he store the booty of future hauls? The Louvre appeared ideal.

# THIRTEEN

# LOC-DIEU ABBEY

I N THE YEAR 1123, not far from an ancient Roman road in France's south-central Midi-Pyrénées region, a small group of Cistercian monks partially drained a small swampy area in a dark, dense forest to make a home for a new abbey. The locals called the area *Locus Diaboli*—place of the devil—for the bloody rituals held there long before by Druid cult members and for the thieves and murderers who later hid in the forest. The monks sanctified the ground by renaming it *Locus Die*, or place of God; eventually it was called simply Loc-Dieu. Later the monks drained much of the remaining swamp around the abbey in the belief that the vapors arising from it during the hot summers made the abbey's inhabitants ill. When the Louvre staff arrived in the summer of 1940, the swampy mist still rose from the pond that remained.

Much of the structure was rebuilt after being burnt down by the English in 1409. During the French Revolution, the building was confiscated as national property and then sold to private owners who transformed part of the structure into a residence. By 1940, when thousands of Louvre paintings arrived, the former abbey was still in the hands of the same family, though they resided there only

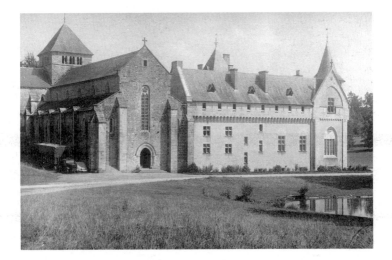

LOC-DIEU ABBEY, 1940

occasionally, having moved to one of their other residences nearby to allow the Musées Nationaux to use the property.

Loc-Dieu Abbey lies just south of the rugged hills and high plateaux of France's Aveyron département, eighty miles northeast of Toulouse, just outside the tiny village of Martiel, six miles southwest of the small town of Villefranche-de-Rouergue. Lucie Mazauric and the other Louvre staff in June's third large convoy from the Loire had almost finished the 300-mile journey when they first heard rumors of an impending armistice. Listening to the radio during their first evenings in the abbey, they heard Pétain's call for a cease-fire. As the prisoner of war toll quickly rose to 1.5 million men, the staff waited anxiously for news of their sons and husbands. They felt, said Mazauric, like medieval fugitives from a plague-infested city.

One recompense, however small, was sleeping quarters that were a vast improvement over those in and near Chambord. The former cloisters of the abbey had long before been renovated to create

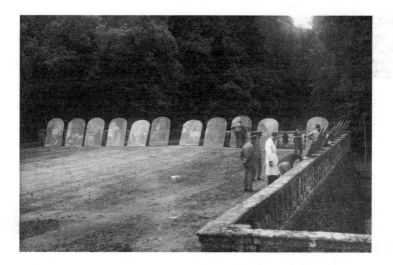

ARTWORK ON THE LAWNS OF THE CHÂTEAU DE SOURCHES

dozens of beautiful, comfortable bedrooms, each furnished with faux-medieval canopied four-poster beds. However, with a head count of 250 people, including many dozens of guards and numerous family members, there was insufficient room at the abbey for all; additional quarters were found in several nearby villages.

Some of the artwork was settled into various outbuildings on the property with green chalk markings on each door providing a clue to what lay within. But most of the art went to the enormous nave of the chapel. The soaring spaces and strong vaulted arches of the ancient abbey seemed the perfect place to safely store the artwork. The curators did not yet know that from the moment they arrived, the abbey had begun posing a serious risk for the artworks, one that had nothing to do with the risks posed by the German invaders.

Jacques Jaujard had requested the staff at each depot to conduct an inventory of their holdings. But with more than 3,100 paintings at Loc-Dieu—eighty-five percent of the total paintings evacuated from the Louvre—and many of them still in their crates from the frantic June evacuation, this was not an easy or quick task. Even a simple count of the crates was difficult. One morning Mazauric and a colleague climbed among the entangled mass of crates in an attempt to count them, only to arrive at a different total each time. Detailing the items within each crate was an even greater challenge since many crates contained a maze of compartments to separate the multiple artworks within. Moreover, each individual painting was wrapped with paper and secured in place with fiber plugs to prevent excessive movement. Removing each painting from all the packing materials to take the inventory took a great deal of time and the huge piles of removed packing materials impeded the process. It was an equally slow process to re-wrap and re-pack each painting. In spite of the difficulties, the inventory progressed. On sunny days the staff opened certain crates outside, as did personnel at the other depots, both curators and artworks benefitting from the fresh air and light.

Daily life may have been calm at the isolated abbey, but the staff were not safe from the ugly specter of anti-Semitism that was growing quickly under new Vichy rules. Jewish curator Charles Sterling was unsuccessfully trying to arrange a country to which he could flee; Philippe Stern, curator of the Musée Guimet, some of whose works were also at Loc-Dieu, was also seeking somewhere to go.

While the turf battle with the Germans over the artworks was unfolding, another seemed about to erupt. On July 15—one day after the German order requiring the declaration of all art with a value exceeding 100,000 francs, the University of Rome published an article demanding that France return all artworks "looted" from Italy by Napoleon, even though any works still in the hands of the French remained there legally under the terms of the treaties

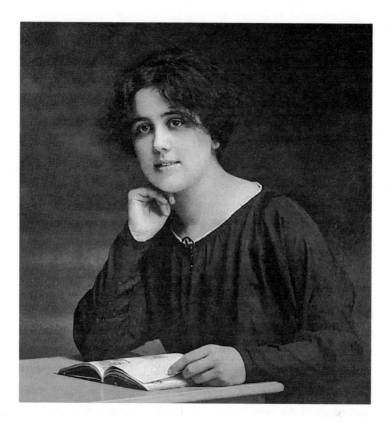

LUCIE MAZAURIC AS A STUDENT

that had ended the Napoleonic wars. The article also demanded the return of all works by Titian and da Vinci—including the *Mona Lisa*—all of which had been legally acquired by the Louvre long before Napoleon. It would be exceedingly easy to return them, the article said, since the French had already carefully packed them. The French arts administration worried that the Italian government itself would make a similar demand. They also worried about the provenance documents for the works in question, since these were stored in the occupied zone at Chambord, where the Germans could easily put them under seal and make them inaccessible in case of Italian claims. On July 22, Lucie Mazauric received secret orders to obtain the provenance documents at Chambord and bring them back to Loc-Dieu.

Just making the travel arrangements was a challenge, since she needed an *ausweis*—an official German travel pass—for passage between the two zones. Loc-Dieu staff could not return to their Paris homes or visit friends or family north of the demarcation line without one. Likewise, Jaujard, based in Paris, needed one to visit the depots in the unoccupied zone. They also needed permission for any trip to transfer artwork between the two zones for conservation purposes. Once Mazauric had her *ausweis* in hand, she headed north. Near the border, she asked some Frenchmen what to expect from the Germans at the checkpoint. "It depends how much beer they receive during the day," her compatriots replied. That day she found the German guards polite enough, but felt humiliated to need travel papers with a German stamp to move about her own country.

Once at Chambord, Mazauric easily located the documents, but then realized they were so extensive that the Germans were sure to spot—and likely confiscate—them when she crossed the border again. Disobeying the orders she had been given, she decided the only safe solution was to copy the most important information and leave the originals at Chambord. For two days and nights, she toiled without sleep, writing it all down in such a way that would be difficult for others to decipher and also concisely enough that she could pack the notes unnoticed in her bags. Once finished, she scattered the originals among the other archives, carefully noting where she had hidden them. She was confident that even a specialist who might come across them would need months to reconstruct it all into any semblance of order.

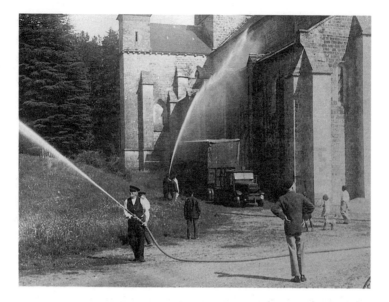

STAFF CONDUCTING FIRE DRILL AT LOC-DIEU, 1940

While the staff waited to see what would happen with the German demand for lists and to return the artworks to Paris—and a possible Italian demand for certain artworks—they went about their business of testing the precious fire safety equipment and watching over the artwork under their care.

In August, curators opened *Mona Lisa*'s case and inspected the painting, which appeared in good condition although there was concern about two wedges inside the case that could cause warping. The curators also noticed that mites had attacked the velvet cushioning of her case. They brushed and aired out the velvet and removed the wedges, then enveloped the painting in new packing material, wrapped it in special paper and hermetically sealed it all to keep out parasites.

The Louvre's paintings had arrived at Loc-Dieu at the beginning of a beautiful, hot summer. The weather seemed delightful to the eye, but quite early in their stay, Germain Bazin had noted that the area appeared humid—a serious risk to the paintings—and said they needed to take precautions by mid-August if the paintings were to safely stay the winter. A subsequent analysis by a government architect said that there were multiple sources of the humidity, including the area's climate, its impermeable soil, the location of the abbey at the bottom of a shallow basin of land and the fact that the abbey had been built directly onto the soil, with no basement or crawl space underneath. And, of course, there was the water itself, only a small part of which was still visible in the form of the pond. Bazin spoke with the locals, who told him what the monks had always known: that the abbey had been built on a swamp. It was easy to confirm; shallow holes were dug and water quickly appeared.

By then, one painting in particular had already received special care. When it appeared that humidity had increased in the chapel where the *Mona Lisa* was stored, the painting was taken to the bedroom of Mazauric and her husband André Chamson, the sunniest room of the building. Even when the painting remained in its special case, "We watched over it," said Chamson, "as we would have done for a sick child." Mazauric hardly dared to walk around, she said, for fear of agitating the air.

New hygrometer readings confirmed what the curators already knew. By early August, some of the meters registered a soggy ninety-five percent, raising fears that the paintings were already damaged. In early September, experts presented Jaujard with two possible solutions: either install enough heating to dry out the moisture or move the paintings elsewhere. A careful examination of the process and costs of installing a heating system was made and the obstacles to such a solution were many. It was not a question of just heating the areas where the paintings were stored; the entire living quarters of the château would need modern heating to remove the fire hazards posed by all the individual fireplaces. Among the many problems of undertaking such a large project was the need for one of the large electrical contracting firms, all of which were located—and now, for all practical purposes, trapped—in the occupied zone.

In mid-September, museum officials decided to move the paintings. Of the several locations suggested, they chose the Musée Ingres in the city of Montauban, which offered a number of advantages. Located only thirty-seven miles southwest of Loc-Dieu Abbey, it would not be a long trip. Moreover, the new location was spacious, its urban setting would provide enough lodgings for the guards and staff, and a fire station was nearby. Jaujard expressed just one concern about the building, which was perched above the banks of the Tarn River: He had been told that the river had caused terrible flooding several times in recent years. When he was reassured that the museum was high enough to avoid flooding from the river, he gave the go-ahead to move the paintings. In fact, the new depot at the Musée Ingres would not suffer river flooding. But a different kind of flood there would almost ruin the paintings just the same.

# FOURTEEN

# VALENÇAY AT WAR

FOR THE STAFF of the Musées Nationaux, as for everyone in France, the realities of war were unsettling. The staff members who had chosen to follow the art had to deal with new and unfamiliar surroundings and, in many cases, isolation from family and friends in Paris. After the armistice, curators—accustomed to the often independent and rarified intellectual atmosphere of their work—also had to adjust to carefully prescribed procedures in order to navigate Nazi and Vichy rules and to protect the art under their care. Following these orders sometimes did not come easily. During the June 1940 evacuations, Jaujard visited Valençay on his way south to check on the movements of art. At the time, a number of senior museum staff members were either stationed at or passing through Valençay. Jaujard called the museum staff together in front of the château, where they could hear the noise of the mass of refugees and see frightened deer—not used to either the noise or activity—running among the bushes, all on the same spot where the duke had welcomed guests to his elegant soirées not long before. As Jaujard was giving instructions, one of the stressed staff members declared,

"We are scholars, not soldiers," Jaujard replied. "Above all, you are citizens; don't forget it."

The château housed the duke and his family as well as many of the curators, assistants, guards and their families. It was also packed to the brim with evacuated art, no small feat given the castle's one hundred rooms. Priceless objets d'art, such as the crown jewels, the scepter of Charles V and the reliquary coffer for Charlemagne's arm, were hidden in the château's wall safe. Crates were stacked in the basement and most everywhere else in the château, including the formal salons.

Some of the most important works of the Louvre were not in the château itself. Michelangelo's *Slaves*, Venus de Milo and Winged Victory of Samothrace—whose immense crate sported a hole cut by the curator of Greek and Roman Antiquities in order to verify its condition and to "visit the captive goddess"—were among some of the items housed in an outbuilding.

Objets d'art and the large Greek and Roman antiquities were not the only Louvre collections at Valençay; the château also sheltered the museum's engravings and Asiatic art collections and works from the museum's David-Weill and Edmond de Rothschild collections, which had been donated to the Louvre several years before the war. There were also items from the Musée des Arts Décoratifs and other French national museums.

On June 23, German soldiers arrived at the château asking about the collections. Two days later the armistice went into effect, putting Valençay just barely in the free zone. That did not stop German soldiers from arriving the same day it went into effect, asking to see the artworks. They were told it was impossible because everything was in crates. Nor did the free zone designation stop officers of the German secret police from arriving the following day, demanding to see the crates stored in the salon. However, no further German interest in the collections was expressed at the time and the works seemed safe enough.

But safety for the art did not mean safety for the curators: by the fall of 1940, both depot head Carle Dreyfus and his assistant Jean Cassou were gone from the château. Cassou had been fired pursuant to a July Vichy law that gave the government carte blanche for a short period of time to fire any civil servant; he was targeted for his outspoken anti-fascist views. As for Dreyfus, the first anti-Jewish law enacted by the Vichy government on October 3 removed many rights of Jews, including the right to hold almost any public service job. When the law—more severe than even the laws promulgated at the time by the Nazis in the occupied zone—came into effect, the duc de Valençay told Dreyfus to leave the château. Dreyfus moved to a nearby hotel for some time; he later went into hiding in the countryside near Valençay, where he would be secretly aided throughout the war by his successor at the château, Gérald Van der Kemp.

Just before war was declared in September 1939, Van der Kemp had been cataloging the Louvre's Edmond de Rothschild collection. He was then called up for military duty and was eventually taken prisoner by the Germans in Normandy. On June 30, 1940 he escaped, then covered hundreds of kilometers on foot in spite of a leg injury to make his way to Valençay, where the Rothschild collection was sheltered.

When Dreyfus was expelled from the château in October 1940, Van der Kemp—aged just 27 at the time—was given the responsibility for some of the country's most important artistic heritage, although his position would not be made official until the beginning of 1941. The official designation brought not only pride; it also allowed him and his wife to move from the single, low-ceilinged room to which they had previously been assigned, facing the cow barn. Their new, prestigious quarters on the top floor of the central pavilion of the château had more space, more light and better air.

Château life for the new head curator was almost dreamlike at first, he later said. With Valençay in the free zone, the château's occupants were relatively isolated in many respects from the war. Van der Kemp had to oversee the ongoing safety and preservation of the art, but otherwise he was free to live as a country gentleman. The duke of Valençay, with whom Van der Kemp would get along well until late in the war, took it upon himself to expose Van der Kemp to the world of upper-class culture, which, Van der Kemp later remarked, would be useful his entire life, particularly given his later rise to head curator at Versailles. Van der Kemp described the duke as distinguished, extremely elegant and preoccupied with his wife and friends. He also described him as "a man of the previous century, occupied mainly with his horses," exercising them daily in the nearby Gâtines Forest, unaware of the eventual and massive Resistance presence among those same trees.

Each morning Van der Kemp rode on horseback through those "immense silent forests filled with savage beasts," he later recalled. "I read enormously. I also hunted. Cut off from the rest of the world, reigning over extraordinary treasures, I was living like a great lord of the seventeenth century, but was also perfectly aware of living at the end of a civilization." And when the Germans would storm into the château later in the war, pin him against a wall, point their machine guns at him and announce that they were about to shoot, he would also be perfectly aware it might be the end of his life.

past the line of Nazi flags flying from the commandeered buildings along rue de Rivoli and made a loop around the Louvre as Hitler expressed his admiration for its design and long perspectives. As the motorcade passed the palace's easternmost side—the Colonnade façade—Hitler exclaimed, "I would not hesitate to characterize this grandiose construction as one of the most brilliant ideas in architecture." By 9 a.m., he was on his way back to Germany.

H itler soon played an almost inadvertent role in preventing the Louvre from taking on a political function. The terms of the armistice with Germany had provided that the French government could have its headquarters anywhere, including Paris, and though government leaders had initially fled to Bordeaux and then the free zone mountain town of Vichy, their original intention was to return to either Paris or nearby Versailles. One advisor to Pétain argued against Versailles, noting that it was a symbol of the monarchy and of the government headed by Thiers during the time of the Commune, against both of which the citizens had revolted. Instead, the advisor recommended another option: the Louvre, noting that it was the perfect museum, "the only one the French people know" and "the most majestic urban palace in the world." The advisor wrote that the French people would respect Pétain for choosing to settle "simply" at the Louvre rather than Versailles and that they would feel that he was "close to them, at home with them." Moreover, the advisor argued—noting that it was not a small point—that Pétain's presence in the Louvre would protect the treasures of the French patrimony against "certain appetites that have begun to manifest themselves," a reference to the looting that had already begun. In December 1940, Hitler put an end to any French plans to return the government to either the Louvre or Versailles. First he dragged out negotiations and then, in contravention of the armistice agreement, he announced that the government could not return anywhere within the occupied zone because it was an "operations area."

As the Germans settled into Paris, Parisians passing by the Tuileries Garden at dawn or dusk could see the changing of the German guards at the main military command post across the street. Inside the gardens, visitors could see German soldiers conducting military drills, handling their weapons and practicing their goose steps. On Sundays, passersby could hear the music of German military band concerts.

The Louvre was also a hive of activity, despite the fact that most of the collections were gone, since the building also served as administrative headquarters for the entire national museum system. Other museum activities went on as well. Curators had to continue looking after the art and antiquities that had been sheltered on site and specialists pursued restoration and preservation activities. For the evacuated items, some of this work could be done at the depots but other tasks needed to be handled in Paris. In addition, an active program of acquisitions continued, as did teaching at the École du Louvre.

It was also inside the Louvre that Jaujard maintained his home base, although throughout the war he would make numerous trips to the evacuation depots to conduct inspections and meet with the staff. Throughout the war, he would send forth a literal mountain of memos, letters and endless phone calls from his office in his battle to save the country's art—and the art of French Jews—while simultaneously complying with endless German and Vichy directives and curators' requests for everything from heating fuel for the depots to shoes for the guards.

Outside Jaujard's office, the Louvre was a loud, dirty construction zone since one of the first Louvre activities that had resumed under the Occupation was a major renovation project that had been planned and authorized several years earlier. Among its major elements were new electrical, heating, lighting, fire and theft protection systems as well as new elevators and windows in some areas, plus renovations to the major galleries as part of a major reorganization to better display the art that would someday return. The project would last throughout the war, creating a massive construction area filled with masons, plasterers, woodworkers, electricians, painters and marble installers, plus unemployed artists hired to help. With a hopeful spirit, it had been decided to continue with the project in spite of the war in order to avoid delaying the reopening of the Louvre when the war was over and the artworks could return. An unexpected advantage of the evacuation was that the absence of the collections made it far easier to conduct the extensive renovations.

I n spite of the ongoing construction work, the Louvre partially reopened at the end of September 1940 under orders from the Germans. The Carnavalet and Cernuschi museums had opened several weeks earlier, as had the Musée de l'Orangerie, one of two small buildings just west of the Louvre at the far end of the Tuileries Garden, where Monet's *Water Lilies* remained on view along with a retrospective on Monet and Rodin.

To mark the reopening of the Louvre, the Germans orchestrated a formal ceremony on September 29, 1940, attended by numerous German military officers, Louvre curators and other French representatives. Kunstschutz head Wolff Metternich gave an inaugural address, directed to the Germans present. He later said it was a chance to "publicly proclaim the principles and the goals" of the German commission to protect the artworks and to make "a vibrant call for their safety to those responsible." He also said it was a happy occasion for him. The curators of the Musées Nationaux, not in the same celebratory mood, all wore black.

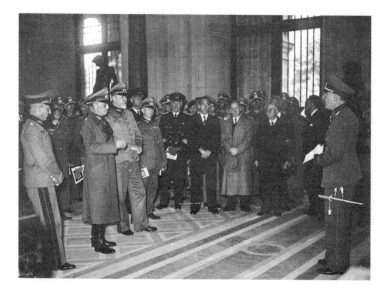

LOUVRE REOPENING, AUTUMN 1940. JACQUES JAUJARD
FRONT ROW, AT LEFT OF MAN IN OVERCOAT,
WOLFF METTERNICH AT FAR RIGHT, GIVING HIS SPEECH

The museum opened to the public several days later. The paint-ing galleries were closed since not a single painting was on display; the vast majority had long since been evacuated and the rest were packed away. A limited number of rooms on the ground floor dis-played some of the sculptures and antiquities that had stayed behind because they were too large, heavy, fragile or unimportant to move. In yet another act of passive resistance by Jaujard, only the items that had remained in place in the galleries, previously protected by wooden framing and sandbags, were on display; he had not brought upstairs a single item that had been taken to the Louvre's basements for safety. Further, some of the sculptures on view—including Venus de Milo—were only plaster reproductions.

The museum was open for five hours on Tuesdays, Thursdays and Saturdays and two hours on Sundays. Entry was free for Germans and one franc for most others except students and artists. Many of the visitors were German soldiers; signs were posted in German asking them not to touch the art objects. Tours in German were organized and "guides with guttural accents escorted respectful droves of dazed soldiers" past the works on display. The German soldiers felt privileged; the French felt otherwise. After a late December 1943 visit to the museum with her young son, painter Jacqueline Gaussen-Salmon would write in her journal: "What misery to see it thus, the old Louvre of our childhood! Empty pedestals, emptier even than last year. Upright as they are, it looks like a decapitated forest. Here and there, lone plaster casts emerge from the desert and from closed doors."

One German, however, did not mind that the Louvre was largely empty; it still contained the piece he most wanted to see. In early November 1940 Hermann Göring demanded a secret visit to privately view one of his favorite works, a sixteenth-century life-size polychrome wooden statue by Gregor Erhart of Saint Mary Magdalene. A sculpture of a nude woman with luxurious tresses flowing to mid-thigh, the work portrays the legend according to which the saint lived alone in a cave clothed only by her hair. Referred to at the time as the *Belle Allemande* (Beautiful German Woman), the Louvre had purchased the piece in 1902 on the open German art market.

To prepare for Göring's November 5 visit, the museum staff cleared building debris from the courtyard by which his vehicle would enter and cleaned the staircase. To block the sight of the construction scaffolding and to provide a suitable background for the statue, they closed the shutters of the room to be used for the private viewing and draped the windows with beige velvet. The *Belle*

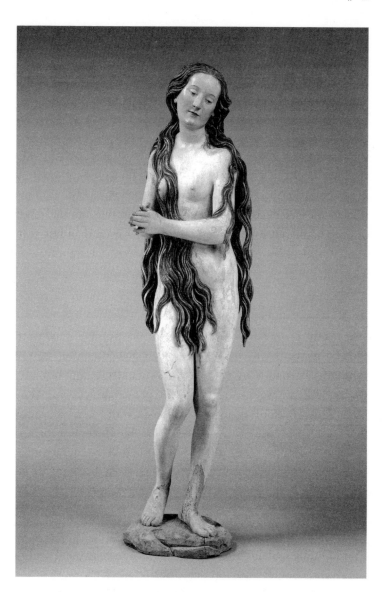

*Saint Mary Magdalene* ("belle allemande") (c. 1515–1520)

LOUVRE, DENON WING, LOWER GROUND FLOOR

*Allemande* was placed on a base and lit softly by the room's chandelier and two small spotlights. Museum officials delayed the museum's public opening time by two hours in case Göring wanted to privately visit other areas of the museum, since it had been stressed that his visit must remain secret.

Göring was accompanied by Ambassador Abetz and an aide-de-camp, Hermann Bunjes, who officially worked for the Kunstschutz, plus two representatives of the Louvre. While Department of Sculptures curator Marcel Aubert discussed the *Belle Allemande*, Göring gazed at the statue, stroking it with his fat hands, Aubert later reported, then commented that he was particularly interested in the statue since he owned a madonna attributed to the same artist. Walter Hofer, curator of Göring's personal art collection, would later say that the statue was "particularly suited to [Göring's] taste, being both German and nude." Regardless of Göring's reasons for coveting the *Belle Allemande*, he would not forget about her. He would visit her again the following spring, having decided that one way or another he would manage to get her.

By the time of Göring's visit to the Louvre that day, he had already begun to lay his hands on the confiscated Jewish-owned art and other items that had come under the control of Alfred Rosenberg's ERR. The previous month, when Hitler gave Rosenberg military support to steal the art, he had quickly sought someplace to transfer the items taken by Abetz and still at the German embassy. A new location also had to be spacious enough to hold the fruits of larger-scale pillaging. On October 4, 1940, Hermann Bunjes approached the Louvre to ask for space in the palace.

Bunjes was a young art historian who had, like Wolff Metternich, taught at the University of Bonn. He spoke fluent French and was familiar with the Louvre, having studied under Marcel Aubert at the École du Louvre. Before long, Wolff Metternich would realize with disappointment that Bunjes was an ally of Göring; later Bunjes would work for Göring directly. When Bunjes asked the Louvre for space, he said it was needed to store items seized from the collections of Edouard de Rothschild. Jaujard, hoping to find a way to keep the works in France, agreed to cede three rooms on the ground floor of the west wing of the Cour Carrée in an area formerly occupied by the Department of Near Eastern Antiquities and seal them off at each end. Later the Germans would requisition several additional rooms. With direct—and discreet—access from the courtyard, the arrangement was perfect for the Germans' purposes. First, they obscured the windows with wood, then the crates began flowing in on Sunday morning, October 6; they continued to arrive intermittently throughout the month. Contrary to Bunjes' statement, the items were not just those belonging to Edouard de Rothschild; they included items from other members of the Rothschild family and from collector Alphonse Kann.

Less than three weeks later, when the ERR's rooms in the Louvre already overflowed with 150 crates of paintings, furniture, carpets, statues and other items, plus hundreds more unpacked ones, the Germans requested yet more space. This time they wanted the small Musée du Jeu de Paume, located 700 yards west of the Louvre at the northwestern corner of the Tuileries Garden. The additional space was perfect. Its secluded location offered privacy from passersby and could easily be monitored from the German military headquarters in the Hôtel de Crillon just across the street. Jaujard agreed to the German request on one condition: that the French could prepare an independent inventory of the items brought there. The Germans were delighted with the new location's privacy and with Jaujard's quick accommodation. Jacques Jaujard was also pleased with the arrangement; he had just planted a spy in their midst.

# SIXTEEN

# MONTAUBAN, 1941

S OME SAY THAT the hilltop town of Montauban, thirty-four miles north of Toulouse, was originally named *Mons Albinus*—white mountain—by the Romans for its silvery willow-covered slopes; others say that the early Gascons named the town for the willows, which they called albas. The modern town was founded in 1144 by the Count of Toulouse, who built a castle on an embankment overlooking the Tarn River. As was common in France, a newer castle was built 200 years later during the Hundred Years war on the ruins of the first, this time by the English "Black Prince" Edward. The prince's château eventually fell into ruin and in 1659 a new Episcopal bishop's palace began to rise in its place. When all church property came into government hands during the Revolution, the almost-pink brick palace became the bustling city's town hall. In the 1800s it became a museum featuring the paintings of the native-born Jean-Auguste-Dominique Ingres. In 1940, the city of Montauban agreed to make room in the voluminous Musée Ingres for the artwork of the Louvre as well.

The move from Loc-Dieu Abbey to Montauban in late September and early October 1940 had been necessary for the

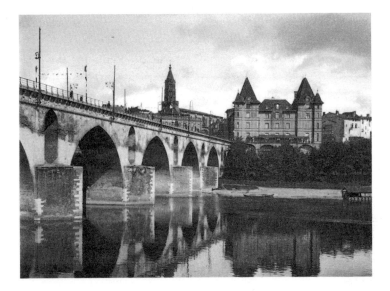

MUSÉE INGRES IN MONTAUBAN, ALONGSIDE TARN RIVER

preservation of the art, but there was a greater sense of calm around this operation than for the earlier evacuations. The biggest problem this time was the lack of trucks, fuel, drivers and supplies for the 47-mile trip southwest. A local French army corps provided trucks and drivers. An early September inspection of the art had found that during the June evacuation, rain had damaged some paintings. This time, the military also provided tarps to cover the artworks en route in case of bad weather. The artworks took to the road again in eleven convoys between September 28 and October 11; this time, there was no rain. On the morning of October 3, three trucks set out. One of them held eleven crates of art with, among other works, *Whistler's Portrait of His Mother* and, in crate LP0, the *Mona Lisa*.

Two days later, several more trucks left for Montauban, one of them carrying only the large rolled *Wedding Feast at Cana* and, luckily, two fire extinguishers. It had been an effort to load the long, heavy *Cana* in its equally heavy crate onto the truck, but the drivers did not expect any further problems for the relatively short ride, all of it flat until Montauban, except for one point where the road headed steeply downhill. The road had not presented any problems for the previous trips, but this time they failed to take the weight of *Cana* and its crate into account. As the driver started down the steep slope, a brake drum overheated, throwing off thick smoke and an acrid burning smell. The convoy stopped and called Mazauric at Loc-Dieu. The truck with *Cana* looked like it might catch fire, they said; send every available guard and all the fire extinguishers. A van with the men and equipment sped off from Loc-Dieu. After hearing no further news and imagining the worst, Mazauric eventually followed on a motorbike, but by the time she arrived at the scene not a soul was in sight. The problem had been resolved and the convoy had continued on, successfully negotiating the hilly streets of Montauban even with the damaged brake.

Once the move from Loc-Dieu was complete, the staff at Montauban—directed by René Huyghe, the head of the Louvre's Department of Paintings—went about the business once again of settling into new lodgings and arranging the artwork. By day, Huyghe kept the *Mona Lisa* in his office. By night, the painting shared a bedroom with either the Huyghes or the Chamsons. From time to time, they opened the painting's case to check that all was still well. They examined the almost 450-year-old work from up close, said Mazauric, "like a doctor scrutinizes a face to analyze even the most minor spot for signs of some secret illness."

While the evacuation to Montauban was underway, Jaujard was in his Louvre office juggling endless concerns. In addition to overseeing the huge construction project and dealing with the many ongoing needs of the depots, he had to obtain permission from the Germans every single time a work needed to travel, whether for restoration or exhibition, and every single time a staff member needed to cross the demarcation line. He was also monitoring the arrivals of pillaged Jewish collections at the newly sequestered rooms in the Cour Carrée while arguing that the looting defied the Hague Convention and trying to deal with the impact of the Vichy anti-Semite laws on his staff. In July 1940, the Vichy government had revoked the citizenship of 15,000 immigrants since 1927, forty percent of whom were Jews. The first specifically anti-Jewish statute in October 1940 excluded Jews from jobs that influenced culture or public opinion (such as teaching, journalism, and film), from many professions and from positions of responsibility in the military, judiciary and civil service, which included the Musées Nationaux. Even more severe statutes would be enacted the following year. Jaujard was also about to begin learning about Vichy priorities for the country's art.

During the Napoleonic wars, it was not just the emperor who had plundered; his troops did their fair share as well. By 1810, French Maréchal Nicholas Jean de Dieu Soult had carted hundreds of works out of Spain, including Bartolomé Esteban Murillo's seventeenth-century *Immaculate Conception*, which depicts Mary surrounded by several dozen cherubs. Upon Soult's death, his collection was put up for auction and the Louvre purchased the Murillo in 1852 for 615,300 francs, then the highest price ever paid for a painting.

On October 12, 1941, Jaujard received a visit from three emissaries sent by the government of Spain, a country still neutral in the war. They expressed a keen interest in the return of the Murillo—tucked away at Montauban—and of an ancient statue, the Lady of Elche, which had been uncovered in 1897 in the Spanish city of Elche and

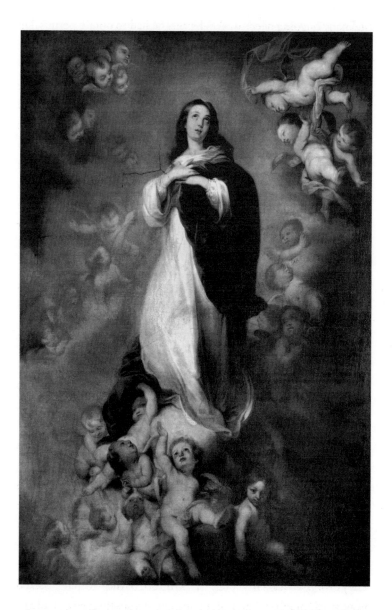

IMMACULATE CONCEPTION, BARTOLOMÉ ESTEBAN MURILLO (C. 1678)

sold to a French collector who in turn sold it to the Louvre. The Spanish representatives also mentioned several other items, some of which had been owned by the Musée de Cluny since 1859. They knew France had acquired the items legally, they said, but felt that the works represented an important part of Spain's cultural history. What could be done? they asked. Jaujard replied that, while he could not authorize any action, it might be possible to arrange a "strictly equivalent exchange" as a "sign of friendship between the two countries." Such exchanges between public collections had been encouraged by a 1932 resolution of the League of Nations, which did not contemplate the measure being used for political leverage. Nevertheless, immediately after meeting with Jaujard, the three Spanish emissaries went off to meet with his superior Louis Hautecœur, the Minister of Fine Arts. What could be done? they asked again. Hautecœur relayed the message to Vichy. It did not take long thereafter for Pétain to announce that he wished to reward Spain for its continued neutrality by ensuring that the Spanish masterpieces were returned.

Three weeks later, on November 6, 1940, Pétain made a trip to Montauban on one of his many brief tours within the free zone during 1940 and 1941, each carefully orchestrated to obtain maximum positive publicity. He stopped to tour the Louvre's depot, where various crates were opened for him. When Murillo's *Immaculate Conception* was displayed for him, he exclaimed, "So many children for a Virgin!"

By the end of November, government officials of the two countries had agreed that the Murillo and the other items requested by Spain would be sent to Madrid in tentative exchange for several alternative items of Spanish origin or of other cultural interest; the Louvre curators had no choice but to agree. On December 6, Huyghe left for Madrid with the Murillo, having agreed that the other items would follow later. The final exchange, approved on the French side by Pétain, was not finalized until June 1941. In the end,

Pétain was not happy that the arrangement had become an exchange; the Louvre, not happy about the arrangement at all, also felt that it had not been an equivalent exchange.

B efore long, it occurred to the Germans that they might also try exchanges as a ploy to get specific items particularly pleasing to their tastes. Hitler's foreign minister Ribbentrop, for one, had long had his eye on *Diana Leaving Her Bath*, one of the Louvre's most prized paintings by Boucher. Even before the war, during a December 1938 trip to France, Ribbentrop had twice visited the eighteenth-century masterpiece at the Louvre, lingering long in front of her. By the fall of 1940, he had already made it known that he wanted the painting by any means. It would not be so easy to do after having been top-pled as head pillager by Rosenberg, but he waited patiently for an opportune moment.

In March 1941, perhaps inspired by the way Spain had obtained the Murillo, that moment came. Ribbentrop asked Abetz to try to obtain the painting. Abetz, in turn, sent his emissary Karl Epting to see Jaujard with a message: the Germans wished to exchange the Boucher for an acceptable work in the German collections. What could be done? Epting asked. Jaujard sent a memo to Louis Hautecœur, informing him of Epting's request and asking what paintings might serve as appropriate options for an exchange. But he also questioned the principle of an exchange itself, given the requesting party.

Abetz, perhaps inspired by the helpful role the Vichy govern-ment had played in the exchange of the Murillo, bypassed Jaujard and instead contacted Admiral François Darlan, Pétain's most trusted associate. What could be done? Abetz asked. Darlan, in turn, went to see Jérôme Carcopino, the Minister of National Education, explaining that an exchange of the Boucher might perhaps lead to

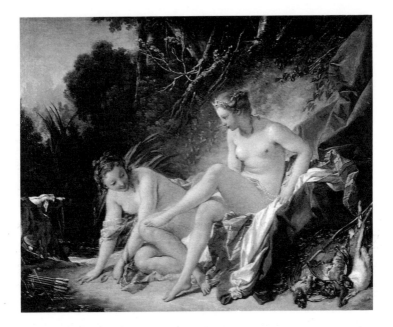

*Diana Leaving Her Bath*, François Boucher (1742)

LOUVRE, SULLY WING, SECOND FLOOR

the release of several thousand French prisoners of war. Darlan told Carcopino that he had noticed that Ribbentrop was "madly in love" with the nude Diana's thighs and he wanted to make Ribbentrop's "dream come true." "Get the painting to Berlin," ordered Darlan.

Epting had not offered a particular work in exchange for the Boucher. Rather, he had simply indicated by way of example that it could come from the Germans' French impressionist collections, leading the French to suspect that they intended to offer a painting the ERR had looted from French Jews. Jaujard had no choice but to begin negotiations for an exchange, though he and other museum officials dragged their feet with respect to identifying an acceptable painting to receive in the exchange. On April 24, 1941, after several

weeks had passed without the identification of an equivalent painting, Darlan issued an order to return the Boucher from Montauban
to Paris. Less than a week later, the painting was in Berlin.
Not long afterwards, Hautecœur happened to see Darlan, who
mentioned the painting. "What do you expect?" he told Hautecœur.
"Ribbentrop wanted the nymphs for his birthday . . . Don't be
annoyed over so little, he'll give you another bad painting in its place."

However, the exchange would not be considered final until the
French agreed to an acceptable trade. The French finally said the
Impressionists were already well represented in the Louvre's collections and that only a painting of the same period and value as
the Boucher would be acceptable. They then narrowed it down to a
work by Watteau, correctly assuming the German museum holding
it would refuse to give it up. By August, Ribbentrop had no choice
but to return the Boucher to Paris. *Diana* would remain at the Louvre
until the following spring, when Jaujard would discreetly send it to a
depot at the château de Sourches. Ribbentrop had not given give up
hope, ordering Abetz to keep searching for an acceptable German
painting to trade and to keep a close eye on the whereabouts of *Diana*.
But he could find no further pretext for an exchange; the painting
would remain safely at Sourches for the rest of the war.

J aujard and the Vichy administration would be at odds throughout the war, but there was one rare issue on which they agreed,
at least in part: how "ownerless" art of Jews who had left France
should be handled. The government helped create a series of regulations and agencies that allowed the Musées Nationaux—with
permission from the Germans—to exercise a right of first refusal to
purchase some of the looted artwork; in that way, the works would
at least remain in France. In the spring of 1941, certain collections
of Maurice and Robert de Rothschild were acquired as part of the

program. By September, the Rothschild items—among them five hundred paintings, an equal number of miniatures and a hundred valuable rugs and tapestries—were at Montauban.

By year-end, the contents of the Saint-Blancard depot, including the Seated Scribe, were also brought to Montauban in order to consolidate oversight. They were located in the Institut Calvin, a separate building near the Musée Ingres. A conservation workshop was also set up near the museum so that the paintings would require less travel for their care.

The year 1941 drew to a close with a false alarm and a piece of long-awaited welcome news. In late November, the architect of the Musée Ingres observed that, due to heavy loads on an upper floor, one of the building's beams was showing worrisome cracks that could cause the ceiling above one of the ground-floor rooms to collapse. This would have been a disaster on its own; it would have been far worse considering that many of the most precious works, including the *Mona Lisa* and the rest of the da Vincis, were stored on the ground floor. The curators felt that the risk was too great to wait for advice from Paris and wanted to move the paintings to another room immediately. However, the curator of the museum did not want to cede another room in the building, even on a temporary basis. After heated discussions, he finally agreed. Paris was then informed of the problem and an architect of the Musées Nationaux was sent to inspect the building; he suggested some preventive measures and the paintings were quickly back in place.

There was also some promising news on the heels of the tragic Pearl Harbor attack: on December 11, the United States at long last declared war on Germany, Italy and Japan. The curators would greet 1942 with hopes for a trouble-free year, but it would not be so. First would come floodwaters and then would come Germans.

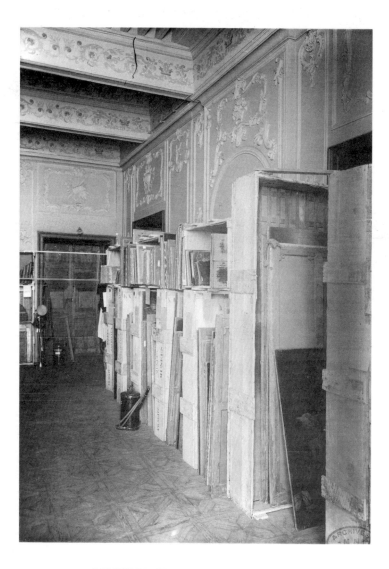

PAINTINGS ARRANGED FOR EASY ACCESS,
LOUVRE ART DEPOT AT MUSÉE INGRES, MONTAUBAN

# SEVENTEEN

# CHÂTEAU DE SOURCES

I N THE ELEVENTH century, two brothers from a family originally named Chaources built defensive fortresses side by side on a site most likely occupied since the Gallo-Roman era in the tiny village of Saint-Symphorien in the Sarthe Département, seventeen miles from Le Mans and 125 miles southwest of Paris. By the mid-1400s, one of the medieval structures was gone; the Marquis de Sourches first visited the remaining one in 1740, located at the end of a long secluded entry drive in the quiet countryside almost a mile north of the village. He fell in love with the panoramic view from the rise of land eastward across the estate's more than 220 acres of grounds and beyond to the distant horizon. The marquis eventually demolished the old château and replaced it with a new limestone palace à la mode, with three floors, 80 rooms and 229 doors and windows. In 1940, the château's large doors and windows welcomed the large paintings of the Louvre and Versailles; in 1944, its vast lawns would be used to send a message to Allied planes flying overhead. The owner, Duke François des Cars, hoped his gesture of allowing

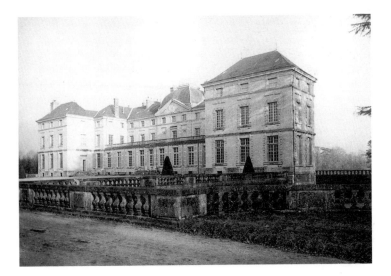

CHÂTEAU DE SOURCES

the partial requisition of his château would keep the Germans at arm's length. But he could not anticipate the Germans' repeated visits to examine a particular piece of art or that they would barge through the door in the middle of the night with machine guns in search of the curator. It would not be the only time German soldiers came with their guns.

During the June 1940 evacuation of the Loire depots, the curators had decided that the very large unrolled paintings from the Louvre and Versailles were too big and fragile to move all the way south to Loc-Dieu, especially given the road conditions. Instead, they grouped them, along with many of the large rolled paintings and other works at the isolated Sourches château. It was ideal as a depot for the large paintings since they could easily fit through the tall doors, reached by only a few steps fitted with a ramp, and it had unusual ground-level access to the basement windows, which

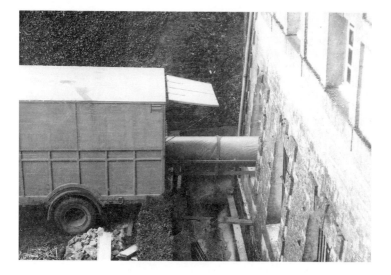

ROLLED ARTWORKS ENTERING THE BASEMENTS,
CHÂTEAU DE SOURCHES

allowed rolled paintings to slide easily and directly from trucks into the building. The basements were huge and dry and their half-meter thick arches were strong enough to withstand even heavy tactical bombs.

Throughout the war, Sourches would be one of the most important art depots. The *Raft of the Medusa* arrived from Versailles on a scenery trailer, the bridges and telephone wires along the route meticulously identified after the problem at Versailles. The large works at Sourches also included, among others, two paintings by Courbet and a group of works, each 13 feet tall, from Rubens' Medici cycle. Sourches also became home to Delacroix's iconic painting, *Liberty Leading the People*, portraying a bare-breasted woman raising the French flag during the Revolution of 1830. The Sourches château sheltered not only many of the large paintings from the Louvre but

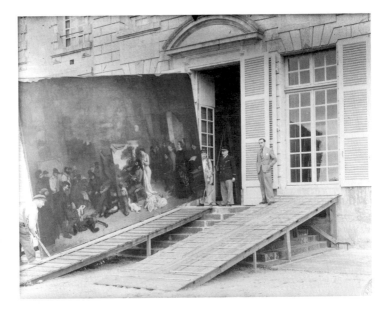

*L'Atelier du Peintre* (GUSTAVE COURBET) ENTERS SOURCHES

also tapestries, furniture and other items from Versailles and works from other museums. It also held smaller paintings such as Boucher's *Diana Leaving Her Bath*.

Items from private collections of several Jewish families were also at Sourches. In 1936 and 1937, George Huisman, then France's director of fine arts, had authorized the future evacuation of important private collections, a number of which were owned by Jewish families. Both the owners and the French fine arts administration knew the collections were at risk; one had only to watch what had happened in Germany.

During the great 1939 evacuation of the Louvre, Jaujard had obtained enough trucks to include a small portion—530 crates—of works owned by the families of several Jewish collectors, among them David David-Weill, a long-time Louvre benefactor and head of the Musées Nationaux board of directors until losing his position as a result of the Vichy anti-Semite laws. Jaujard had also obtained falsified pre-war stamps and applied them to contracts he drafted purporting to show that certain Jewish collectors had donated their art to the Louvre before the war. The Germans would simply ignore the documents.

While the Jewish-owned art was spread among the depots, one of the biggest lots comprised the 130 crates from David-Weill at Sourches. On January 20, 1941, a group of German police and military authories arrived at Sourches demanding a list of the contents of the David-Weill crates. On April 8, Wolff Metternich warned Jaujard by telephone that the ERR was about to confiscate the collection, having called in the slim hope that the French could find a way to stop it. But they could not: three days later, four German trucks arrived at Sourches and loaded up the 130 crates containing nearly 2,900 paintings, engravings, sculptures and other items. Destination: first the Jeu de Paume Museum in Paris, then Germany.

The Sourches seizure was just the beginning. In July and August 1941, the ERR seized Jewish-owned artworks at the Moire, Brissac and Chambord depots. Wolff Metternich had also called Jaujard four days ahead of the Chambord seizure but again both men were helpless to prevent it. The Germans confiscated not only most of the families' evacuated art but also much of the rest of their collections located elsewhere. During the course of the war, but in large part by 1942, four families alone—Wildenstein, Rothschild, Kann and Seligmann—would be looted of more than ten thousand objects located in Paris, the depots and elsewhere in France.

Sourches came to have another, very special, piece of art coveted by the Germans: the famous Bayeux tapestry, a 225-foot-long embroidery of wool on linen depicting the conquest of England in 1066 by William the Conqueror, Duke of Normandy, at the battle of Hastings. Created within a decade of the event, the tapestry had survived repeating pillage of the city of Bayeux during the Hundred Years War. It had survived the violent religious wars of the sixteenth century, including the 1562 sacking of the Bayeux Cathedral. The tapestry had also escaped destruction in 1792, when France's revolutionary government declared that all works of art reflecting the history of the monarchy were to be destroyed. Likewise, it remained safe during the Franco-Prussian War of 1870–1871 and World War I. The tapestry had survived a thousand years of intermittent war, revolution and neglect, nestled in the small town of Bayeux all that time except for a brief exhibition in Paris during the time of Napoleon. But by the eve of World War II, the Germans had already targeted it and throughout their occupation of France they would not give up their quest to get it.

In 1935, Heinrich Himmler, overseer of the Gestapo and the SS and an avid collector of both purchased and looted art, set up a research group called the Ahnenerbe, whose purpose was to prove— whether by truth, distortion or outright fabrication—Hitler's belief in the existence of a lost Aryan master race from northern Europe from which, according to Hitler, modern Germans were descended. As part of this quest, one mission of the Ahnenerbe was to identify and track down purported Aryan art and artifacts. As early as July 1939, the Ahnenerbe had taken the position that, since the Normans who had conquered England in 1066 were Vikings originally from northern Europe, the Bayeux tapestry was of Germanic origin, not French, and therefore eligible to be claimed as a German national monument. The Ahnenerbe faced a stumbling block to immediate plunder, however: the tapestry was officially a French national monument, entitled to protection by the Hague Convention.

On September 1, 1939, the almost 900-year old tapestry was removed from its exhibition case in Bayeux's former Palais des Evêques (Bishops' Palace), rolled onto a special mechanism, sprinkled with moth powder and crushed pepper, wrapped in two large sheets, tied and inserted into a custom-made, zinc-lined crate. The crate was set into a specially constructed concrete shelter in the dry, thick-walled, and presumed bombproof basement of the Palais des Evêques. The tapestry remained in the calm, safe darkness of its basement shelter until France fell to German forces in June 1940. Nazi attention soon turned to the tapestry.

Between September 1940 and June 1941, Germans demanded access to the tapestry a dozen times. An SS cameraman came to shoot the tapestry for two propaganda films. After all, how better to illustrate Hitler's goal of conquering England than by a work of art portraying the previous "Aryan" conquest? The most worrisome attention, however, was spearheaded by Himmler, who in early 1941 called for a detailed scientific investigation of the tapestry in his Ahnenerbe quest to prove Aryan origin and justify the tapestry's confiscation. From June through August 1941, German experts came to Bayeux to study and photograph the tapestry as part of work on a future multi-volume publication about the tapestry and an artist sent from Berlin began work on a detailed reproduction of the tapestry in pen and watercolor.

It was evident to Wolff Metternich that the tapestry was at risk. To provide a possibly stronger buffer for the tapestry, he suggested to Jaujard in August 1941 that it join the Louvre works stored at Sourches. The move may have been intended for the tapestry's protection, but its journey to Sourches would sorely test its thousand years of luck.

The Kunstschutz, although having ordered the move, did not provide fuel for the 220-mile round trip. Bayeux authorities solved the problem by borrowing a 10-horsepower van from a local trades-man whose engine, like many others in France, had been converted into a gazogène one, powered by burning wood or charcoal.

The tapestry's departure was set for 5 a.m. on August 19. Monsieur Cervotti, Bayeux's police commissioner, and Monsieur Falue, keeper of the tapestry, waited in vain for the driver to arrive. They finally walked over to the town's main street, where they found the driver struggling to start the van, which had only just recently been equipped with the gazogène converter. After finally getting it going, they headed to another spot in town to load twelve sacks of charcoal and a fire extinguisher. Just after 7 a.m.—already two hours late—they departed. Four hours later, the three men, the small van and its precious cargo reached Flers, only forty-two miles from Bayeux.

Not having eaten since before dawn, they decided to stop for lunch and turned off the van's motor to conserve fuel, leaving the priceless tapestry aboard. When they returned, the van would not start. For twenty minutes, the driver stoked and poked and prod-ded. Finally, after several exploding sounds, the driver, covered with black soot and sweat, managed to start the van and off they went. But not for long. At the edge of town the road inclined, causing the van to falter so much that they feared the motor would again give out. Cervotti and Falue jumped out and pushed the van up the hill. Once over the summit, the van started speeding downhill. Cervotti and Falue ran after the runaway van and caught up only when it reached level ground. The rest of the journey continued in this pre-carious manner until the men, tired and dirty, reached Sourches around 4 p.m. after the nine-hour, 109-mile trip. They handed over the tapestry to Maurice Sérullaz, the assistant head of the Sourches depot, whose first act was to affix red circles to the crate to indicate its priority for evacuation in case of fire or other danger.

In January 1942, the Ahnenerbe wrote to the Kunstschutz requesting access to the tapestry at Sourches. The request was answered by Bernhard von Tieschowitz, Wolff Metternich's second in command and of the same mind as his boss regarding the protection of French museum collections. Tieschowitz responded that since the Sourches château was unoccupied and unheated—neither of which was true—such a project should be delayed until better weather. The tapestry was safe at Sourches for the time being, but Himmler was just waiting; later, he would act.

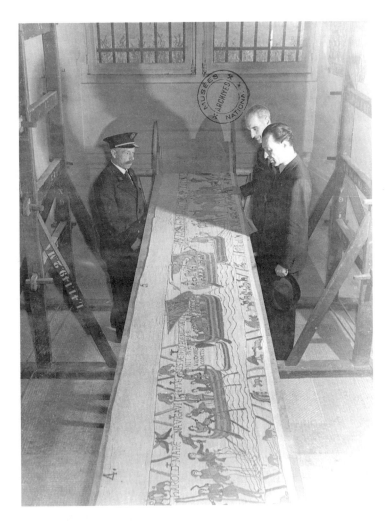

BAYEUX TAPESTRY, JACQUES JAUJARD AT FAR RIGHT

# EIGHTEEN

# MONTAUBAN, 1942

Though Wolf Metternich could not prevent seizures of artworks by other German agencies, he continued to assist Jaujard in any other way he could. By 1942, when the art depots were scrambling for heating fuel and every other sort of material, Wolff Metternich did his best to facilitate their supply. He also continued to provide precious travel passes for both curators and art.

But in one instance, Wolff Metternich's permission was specifically not requested to transport a piece of art. In May 1942, two individuals who had inherited a seventeenth-century painting by Le Brun of Pierre Séguier, a former chancellor of France, contacted museum officials. The heirs, fearful that the Germans might take the painting, inquired whether the Musées Nationaux might be interested in it. Museum officials arranged a modest payment and paperwork indicating it had been a gift. The painting was located at the former depot of Chèreperrine, owned by one of the heirs to the painting. But a problem remained: German permission was needed to move any valuable piece of art and the French did not want to draw German attention to the transfer. Furthermore, the size of the painting—almost 10 feet

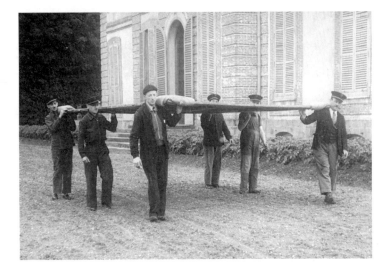

MOVING *CHANCELLOR SÉGUIER AT THE ENTRY OF LOUIS XIV
INTO PARIS IN 1660* FROM CHÈREPERRINE, MAY 1942

by 12 feet—did not lend itself to a discreet move; it called for a high, covered truck, which would be too noticeable. Instead, curators found a flatbed truck, then constructed a crate with the exact dimensions of the painting to lay flat on the truck. They assumed that inquiring eyes along the way would assume the truck was transporting a mirror. The painting covered the twenty-five miles from Chèreperrine to Sourches uneventfully and the men involved in the operation had the small joy of having kept a painting from the Germans.

The painting may have remained safe from the Germans, but Wolff Metternich, on the other hand, did not. From his very first days on the job, he had helped the French in many ways, from obtaining travel passes to finding fuel for vehicles to move artworks. He had even obtained the release of Georges Salles, the curator of the Louvre's Department of Asian Arts, from a prison camp. He had also been instrumental in protecting the works of French museums from German lust. In the early months of the German occupation, Wolf Metternich had repeatedly undermined Abetz's efforts to plunder the art at the depots. He had established procedures that forbid the German military to enter the depot and had warned French authorities of upcoming ERR raids. Above all, by the end of 1941, he had obtained a promise from Joseph Goebbels that the Germans would not try to remove the French national collections from France until the end of hostilities, though the promise would later be broken. By June 1942, Wolff Metternich had become such a thorn in the side of the Nazi looters—especially Göring—that he was forced to resign, reportedly on the express orders of Hitler. However, in a stroke of luck for France, the Germans replaced Wolff Metternich with Bernhard von Tieschowitz, the somewhat similarly minded deputy head of the Kunstschutz. The French museum system would continue to have at least some German assistance.

The summer of 1942 was also a time of unprecedented action against Jews by both Germany and Vichy in the occupied zone and in the theoretically "free" zone. The first major roundup of Jews had taken place in Paris the previous May when almost 4,000 men were sent off to internment camps in France; they were deported to Auschwitz in 1942. Between June and September 1942 alone, almost 37,000 Jews were deported from France to Germany, 7,000 of them from the "free" zone.

By then, the depot at Montauban had already lost a number of Jewish guards and administrative personnel because of the multiple anti-Jewish laws that Vichy had passed in 1940 and 1941. Jaujard had sent most of the Louvre's Jewish guards to the free zone early in the German occupation to protect them but the Vichy Jewish

statutes had gradually forced them out. Jaujard's assistant Suzanne
Kahn also lost her job as a result of the anti-Semite laws, as did several others. Charles Sterling, a Louvre curator and highly regarded
medieval art historian who had followed the art to Loc-Dieu and
then Montauban, had stayed into 1942, though he had been forced
from his position as a functionnaire. However, he managed to leave
France before the end of the year for New York.

Vichy's complicity with respect to undermining national art collections was subtle at the beginning of the Occupation. The
first hints of collaboration had appeared with the Spanish exchange
initiative in late 1940, then more openly with the "exchange" of
Boucher's *Diana* in mid-1941. Their complicity became more brazen
in the summer of 1942, though it involved a work that did not belong
to the French. The Ghent altarpiece, also known as the *Adoration of
the Mystic Lamb* for the theme of its largest panel, is an early fifteenth-
century polyptych by van Eyck, with large oak sections—in total almost
12 feet high and more than 15 feet wide—portraying Biblical scenes.
The work is one of the most famous panel paintings in the world.

In 1794, Napoleon's men snatched several of the central panels
from the altarpiece's home in a Ghent, Belgium (then Flanders)
cathedral as war booty and carted them to the Louvre; they were
returned to Ghent in 1815 after Napoleon's fall. A year later, the
cathedral sold several panels that in 1821 came into the hands of King
Wilhelm III of Prussia, who installed them in a Berlin museum.
Germany returned the panels to Ghent in 1919 as part of war reparations under the Treaty of Versailles.

In May 1940, as the Germans invaded Belgium, Jaujard agreed
to shelter the altarpiece and a group of other Belgian paintings in a
small museum in the château de Pau, located in the far southwest
of France near the Spanish border, a safe distance from German

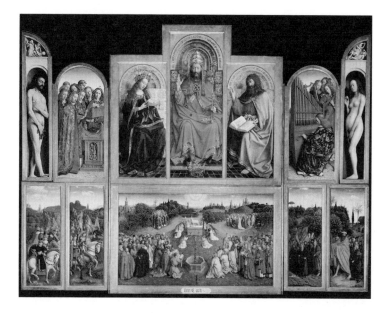

GHENT ALTARPIECE, JAN VAN EYCK (C. 1432)
MYSTIC LAMB PANEL AT BOTTOM CENTER

hands, or so they believed. They could not know that it was not safe at all: the entire altarpiece—not just the panels Germany owned until 1919—had been named in the 1940 Kümmel report, the secret German list of artworks abroad that the Nazis claimed as their own. They were just waiting for an opportune time to grab it.

In August 1941, a Kunstschutz employee had called Jaujard on behalf of Wolff Metternich to warn that some Germans might be coming to Pau in an attempt to take the altarpiece, purportedly back to Ghent. The Kunstschutz representative passed along a suggestion from Wolff Metternich that Jaujard should instruct the museum's curator to refuse to hand over the altarpiece without written authorization signed by three individuals: Jaujard, Wolff Metternich and either the mayor of Ghent or the Belgian director of fine arts. Jaujard and Wolff Metternich then quickly drafted an agreement to that effect.

The Germans showed no further apparent interest in the altarpiece and one could have concluded they had forgotten about it. But they had simply waited: exactly one year later after the Kunstschutz warning, one of Hitler's advisors, Ernest Buchner, swooped in and took the masterpiece. He chose his timing with care. Wolff Metternich had recently been removed as head of the Kunstschutz, Jaujard was away on vacation and his superiors in the Fine Arts administration were busy preparing for a museum opening. On August 1, 1942, a quiet Saturday, Buchner appeared at Pau and informed the curator that he had instructions to take the altarpiece back to Belgium. For some reason, the museum's curator did not follow the protocol that had been previously arranged. Instead, when he could not reach anyone in the fine arts administration, he contacted the government in Vichy for guidance. Prime Minister Pierre Laval, an avid Nazi collaborator, telegrammed the curator with orders to turn over the altarpiece to Buchner. On August 3, off it went—not to Belgium, but to Germany.

When Jaujard's boss and head of the French fine arts administration Louis Hautecœur, found out, he protested to his own superior, Abel Bonnard, Minister of National Education. The complaint fell on deaf, collaborationist ears. "When the head of the government gives an order," Bonnard told Hautecœur, "you are to execute it, not discuss it."

When Jaujard returned from his leave and learned of the kidnapping of the altarpiece, he was furious but kept an official silence in order to respect Belgium's request to keep the incident confidential while they tried to negotiate with the Germans for the return of the altarpiece. But he would not keep silent for long.

On August 30, 1942, another problem arose, this one at Montauban. At 5:30 p.m., a violent summer storm, some said a tornado, suddenly pounded the depot with rain and hail. Within seconds, an avalanche of rain filled storm sewers and the overflow formed a river that headed straight down the sloped road towards and then into the ground floor of the depot. The water instantly flooded every room but one on the ground floor and began to soak the Louvre's paintings.

Huyghe was away, as were Chamson and Mazauric, leaving curator Maurice Sérullaz, visiting from Sourches, and the night guard alone to deal with the sudden flood. Sérullaz quickly opened the French doors on the side of the building facing the river to let the flood water flow through and drain out. He called in off-duty guards and recruited additional assistance from Huyghe's wife, the fire department, the police department and the town hall. They raised the paintings that had been at ground level and swept aside and sopped up the water with mops and towels supplied by the nearby hospital.

Due to their quick action, only sixty-nine paintings were damaged, none of them seriously, although a restorer would be needed to make repairs. Among the works affected were Manet's *Olympia* and works by Titian, Goya, Velasquez, Raphael and Veronese. The *Mona Lisa*, on the other hand, was safe and sound in René Huyghe's tiny office—the only room on the entire ground floor that had not been flooded.

Life at Montauban returned to tranquility for a time, though the calm did not last. On November 8, 1942 the Allies landed in North Africa. Three days later, the German army invaded France's free zone. Jaujard and the curators at Montauban immediately knew they needed to evacuate the art and antiquities yet again since

Montauban was a likely magnet for Allied bombing and aerial combat. The town lay right along the major road and rail arteries linking the Pyrenees, the Mediterranean and Paris. Moreover, the Tarn River ran alongside the depot and the Canal du Midi was nearby; both were important waterways and thus also potential military targets. The bridge across the Tarn, just outside the depot, was another important transportation link. They also knew the town could become a German stronghold. The day the Germans invaded the free zone, the staff at Montauban wrapped the *Mona Lisa* and readied her for immediate travel if needed.

One morning at dawn, the police prefect of Montauban warned Huyghe and Chamson of the Germans' imminent arrival. The two men went to the local barracks to offer their services and were told to return the following day. By the time they returned, Germans had already overrun the barracks and emptied the food stocks held in reserve for the local population. From the windows of the museum, the Louvre staff watched endless columns of Germans troops arrive. As the enemy settled in, they strolled around town, snapping photos like tourists with "cameras more magnificent than their submachine guns."

The same day *Mona Lisa* was packed, Jacques Jaujard sent a request up his chain of command: Could we try to notify the British and American governments of all the art depot locations to avoid inadvertent bombing? An answer came back from the Vichy government: "No."

The Montauban staff began to pack up the other artworks, though they knew an immediate evacuation was not possible given German troop movements. In the meantime, Huyghe and Chamson began to search the countryside for a safer location for the art. They found several possibilities, none of them ideal, including the small château of Loubéjac, only six miles from Montauban. It would hold only a small part of the collections, but it would be a start. While the museum staff were waiting for the paperwork, they worried that the Germans would requisition the château for themselves. To stake a French claim first, on December 5 they moved just nine crates to Loubéjac; thirty additional crates followed on December 21. André Chamson took up residence at the new depot while the staff remaining at Montauban continued to pack. Meanwhile, the curators became increasingly concerned about the German presence and justifiably so; in the middle of one night, police searched the Chamsons' residence.

As 1942 came to an end, Jaujard's plate was unpleasantly full. The Germans now had direct control over the depots in the former free zone. The risk of battle in the area loomed but he had not yet found a solution for moving the thousands of paintings and antiquities at Montauban and Vichy authorities were refusing his requests to notify the Allies. Moreover, the Ghent altarpiece affair had taken an ugly turn within the French administration and Jaujard's job was in jeopardy. While he had initially agreed to remain silent on the matter, he changed his mind after the kidnapping became public and created a furor in the international press. In November, he spearheaded an official protest by the curators against the Vichy complicity in helping the Germans steal the altarpiece. The curators voted for a demand to return the altarpiece to Belgium; the vote was unanimous but for one person who felt that such an action could put their jobs at risk. He was right. Bonnard was enraged by Jaujard's role in the protest. Bonnard, an avid collaborator whom Chamson described as "more Nazi than the Nazis," accused Jaujard of acts of rebellion and on December 21 issued him an official reprimand for insubordination. The curators responded by threatening to resign en masse if Jaujard was fired, which only further infuriated Bonnard.

Yet on December 30, Jaujard gathered together the staff of the Musées Nationaux and spoke of the gratitude, joy and affection he felt each day working with them and thanked them for all the work they had done to preserve the country's artistic heritage. "What a magnificent obligation we have, what a privilege," he told them. "We have had to watch over it, to act, to battle," he said, "to conserve, protect, to save this supreme wealth that comprises artistic master-pieces of all time. So far, we have kept it sheltered from all dangers." But he went on to acknowledge the uncertain future, noting that "the difficulties that we have surmounted are perhaps not comparable to those that we will have to confront." He would be proved quite right.

# PART
# IV

# NEW BORDERS, NEW BATTLES

*November 1942 to December 1943*

# NINETEEN

# INSINCERE INTENTIONS

**A**FTER HITLER'S JUNE 1940 unexecuted order to "safe-guard" the French national collections, he had taken no subsequent action to obtain them. There was no urgency, he had originally thought, since he believed he would get all the French art he wanted upon his ultimate victory and a subsequent peace treaty. But towards the end of 1942, with the Allies in North Africa and the United States in the war, Hitler's plans for world conquest were looking less likely and it seemed an opportune time to accelerate the acquisition of certain French artworks for his dream museum at Linz. Göring was also anxious to expand his vast personal collection. He thought he might succeed on both Hitler's behalf and his own with a purported "cultural exchange" initiative where Ribbentrop—with *Diana Leaving Her Bath*—had not.

Knowing that Jaujard would be an obstacle to such a plan, Göring simply bypassed him, going in late November 1942 directly to Vichy Prime Minister Pierre Laval, who gave his approval in principle for an exchange program. With Vichy clout in hand, Göring sent his emissary Hermann Bunjes into action. On December 17, Bunjes informed Jaujard that the German government wished to negotiate an exchange of artworks between French and German museums, noting that Laval had already approved. When Jaujard asked for an example of French-owned art that would interest the German museums, Bunjes had a quick reply: the *Belle Allemande*. This was the carved wooden statue of Göring's dreams—and he did not intend it for any German museum. Jaujard was well aware that the exchange proposal was just a scheme to steal French artworks, only "surrounded by smiles," as a Louvre curator put it. While Jaujard could not outright refuse a German "request" or disobey a complicit government that had already approved it, he did manage to extract a critical concession from Bunjes that any exchange would involve no more than ten items.

Negotiations began on January 7, 1943, with Bunjes representing the Germans and Jaujard and Louis Hautecœur representing the French. Bunjes assured them that Germany was not remotely interested in seizing French property, adding that even the Jewish property taken by the Germans did not yet have a destination and that Hitler would make such a determination later. This slickly worded reassurance could give the impression that the seized Jewish property was still at the Jeu de Paume, though Jaujard knew otherwise from his spy at the museum that the seized Jewish property had begun leaving for Germany almost two years before.

Bunjes had a list of seven desired French pieces. Not surprisingly, the *Belle Allemande* was on the list. Another item was the *Presentation in the Temple*, the central panel of a fifteenth-century altarpiece known as the *Seven Joys of the Virgin*, created in Cologne by the Master of the Holy Kinship. But the first item listed was one of the most prized works of Paris's Musée de Cluny, a spectacular eleventh-century decorative altar frontal piece known as the Basel Antependium.

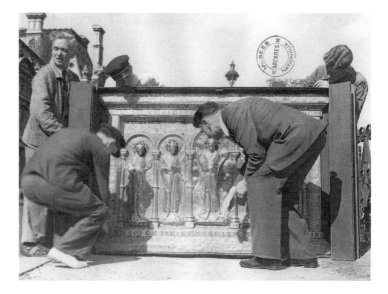

CURATOR AND GUARD INSPECT BASEL ANTEPENDIUM FOR
DAMAGE, IN LOUVRE'S COUR CARRÉE AFTER WAR'S END

Made of solid gold panels affixed to an oak core, the masterpiece had been legally acquired by France in 1854, though it was listed in the Kümmel report. Both Jaujard and Hautecœur were vehemently against exchanging the Antependium and it was seemingly removed from the list of works under consideration for an exchange. They could not know that, to avoid confrontation with Göring and his relentless desire for the altar, the Vichy government would later add it back. Moreover, the exchange proposal would set off almost a full year of pressure from the Germans and resultant foot-dragging by Jaujard that would enrage Bonnard and not only endanger Jaujard's job but also lead him to fear for his safety.

# TWENTY

# CHÂTEAU DE MONTAL

I N THE MEANTIME, Jaujard and the curators had to find a new, safer depot to replace the large space in Montauban. They searched for almost two months, but every potential château had a flaw, from difficult access to dampness and from inadequate size to insufficient lodging for guards. And some owners simply did not want to give up any of their creature comforts, even if it meant security from possible Nazi requisition. In early January 1943, the Chamsons, accompanied by Jaujard and his wife Marcelle, scoured the countryside within a reasonable distance of Montauban in search of a new depot. They finally spotted the château de Montal, eighty miles northeast of Montauban.

In the late fifteenth century, Lord Robert de Balsac had acquired a medieval manor on the heights overlooking the Dordogne Valley in the tiny hamlet of Saint-Jean-Lespinasse. Early the following century, his daughter, the widow of Amaury de Montal, rebuilt the structure in Renaissance style in anticipation of her son's return from waging war in Italy for France's King François I. She had the new château adorned with elaborate architectural sculptures; when she learned of her son's death at war, one of the sculpted stones

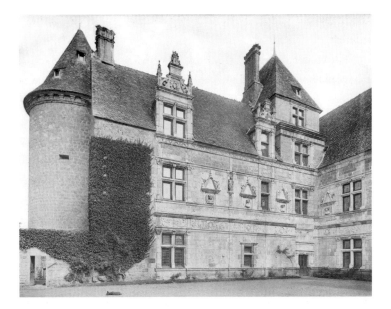

CHÂTEAU DE MONTAL

was engraved *Plus d'espoir:* Hope no more. Ownership of the château eventually fell away from the family and it passed from one owner to another. Between 1881 and 1903, the sculpted decor was auctioned off and then later bought back by art patron Maurice Fenaille after he acquired the château in 1908. In 1913, he donated the château to the French government, conditional upon its use by himself and his children. In January 1943, when the Jaujards and Chamsons came upon it, not only did it meet all the requirements for an evacuation depot but the current resident, Fenaille's daughter Madame de Billy, agreed to lend the entire château to the Musées Nationaux.

The château de Montal offered multiple advantages. It was relatively isolated, it posed a low fire risk and the nearby small town of Saint-Céré and neighboring villages contained enough lodging for the numerous guards, without being so large as to draw military interest.

The château's ground floor had four main large, vaulted rooms that could hold almost all the paintings. The smallest crates could be sheltered in an equally large space on the floor above. But it was still not large enough to hold all the evacuated treasures of the Louvre or to provide enough maneuvering space to open crates for conservation purposes. As a result, supplemental châteaux were found. The large rolled paintings would go to a small château in Bétaille, located ten miles from Montal; other paintings would go to a small château in nearby Vayrac. Also nearby was the château de Lanzac, which sheltered the art belonging to the Musée Ingres.

E ven though the new Louvre depots were identified before the end of January, 1943 it took time and effort to organize the move. First, Jaujard had to obtain both Vichy and German permission, the Kunstschutz needed to make inspections and funding from the Vichy government had to be arranged. More intensive effort than ever was needed to obtain enough manpower, vehicles, fuel and supplies for the move. Moreover, Montal needed renovations to provide access for the large crates. Thus, though the decision to leave Montauban had been made in November 1942, the move to Montal did not take place until March 1943.

Almost eight hundred pounds of packing material arrived at Montauban on March 1. The first convoy was loaded the next day; it headed out at 7 a.m. on March 3 with police motorcycle escorts. Since gasoline-powered trucks were no longer available, the more dangerous and unreliable gazogène-powered vehicles were used. The scenery trailers that had previously transported the heavy, long rolled paintings had long since returned to Paris; this time, workers transported the *Wedding Feast at Cana* and the other large rolled works to their newest temporary home at Vayrac on a gazogène-powered cattle truck. Yet again, the move ran into a hitch. A police officer stopped them along the way and accused them of transporting cannons and airplane parts. But by March 13, sixty-five truckloads of art and antiquities had safely navigated the steep hills of the Dordogne to bring part of the Louvre treasures to their next homes. *Mona Lisa* was now tucked away at Montal.

Montal and the two satellite châteaux, Bétaille and Vayrac, could only fit the Louvre's 3,500-plus paintings. The Seated Scribe and the other Egyptian antiquities at Montauban that had been moved to Loubéjac in December were relocated yet again in April to another château, La Treyne, located twenty-four miles west of Montal on a rocky promontory overlooking the Dordogne River. La Treyne also became home to the museum's objets d'art and drawings, part of the Louvre archives and several crates from the Musée Guimet, as well as the Maurice and Robert de Rothschild collections that had been discreetly acquired by the state in 1941. One day a young staff member visiting La Treyne from the Louvre's Department of Paintings spotted the crates in the château's *grand salon*, pointing out that they bore the recognizable insignia of the Rothschild family. The next day, the depot staff scraped down the crates to erase any identifying trace. They did it just in time; only days later, a German inspector arrived. He looked around for an hour, noticed nothing special and left.

I n 1939, it was not only the Musées Nationaux that had conducted evacuations. France also had several hundred provincial museums; the contents of those considered most at risk had been evacuated to over one hundred depots spread across the country. It had been a wise move, since forty-nine provincial museum buildings were partially or entirely destroyed during the Germans' advance

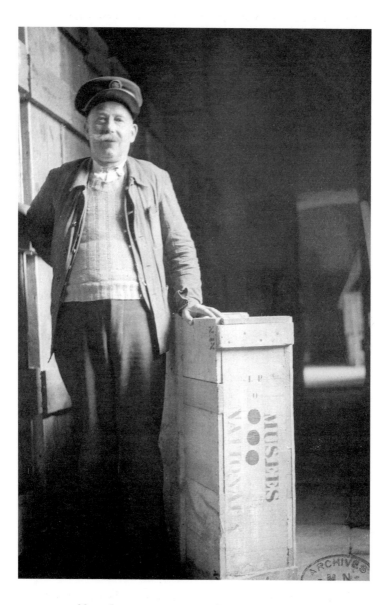

*Mona Lisa* IN CRATE AT CHÂTEAU DE MONTAL

through France in May and June 1940. In 1941, additional provincial museums evacuated their collections and new legislation brought the country's provincial museums under state control, though the legislation was not fully funded until 1943. The new arrangement added even more responsibilities to Jaujard's already heavy load. Additional provincial evacuations took place in 1942. In March 1943, amid concern about potential military operations in southern France, provincial collections from Avignon, Lyon, Marseilles and other southern cities were evacuated farther inland, a number of them to locations within driving distance—some just barely—of the Louvre's depots, giving the curators far more inspection work to do.

By 1943, La Treyne depot head André Chamson was responsible for regular inspections of eight depots. With each new inspection, Chamson, like all the other curators, was reminded that the work could be for naught if wayward German troops raided a depot. Occasionally, though, the curators received a bit of reassurance that all was well, at least for the moment. During Chamson's first inspection of a Benedictine monastery sheltering works from the museums of Narbonne and Carcassonne, he was invited to join the monks for lunch. The meal took place in the monks' customary silence, though the young abbot read a passage from the Bible that Chamson recounted as follows: "'Then Caesar ordered him to come before him and told him: Deliver to me that which has been entrusted to you or I shall put you to death. And he replied, 'You can put me to death but I shall never surrender that which has been given unto my protection.'" Chamson nodded to the abbot in gratitude.

While the curators in the countryside looked after the evacuated treasures, Jaujard continued to battle in Paris with the Germans over the exchange proposal. He managed to whittle down the total of items under consideration. He had curators write long, technical reports explaining why each work suggested by the Germans was too valuable to give up. In March, he refused to send the Basel Antependium from Chambord to Paris for a requested viewing by Göring, arguing that the thousand-year-old altar was too fragile to travel and could not leave Chambord unless Pétain himself gave permission. Göring eventually sent his representatives to Chambord in June to inspect it there instead. But in early July Bonnard ordered the return of the altar to the Louvre for another anticipated viewing request by Göring. This time, Jaujard could not refuse the direct order and the work went to Paris. The battle with the Germans—and the Vichy government—over the "exchange" of art had only just begun.

# TWENTY-ONE

# A CHÂTEAU LIFE

SOME WARTIME BATTLES are public; more private ones lie below the surface. So it was with the staff of the Musées Nationaux as they protected the art and antiquities of the Louvre. If any French citizens had given thought to the curators who had taken up residence in the elegant châteaux, they may have been envious, but in most ways the curators' lives were not remotely as glamorous as they might have seemed.

Away in the countryside, depot employees were subjected to far less daily contact with German troops, but they also had far less contact with friends and family. In addition, their empty Paris-area homes were potential targets for German requisition, which required repeated intervention by Jaujard and Wolff Metternich to prevent. Residences not eyed by Germans could be targeted by squatters, as was the Chamsons' Paris pied à terre.

At the châteaux, the curators' existence was half-aristocrat, half vagabond, said Mazauric. They may have worked and sometimes lived in sumptuous quarters, but they used chipped plates and second-hand bedding Jaujard had managed to find. When curator Hans Haug took over the Cheverny depot, he was told to bring his own sheets. As the war went on, elegant bedchambers offered little compensation when they were frigid from lack of heat. And curators who had spent their days in the hallowed halls of the Louvre, Versailles and other museums in the sometimes rarified atmosphere of art curation now found themselves moving crates, arranging for weapons and ordering supplies of snake bite anti-venom.

In the châteaux where owners or their representatives were resident, the staff had to learn to mix with the upper crust. At Valençay, Van der Kemp developed an easy relationship with the duke. Curators at other châteaux generally also found ways to relate to the owners. "We had to acquire some notions of hunting vocabulary," Mazauric said. "Thirty or forty technical words well placed in the conversation sufficed to make us worthwhile conversation partners."

For the most part, depot staff and château owners got along well or at least stayed out of each other's way, but occasionally there was friction. Sometimes it was minor; other times it was anything but. During the June 1940 evacuation, as Louvre attaché Christine Desroches Noblecourt was taking the Egyptian antiquities from Courtalain to Saint-Blancard, a new depot manager arrived at Courtalain with a glamorous but garish girlfriend in her sports car, which she had offered as an escort vehicle for one of the convoys. The marquise of Courtalain initially refused to let the girlfriend in. When Desroches Noblecourt pointed out that they could not leave the next day without the woman's car, the marquise haughtily retorted, "What, you're taking sides with her against me?" The tension escalated when Desroches Noblecourt returned to Courtalain several days later. First, the marquise gave her a frosty reception. Later that evening, she said to a dinner guest, "Paris will be saved; I had masses said for the hills that surround the city." After Desroches Noblecourt scornfully replied "Do you really think your masses are

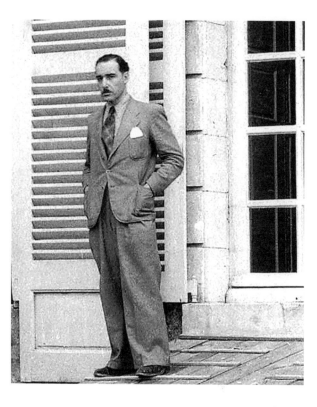

GERMAIN BAZIN AT THE CHÂTEAU DE SOURCHES

going to stop the invasion?" the guests refused to speak to her for the rest of the meal.

But minor sniping of that sort paled in comparison to the all-out war that the owners of the château de Sourches conducted against the Musées Nationaux. In June 1940, when Germain Bazin, the newly appointed head of the Sourches depot, arrived at the château, Duke François des Cars welcomed him at the front door with a warm, "Monsieur, you are at home here." The relationship went downhill from there.

Like a number of the châtelains that had opened their castles to the Musées Nationaux, the duke and duchess had done so primarily to prevent the occupation of Sourches by Germans. Most château owners may not have been thrilled to share their domains, but the des Cars began to openly chafe at the arrangement within just a few months of signing the requisition documents in May 1940. At the end of September, they agreed to provide a certain quantity of wood for heat for the depot's use, but a week later, they reduced the promised quantity by more than eighty percent. A day after that, the duke refused to provide the electric saw needed to cut the wood. In early December, he threatened to cut off water and electricity to the rooms used by the depot unless a new payment arrangement was made. He kept his threat: on December 30 he removed the electric meters. Four days after that, he demanded four rooms back. The demands continued non-stop throughout the winter and into the spring and summer of 1941. In July the duke asked Bazin to forbid the guards from inviting family members during their vacations because the château was not a "retirement home for the personnel of the Musées Nationaux." Less than two weeks later, the pond holding essential water in case of fire was empty and the duke would not promise when it would be refilled. He again disputed the agreement about the supply of wood and again threatened to cut off the depot's water. Another two weeks later, the duchess said she urgently needed to reclaim yet another room, then simply stuffed it with unused furniture. Two weeks after that, the duchess said there was no room for the visiting Jaujard. The endless demands went on. The last one from the duke came on November 10, 1941 when he reiterated a request that Bazin relinquish the kitchen facilities he had been given. Less than two weeks later, the duke died. Two months of calm ensued, after which the duchess once again began making demands, this time supported by the duke's brother. Demands and disagreements would continue past the end of the war and even after the depot closed down in 1947, when the duchess and her brother-in-law would sue the Musées Nationaux. The lawsuit would go on until 1953.

If outsiders idealized the château life of the Louvre curators, they surely overrated the quality of life of the guards. Some had rooms in the châteaux or outbuildings, but many of the rooms were so spartan that Germain Bazin said they were like cells. A number of the guards were older men, many of them injured veterans from World War I; Bazin appealed to Jaujard to try to find them at least a comfortable chair. Other guards had to bicycle from nearby villages in hot summers and cold winters. They earned little and sometimes worked more than sixty hours a week, much of it on outdoor patrol, and wore increasingly shabby uniforms and shoes, both of which Jaujard tried to have replaced.

The guards and firemen patrolling the Louvre had it far easier by comparison; their biggest problem was often simple boredom. Only young and fit men could serve as firemen. Every shift had two two-man patrols, each starting from a different point and following a complicated itinerary that took them throughout the palace. The men surveyed the roofs of the palace and walked the endless attics with enormous oak beams overhead. They patrolled the dark basements by a flashlight's dim glow, passing along the medieval foundations of Philippe Auguste's original fortress and through large rooms stuffed with statues and other items evacuated from both the upstairs galleries and other museums. To break the monotony of the long hours of patrol, they found ways to amuse themselves. Sometimes one of the men would hide behind a statue or in one of the endless dark corners and wait for his shift partner to come along, then jump out and scare him half to death by pretending to be Belphégor, the phantom of the Louvre in a 1927 horror story. A chase would then ensue as they clattered down the venerable parquet halls until reaching the public spaces, where they would return to a slow, dignified walk.

Curators at the depots had little time to get bored. They looked after the artwork and ensured the smooth operation of the depots, including tasks that ranged from assuring guard coverage to arranging and conducting the ever-important fire drills. They corresponded with Jaujard and local German municipal authorities to be sure signs were in place forbidding troops to enter. The signs would be respected for now; later it would be a different story. Several of the curators also continued their scholarly research and some returned to Paris from time to time to conduct courses at the École du Louvre; André Chamson turned to his writing. Many of them, including Chamson, also found time to join the Resistance.

Life at the depots was not all work. At Montauban, the Chamsons and Huyghes received friends and visitors that ranged from writers, journalists and publishers to artists and art historians. The Chamsons also had their young daughter Frédérique to raise. It was not a typical childhood to have everyday exposure to some of the world's most spectacular art, including, from time to time, the *Mona Lisa*. In the afternoon after school, Frédérique visited her mother at work at the depot, where Mazauric would give her a few coins to get a small treat at the neighboring pâtisserie. After she returned, her mother would pull out one of the unwrapped, unframed masterpieces and discuss it with her daughter.

Like all French residents during the war, the curators and their families battled to find enough to eat. After the Chamsons moved

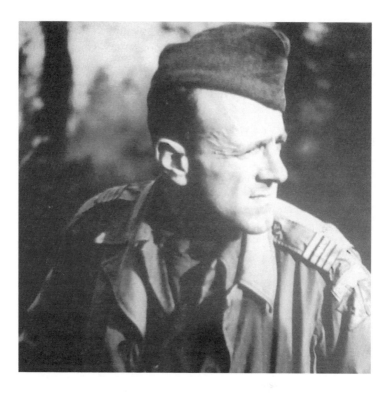

ANDRÉ CHAMSON

to La Treyne in 1943, they had the opportunity to buy a cow, giving them hope for better nutrition and relief of André Chamson's ulcer. At an agricultural fair, they chose a beautiful cow and named it M.N., for "Musées Nationaux." When the animal soon stopped giving milk, they learned it was a beef cow. They returned to the fair with a farmer who helped them choose another cow, this one skinny and ugly, but which would give plenty of milk until the end of their stay. Some of the Louvre's guards had a different meaning for the initials M.N.: *mal nourri*, or "malnourished."

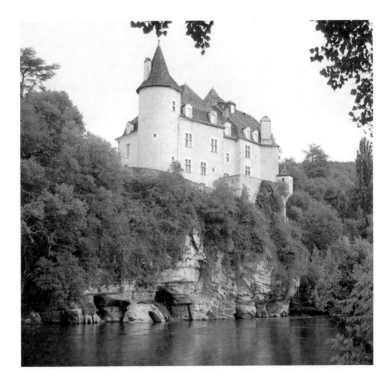

CHÂTEAU DE LA TREYNE

Jacques Jaujard juggled so many battles, he appeared to be in multiple places at once. In Paris, he attended one meeting after another, including curators meetings, those of the Réunion des Musées Nationaux (an umbrella organization responsible for, among other things, acquiring and displaying artworks for the French national collections) and its subcommittees and others with his spy at the Jeu de Paume. He met with his superior, Louis Hautecœur, and had numerous meetings with Göring's representative Hermann Bunjes about the exchange proposal. In addition, he continued to make endless phone calls and issue endless memos, letters and reports that went to and from the curators on every conceivable topic from guns to guards. Memos kept him abreast of events at each depot; many were of grave importance, others a bit less so. In January 1942, with qualified staff scarce, Germain Bazin at Sourches wrote to Jaujard that a new guard was needed—a "younger and more intelligent" one—who could take care of vehicle maintenance. Jaujard found a candidate and arranged the paperwork. At the beginning of March, Bazin wrote to Jaujard that the new guard was worse in aptitude and intelligence than the previous one and that he appeared to be "ignorant of the most basic principles of the workings of a motor and the mechanism of a vehicle." Jaujard replaced the guard. Five weeks later, Bazin wrote to Jaujard that the new guard was not up to par and that he was worried about expensive repairs that would result from damage "by the hands of a man so inept and unintelligent."

Jaujard's memos and phone calls also went to and from the Kunstschutz to enforce rules intended to prevent troops from entering the depots and to push back efforts of German troops to commandeer outbuildings and grounds at depot locations. Jaujard also worked with the Kunstschutz to obtain vehicles and gas, telephones, heating fuel for the depots and fuel for the motorized fire-protection water pumps, all of which became harder to come by as the war went on. He also made countless trips to the depots across France, not only those holding items from the national museums but also almost sixty provincial depots. In 1943 alone, he made six trips totaling more than eleven weeks of travel to southwestern France to find replacement depots for Montauban and to inspect all the Louvre depots. Beginning in 1943, he also fought to obtain exemptions for young men from Vichy-imposed forced labor rules, which in many cases would save their lives.

# TWENTY-TWO

# RESISTANCE

I N HIS FAMOUS June 18, 1940 speech, Charles de Gaulle called the French people to action with the words, "Whatever happens, the flame of resistance must not and shall not go out." He invited the French soldiers who had been evacuated to Britain to join his new London-based *Forces françaises libres* (Free French Forces). But of the 115,000-plus soldiers that the British had recently evacuated from the far northern French coastal town of Dunkirk, less than 3,000 had joined de Gaulle by August 1940. In addition, he had only grudging support from England and none from the United States. Churchill supported the Free French movement but disliked the arrogant, inflexible de Gaulle; Roosevelt said de Gaulle aimed to be another Napoleon and wanted nothing to do with him.

Resistance within France was equally slow to take root, although from the very beginning of the Occupation, a small number of people had begun to organize, among them employees of the Musées Nationaux. Initially, Resistance numbers remained small since, early in the Occupation, there was little hope of assistance from the outside world and without it, resistance against both the Germans and the complicit Vichy government seemed futile to most. Also, many

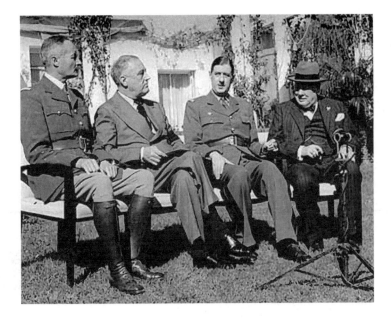

FROM LEFT, HENRI GIRAUD, FRANKLIN D. ROOSEVELT,
CHARLES DE GAULLE, WINSTON CHURCHILL, JANUARY 1943

people, including those in the powerful Communist party in France, had no more enthusiasm for de Gaulle than they did for Pétain. Referring to them both, a Communist poster in January 1941 read: "France wants neither cholera nor the plague." But little by little, internal resistance began to grow. It meant many things. At first, and for most people, it meant small, solitary acts like subtly jostling German soldiers on the sidewalks, ripping down German posters or deliberately slowing a delivery. More actively, it could mean hiding people or participating in strikes. Still more active resistance ranged from publishing underground newspapers to passing military information to the Allies and from sabotaging industrial production, phone lines and railways to carrying arms.

By July 1943, de Gaulle's Free French Forces had swelled to 50,000, still just a fraction of what it would be a year later. Inside France, the active Resistance had grown by 1943 to hundreds of thousands of men and women, many of them not remotely in support of de Gaulle. Originally composed of numerous unaffiliated groups both large and small, by early 1943 many disparate Resistance groups had begun to form working coalitions to increase their capabilities. In February 1944, many of them would unify to form the French Forces of the Interior (*Forces françaises de l'Intérieur*, or FFI).

E arly in the war, resistance had been primarily an urban activity. In larger population centers, there were more like-minded people and they could easily blend into city anonymity. Towns also had more resources for the production of explosives and clandestine and forged documents as well as more networks of individuals to distribute them. But the geographic distribution of the Resistance began to change dramatically in February 1943 after Vichy enacted its *Service du travail obligatoire* (STO) scheme, a forced work program that subjected French males in their early twenties to deportation to Germany to replace German workers who were being drafted in large numbers for military service at the Russian front. To avoid the program, young Frenchmen by the tens of thousands went into hiding in the thinly populated hills, forests and mountains of rural France, which contained few occupation troops but much natural cover that made even aerial reconnaissance difficult. These men came to be known as the *maquis*, from the Italian word for dense Mediterranean evergreen bushes, which evolved into the Corsican expression *darsi alla macchia*—take to the maquis—the act of fleeing one's village into the rugged Mediterranean hills and their tall macchia scrub vegetation, which men might do to escape authorities or vendettas. The isolated, steep and forested hills and river valleys surrounding the Louvre's Montal depot and the others nearby were particularly well suited for maquis activity. The depot staff came in contact with the maquis almost immediately after the Louvre moved its treasures to the area in 1943 and many of them joined up.

During walks in the secluded forests around La Treyne, André Chamson and his wife found containers of weapons that the Allies had begun to parachute in for the Resistance. Before long, Chamson was leading a double life as "commandant Lauter" of a local maquis cell. To meet with them, Chamson sometimes headed off into the forest. Other times, he liaised with them via a female contact who came to see him at the depot. When she arrived, the woman required Chamson's wife to leave the room; for the maquis, secrecy could mean the difference between life and death.

A number of other curators were also in the maquis. Numerous guards were as well, many of whom were deserters from the STO forced work program. Maquis members at the depots began to store leaflets, cash, armbands, weapons or ammunition in their quarters and even among the crates of art, which caused great concern to Jaujard, since discovery of these items during a German search would almost certainly mean confiscation of the artwork as well.

As Resistance activity blossomed during 1943, the Germans began to suspect that the depots of the Musées Nationaux were being used to store clandestine supplies. By October, they began to take action. Until then, a protocol between the Musées Nationaux and the Kunstschutz had stipulated that no German, civil or military, could enter any of the art depots without advance and specific high-level authorization, both French and German. On October 5, 1943, Tieschowitz came to the Louvre to warn Jaujard that, effective immediately, local German military authorities could search any depot and open any crate to look for Resistance leaflets, unauthorized weapons and munitions. Although Jaujard repeatedly warned the depot heads not to keep such material at the depots, he knew the warnings sometimes fell on deaf ears. On one occasion, when he learned the Gestapo was about to search the depot at the abbey of Saint-Guilhem-le-Désert, he immediately sent André Chamson on an urgent mission to warn the abbey's priest, who quickly emptied a crypt full of submachine guns and a recently landed British parachutist.

While most Musées Nationaux staff involved in the maquis kept their activities secondary, René Huyghe, head of the Montal depot, led an active, high-profile double life as a maquis leader that caused Jaujard great concern. When an errant guard made off with Huyghe's stash of weapons, Huyghe and several maquis helpers kidnapped the man and brought him to the château. While Huyghe distracted the depot guards, the helpers smuggled the prisoner up to the château's attic. After the man admitted he had stashed the weapons in Paris, Huyghe personally set off to retrieve them, calling on Jaujard for help. Until Huyghe returned with the weapons—an operation at great risk of German discovery—the hostage remained in the attic under maquis guard, just above the *Mona Lisa* and the other most valuable paintings of the Louvre. His meals were supplied by Huyghe's mother, who had agreed to bring the food upstairs, but only on the condition that he would be properly fed.

Huyghe went out on a limb in other ways. With the help of a local municipal official who was also in the Resistance, Huyghe arranged false identity papers for eight young men who had been sentenced in absentia to death for fleeing German military service and then he hired them as guards at the Montal depot. Since the Germans knew that every depot employee had to have an impeccable dossier, they had little reason to question the men's presence.

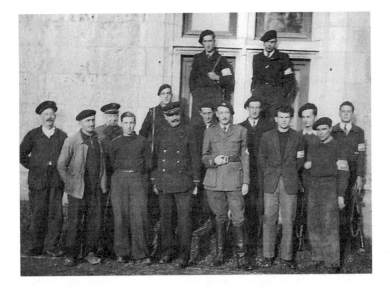

RENÉ HUYGHE (FRONT, THIRD FROM RIGHT) WITH HIS BAND OF MEN

The Louvre staff's Resistance activities extended far beyond aid to STO defectors and the maquis. Some staff members, such as Christiane Desroches Noblecourt, an attaché in the Louvre's Department of Egyptian antiquities, served as couriers. After evacuating the Egyptian treasures from Courtalain to Saint-Blancard in the spring of 1940, she initially returned to Paris, where Jaujard made her acting curator of the department. Having joined a fledgling Resistance group just days after de Gaulle made his June 1940 speech, she soon began to leverage her museum position to crisscross France with messages for the Resistance. Crossing the demarcation line between the occupied and free zones required an *ausweis*, but the Kunstschutz was liberal about arranging passes for museum staff upon Jaujard's request. Though the Saint-Blancard depot was in the able hands of more senior staff, Desroches Noblecourt occasionally asked Jaujard to arrange an *ausweis* to "inspect" the depot. Knowing full well she had other destinations in mind once she crossed into the free zone, he responded with a smile, "You're right, your crates need you. What professional dedication!"

The Resistance was also active at the Valençay depot. André Leroi-Gourhan, an assistant curator of the Musée Guimet, was asked by Jaujard and the head curator of the Guimet to go to Valençay, ostensibly to help out with the Guimet art collections in storage at the depot but also to contact the Valençay area maquis to help assure they would not provoke any actions against the Germans near the château and thus put the art collections at risk. Leroi-Gourhan made contact with the maquis as instructed, but rather than simply warning them off, he joined them. Leroi-Gourhan also recruited several other members of the depot staff into the group, which was aptly baptized "*le maquis de la Vénus.*"

The BBC transmitted coded messages to advise the area's maquis of incoming deliveries to the duc de Valençay's forests and others nearby; listeners over the airwaves heard, among other phrases, "*La Vénus de Milo tricote*" (Venus de Milo is knitting) and "*La Victoire de Samothrace fait du vélo*" (The Victory of Samothrace is riding a bicycle).

Gérald Van der Kemp, the Valençay depot head, also helped by relaying information to the area maquis, an easy job since the surrounding forests were full of them. In 1940, Churchill had created a top-secret service called the Special Operations Executive (SOE), whose goal was to "set Europe ablaze" by conducting subversion and sabotage in the occupied territories and by providing aid to local Resistance movements. The SOE's F Section parachuted its first member into the Valençay area in May 1941. By 1943, the F Section had grown to over a thousand members. Unbeknownst to the duke, they often met in his forest, where they also received parachute drops of weapons and supplies.

Van der Kemp was comfortable acting as a relay to the maquis but feared that doing more would expose the château, its inhabitants and the artwork to Nazi reprisals. He was horrified when he found out that Leroi-Gourhan had stockpiled Resistance weapons in a grotto on the château's grounds and armbands of the FFI in the château's attic, and demanded that Leroi-Gourhan get rid of them. Van der Kemp's anxiety would turn out to be well justified.

L ike many others in France, a number of Louvre staff members were also involved in the underground press that had begun to sprout in the earliest days of the Occupation, since the regular press was censored in both the occupied and "free" zones. The Gestapo actively sought out those involved and anyone caught was subject to arrest, deportation or worse. While at Montauban, André Chamson wrote an underground book, *Le Puits des Miracles* (The Well of Miracles). Each morning he took the pages written the evening before and carefully tucked them in the hollow of a tree to avoid their discovery in case his family's apartment was searched. Jaujard's wife smuggled the very last pages of the manuscript to Paris, hidden in her toothbrush holder.

W ithin months of the Germans' arrival in Paris, underground groups had begun to sprout in the city. The groups were usually small, since Nazi eyes were everywhere and large gatherings ran a higher risk of being noticed by Germans and denounced by collaborationist neighbors or coworkers. Some of the first and most active members of these groups were employees of the Musées Nationaux and a number of their clandestine activities took place right under the nose of the Nazis in the endless rooms and shadowy halls of the Louvre itself.

One early Resistance leader was art historian and Musées Nationaux curator Jean Cassou. After assisting with the evacuation in the fall of 1939, he had served as Carle Dreyfus's assistant at Valençay before being called back to Paris in the summer of 1940. Very quickly, he helped form one of the first Resistance groups in France, the *Français libres de France*—Free French of France. The small circle also included, among others, the Louvre's Christiane Desroches Noblecourt and Agnès Humbert, a curator at another museum under Jaujard's purview who had also assisted with the 1939 Louvre evacuation. By early October, Cassou and Humbert were part of the larger Musée de l'Homme resistance network and both had been fired from their jobs, two of 35,000 victims of a July Vichy law that gave government ministers three months to dismiss any civil servant, a quick and effective way to purge the administration of anyone disloyal to the new order. Jaujard had been handed the unpleasant task of carrying out the two dismissals but had been given no reason for them.

Jaujard could not save the jobs of Cassou or Humbert, both of whom were eventually arrested and imprisoned for their resistance activities. Jaujard also could not protect the jobs of Jewish colleagues from the impact of Vichy anti-Semitic statutes. Among those who lost their jobs as a result of these laws were Carle Dreyfus, curator of the Louvre's Département des Objets d'art and initial depot director at Valençay and David David-Weill, head of the national museum system's board of directors. Both men went into hiding for the duration of the Occupation. Also a victim of the statutes was curator Charles Sterling, who left in 1942 for New York, where he joined the Metropolitan Museum of Art.

Jaujard was, however, able to save other jobs and in some cases, lives. Sometimes he used facts to his advantage. After the STO forced labor program came into effect in 1943, Jaujard managed to exempt a number of young men from the program by stating that the strong young workers were needed because too many other depot guards were elderly, suffering from war injuries, or had other infirmities. Other times, Jaujard simply lied. He knew his deputy Joseph Billiet was a Communist, yet when Jaujard was told in August 1941 to purge his staff of Communist sympathizers, he reported that, to his knowledge, there was no such person on his staff. Sometimes he called upon his good relationship with the Kunstschutz. In 1944, Jaujard's former secretary Suzanne Kahn, who had lost her job due to the anti-Semite laws, and her husband were rounded up by the Germans at the Drancy internment camp and faced imminent deportation to Germany. Jaujard successfully prevailed upon the Kunstschutz to keep them in France, citing special care needed for her husband's broken leg.

Jaujard turned a blind eye to the underground press activities percolating behind the closed doors in the Louvre itself, just steps away from the Germans guarding the sequestered area of the palace. Jaujard's deputy, Joseph Billiet, founded an underground journal, "L'art français," denouncing the pillage of Jewish property and the Vichy silence that followed, the theft of the Ghent altarpiece and the actions of certain French leaders. Claude Morgan, an employee of the Musées Nationaux, drafted the early issues of an underground paper, "Les lettres françaises," from his Louvre office. And those first issues spun off the Louvre's own duplicating equipment using paper provided knowingly by the museum. This provided precious help since both printing equipment and supplies were in short supply and trying to obtain illegal ones was a dangerous proposition. Morgan's office also hosted meetings of the clandestine paper's editorial committee.

It was one thing to publish underground works; it was another to unobtrusively store and distribute them. Morgan stockpiled finished copies of "Les Lettres Françaises" in the obscurity of the Louvre, as well as copies of books published by the underground literary publisher, Les Editions de Minuit (Midnight Editions), which other Resistance members had delivered to him in small, inconspicuous bundles. From the Louvre, transfer was easy: it was just a moment's walk to the Pont des Arts, a narrow pedestrian bridge crossing the Seine. Just on the other side, the books were passed along to Resistance members—meetings that risked torture and death for all.

The Louvre sheltered more than just Resistance publications. Its endless labyrinth of underground rooms stretching almost half a mile from the Saint-Germain l'Auxerrois church to the Tuileries also served, with Jaujard's knowledge, as a safe house for Resistance members in hiding, Allied parachutists and Jews. Resistance members on the run also found shelter in Jaujard's Louvre apartment. For several weeks in August 1943, he and his wife hosted Pierre Dalloz, a founding member of one of the important maquis groups, Vercors. When Jaujard began to fear for Dalloz's safety, he whisked him off to the Paris apartment of his assistant Jacqueline Bouchot-Saupique and her husband. Jaujard also welcomed Jean Cassou while Cassou was on the run, showing him the key hidden under the front doormat so that Cassou could enter even in Jaujard's absence. Jaujard's apartment also hosted some of the meetings of the Conseil National de la Résistance, the body created in mid-1943 to coordinate various Resistance groups.

The day after the Germans invaded free France in November 1942, Jaujard had requested permission from Vichy authorities to notify the British and Americans of the depot locations, in order to prevent inadvertent bombing of depots and of items in transit. After receiving no response, he asked again several weeks later. The request made its way from one government department to another.

Finally, on December 31, the Vichy Minister of Foreign Affairs refused the request. Jaujard learned through the grapevine that the Minister had scribbled in the margin of the request, "Proposal irrelevant, no follow-up needed." In April 1943 and again in April 1944 Jaujard would renew his request. Each time he would receive an official refusal; permission was finally granted in June 1944.

But Jaujard had not waited for permission. In yet another of his many acts of quiet resistance he had taken matters into his own hands immediately upon receiving the first refusal at the end of 1942. He and staff member Christiane Desroches Noblecourt had secretly drafted a detailed list of depots and locations, which he then turned over to curator—and Resistance member—Robert Rey, who managed to relay the information to London.

It had been arranged that the BBC would broadcast coded messages to let Jaujard and the others know that London had received the information. Before long, the airwaves carried the message, "Van Dyck thanks Fragonard." In April 1943, when some artwork had to be moved, Jaujard again asked authorities for permission to notify the Allies. After another refusal came, Jaujard and Rey got to work. Soon, puzzled radio listeners heard the message: "Mona Lisa is smiling." Jacques Jaujard, also listening, smiled too.

# TWENTY-THREE

# THIEVES AND SPIES

O F ALL JAUJARD'S actions, perhaps the most daring was planting a spy in the Germans' midst. His spy was even more daring; she faced the daily risk of imprisonment and execution if discovered. In early October 1940, the Germans had asked for space at the Louvre in which to store the art, furniture and other items seized from Jewish collectors. Three weeks later, when the three allotted rooms in the sequestered section of the Louvre overflowed, they wanted still more space, this time the entire small Jeu de Paume Museum, located across from the Louvre in the northwest corner of the Tuileries Garden, bordered by place de la Concorde and rue de Rivoli. The small building, constructed in 1861 as a games court for Napoleon III, had housed various temporary exhibitions and a permanent collection of modern foreign art. The location was perfect for the ERR's looting operation since it was isolated from the street and curious eyes on two sides by the walls of the Tuileries Garden, allowing trucks to discreetly come and go. The building was also easy to protect since it was almost right across from the Hôtel de Crillon, the German military headquarters. Göring would also have the building heavily guarded by Luftwaffe and Gestapo officers.

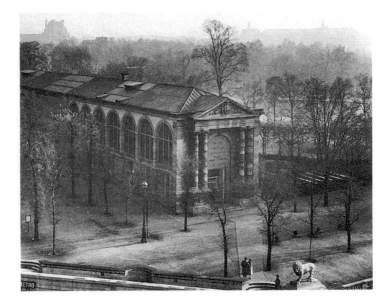

MUSÉE DU JEU DE PAUME, LATE 1940S, LOUVRE IN BACKGROUND

In ceding use of the building, Jaujard had one condition—that the French and Germans would make parallel lists of seized items. To make the French list, Jaujard designated Rose Valland, an unpaid worker with several degrees in fine arts and art history. She had volunteered at the Jeu de Paume since 1932 and had been the museum's administrator from just before the declaration of war in September 1939 until the Germans arrived in Paris the following June. In addition to assigning Valland responsibility for the list, Jaujard gave her another mission: to find some way—any way—to remain at the Jeu de Paume, in hopes of keeping track of what the Germans were doing. Jaujard knew that many of the seized assets would be sent to Germany and the French could not prevent it, but he hoped that by identifying items as they were brought in and possibly learning where they went, the information might help in their recovery after the war.

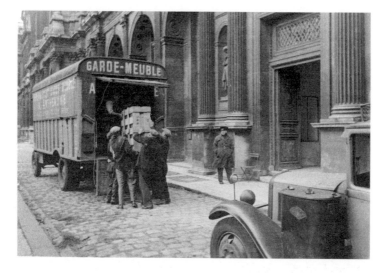

TRUCK IN LOUVRE'S COUR CARRÉE, BRINGING SEIZED
ASSETS TO SEQUESTERED AREA OF THE MUSEUM
(BUNDESARCHIV B323 BILD-311-009/O.ANG.)

On November 1, Göring's Luftwaffe men rushed more than 400 crates of seized assets into the building. The following morning, they roughly unpacked them, haphazardly stacking paintings against walls as Valland began to prepare the French list as best she could, assisted by several colleagues. It quickly became evident to her that the Germans had no intention of preparing a dual inventory. Had there been any doubt, it was eliminated just after noon when Hermann Bunjes—nominally a Kunstschutz employee but in practice an enthusiastic aide of Göring—came along, slapped closed the notebook in which the French were making their list and told her and her colleagues to leave and not come back. The others left but, following Jaujard's instructions, Valland simply ignored his order, taking the position that it did not apply to her since the permanent collections of the museum still needed tending and the building's maintenance staff still needed supervision, both of which had been her responsibilities before the Occupation. Baron Kurt von Behr, chief of the ERR's operations in France, made the mistake of allowing her to stay.

The first several days in the new Nazi art depot were a frantic blur of activity. Valland soon learned why: Hermann Göring was coming from Germany to inspect the booty. On November 3 he arrived, accompanied by Luftwaffe men, ERR authorities and his own personal art curator, Walter Hofer. Sporting a long overcoat and a wide-brimmed fedora, his trademark cane in hand, Göring spent the entire day at the museum. Two days later, in addition to feasting his eyes on the *Belle Allemande* at the Louvre, he returned to the Jeu de Paume, where he joyfully examined the spoils again. By day's end, Göring had indicated the disposition of various items. One category comprised artworks he had set aside for Hitler; a second category was a list of artworks for himself. Further items were tagged for German museums or elsewhere.

Before long, under Valland's watchful eyes, the fruit of additional confiscations of Jewish-owned assets arrived; most were then catalogued and prepared for shipment to Germany. By the end of January, the German military commander of France felt compelled to write to his superior of his disapproval of Göring's actions, noting among other things, "[T]he whole question of the confiscation has already stirred up plenty of dust. I myself am of the opinion that it ought to stop now, and that any further seizure ought to be refrained from." But Göring had Hitler's support and just several days after the commander's protest, Göring was back at the Jeu de Paume to pick more fruit. On February 5, Wolff Metternich and his assistant Tieschowitz arrived and announced that they were, as representatives of the Supreme Army Command, responsible for the safety of the sequestered works. Göring made them leave.

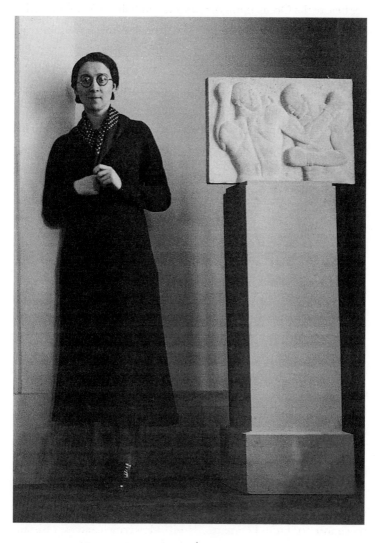

ROSE VALLAND AT MUSÉE DU JEU DE PAUME

Several days later, a train with twenty-five baggage cars loaded with looted artwork, antique furniture, Gobelins tapestries and other items took off for Berlin. The top masterpieces handpicked by Göring—nineteen crates designated for Hitler and twenty-three for himself—were loaded into two baggage cars hitched to Göring's private train. As his train headed to Germany, the roar of its Luftwaffe-provided fighter plane escort echoed through the French countryside. Aboard were Vermeer's *Astronomer* and works by Rembrandt, Fragonard, Boucher and other masters. Göring's hand-written instructions for the shipment sounded like a restaurant order: "All the paintings marked 'H' are for the Führer . . . . Everything marked "G" is for me."

By the summer of 1941, Valland was getting a salary for the first time and Göring had made five additional trips to Paris and arranged for perhaps three-quarters of the war's entire plunder to be shipped to Germany. He made four more trips to the Jeu de Paume in 1942; all carefully noted by Valland. In mid-1943, seizure activity slowed considerably when Hitler removed Rosenberg—and thus also Göring— from control over the ERR. Most of the subsequent activity at the Jeu de Paume would involve cataloguing seized items still on the premises and preparing their shipment to Germany. All told, between March 1941 and July 1944, 4,174 crates holding almost 22,000 pieces of pillaged art left France for Germany, not to mention hundreds of thousands of other items, including jewelry, tapestries, antique furniture, and other treasures taken from individuals and libraries.

A s seized items arrived at the Jeu de Paume and as they were shipped off to Germany, Rose Valland was watching. By day, she found every excuse possible to circulate around the building to observe the Germans' activities. She looked after the French artwork that belonged to the museum before the war and checked

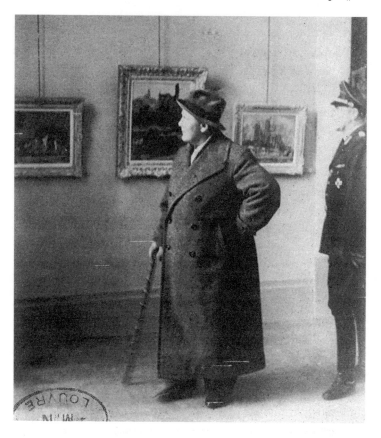

HERMANN GÖRING AT MUSÉE DU JEU DE PAUME

the electric and fire protection systems. Plain-looking and plainly dressed, the quiet 42-year-old with the large round glasses drew little attention from the Germans as she moved about, making careful mental notes of everything she saw. She plucked documents out of wastebaskets. She eavesdropped on conversations as the Germans spoke freely in front of her, unaware that she was fluent in German. The locations of the German depots were noted in a book that was always left on a table and, above the table, a list was posted with the day's shipping orders and destinations. And the records being compiled by the ERR were not locked up. Valland made good use of her access to all of these. She also got hold of the watchman's logbook.

Valland also had other sources of information. The guards told her whatever seemed interesting and she befriended the head packer and one of the drivers to find out what they were doing. Two guards in the Louvre passed along information about ERR processing activities in the sequestered rooms of the Cour Carrée, where she was forbidden to go.

By night, she used her spectacular memory to make secret notes of her findings. She also sometimes managed to sneak out negatives of ERR archival photographs and had prints made, then slipped them back in the following morning. Every few days, Valland passed along some details during her normal meetings with Jaujard or his assistant Bouchot-Saupique. Jaujard managed to relay some location information to members of the Louvre's resistance network, who in turn passed it into Allied hands. As a result, before the war was over, the Allies knew where some of the looted art had been initially transferred and avoided bombing these locations.

From the moment she began spying at the Jeu de Paume, Valland knew the great personal risk involved; had she been caught, she would have been imprisoned or sentenced to death. Yet she would continue her deception for four years. In February 1944, she would have a particularly close call when a Göring representative at the Jeu de Paume caught her trying to decipher an address. Looking her straight in the eyes, he told her that she could be shot for speaking about the building's activities. Ever calm, she simply responded, "Nobody here is stupid enough not to know the risks."

While the overwhelming majority of the looted artwork went to Germany to enrich the collections of Hitler and Göring, other items—particularly those not in keeping with Nazi ideology—were sold to obtain hard currency or to obtain works considered more desirable. Certain other works were traded with the same goal. By far the biggest category of unacceptable art was what Hitler called *entartete Kunst*, or degenerate art. This included modern art, especially abstract works, but also more generally art from Impressionism forward, plus works by any Jewish artist. Among the many artists producing work considered "degenerate" were Klee, Picasso, Modigliani, Kandinsky and Chagall, but also Vincent van Gogh. In 1937, Nazi officials purged German museums of over 16,000 "degenerate" works. "Degenerate" artists were removed from positions as teachers and were forbidden to exhibit or sell their work or even to buy art supplies. In many cases they were not allowed to paint or sculpt at all and many of their works were seized and destroyed.

The same fate was in store for some of the stolen "degenerate" art stored in the sequestered rooms of the Louvre alongside furniture and other items that had been ripped from Jewish homes. On July 19, 1943, a group of ERR agents met in the sequestered rooms to convene what amounted to a trial of the "degenerate" art. They set aside some paintings—including works by Courbet, Monet, Degas and Manet—to trade for more "acceptable" ones and designated other paintings for possible sale, among them works by Bonnard, Vuillard, Matisse, Braque and Dufy.

The rest, considered "dangerous," were slated for destruction. On July 23, 1943, in the sequestered rooms of the Louvre, Nazi agents with knives in hand slashed more than 500 paintings, from Jewish family portraits to works by Miro, Klee, Ernst, Picasso and others. Then they loaded a military truck with the debris, hauled it to the Tuileries Garden and set it ablaze. The column of smoke rising into the Paris sky remained visible for hours afterwards, until it disappeared into the inky darkness of the nightly German-ordered blackout.

NOTE FROM ROSE VALLAND REGARDING THE JULY 23, 1943 BONFIRE

## TRANSLATION

### 23 JULY 1943

THE PAINTINGS MASSACRED IN THE SEQUESTER OF
THE LOUVRE WERE TAKEN BACK TO THE JEU DE PAUME
(A TRUCKLOAD, ABOUT FIVE OR SIX HUNDRED) AND BURNED
UNDER GERMAN SURVEILLANCE IN THE GARDEN OF THE
MUSEUM FROM 11 A.M. TO 3 P.M.
IMPOSSIBLE TO SAVE ANYTHING.

# TWENTY-FOUR

# FROM HEAVEN AND EARTH

T HREE MONTHS AFTER the Germans arrived in 1940, food rationing went into effect; by year's end, food shortages had already appeared. Even the famed market street, rue Mouffetard, had little food to sell. By the dawn of 1942, both heating fuel and food were difficult to find. That January, when Louvre staff member Magdeleine Hours gave birth, her cousin brought two logs tied with a blue ribbon for her fireplace so she might have a bit of heat. Gifts from her museum colleagues included a pound of butter and some carrots from the Louvre's canteen. By 1943, almost everyone was habitually hungry; only those wealthy enough to buy on the black market could eat plentifully. In 1943, when the official price of a kilo of butter was just over sixty-two francs, a willing buyer of that rare commodity could sometimes obtain it for six or seven times that much. But the severe shortages often made food staples impossible to find even if one had the ration cards to obtain them.

There were many reasons for the shortages. Transportation was severely restricted, which exacerbated supply problems in cities and

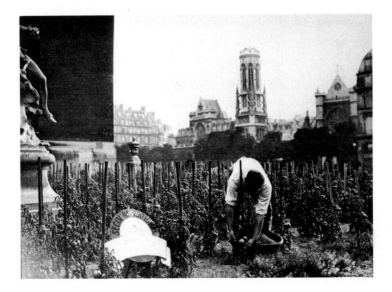

TOMATO PLANTS IN THE WARTIME GARDENS OF THE LOUVRE

other areas that did not locally produce a diversity of food items; in the southern area of Hérault, people were living on a diet of chestnuts and potatoes. The Allied invasion of North Africa in November 1942 had cut France off from trading partners. There was less labor for agriculture since men had gone off to war and women to factories and other production resources such as fuel had been diverted to German military use. Moreover, much of the food that was produced either disappeared into the black market, was requisitioned for the German military and administrative machine in France or shipped to Germany to ease food shortages there. When the Germans arrived in Montauban in November 1942, they immediately confiscated the entire city's stock of food reserves. To have any hope of finding a small bit of cheese, Mazauric had to go out at dawn. Rutabagas, or swedes—which before the war were fed only to cattle—were one of the few plentiful foods in Montauban, as were overripe peaches that the Germans could not transport.

As hunger mounted, so did creativity. By 1943, many public spaces in Paris had been transformed into vegetable gardens. The Saint Cloud racetrack at the western edge of the city was turned into six hundred individual working gardens. Clearings in the woods along the city's periphery were planted as well, as were the Longchamps racetrack, the esplanade of the Invalides and parts of the two giant parks flanking the city, the Bois de Boulogne and Bois de Vincennes. So too were some former ornamental gardens at the eastern corners of the Louvre, which began to sprout thousands of leek and tomato plants.

The Louvre gardens were not the only area of the grounds to provide sustenance. A small post of five firemen was stationed in a large ground-floor room of the palace along the Cour Visconti, an inner courtyard near the Grande Galerie, not far from the Pont des Arts. The sparsely furnished room held only a bed for each man plus a table and two benches and, in one corner, a small gas burner for reheating their meager meals. They decided more food was needed. Avoiding the watchful eye of guards, one of them fished large goldfish and old carp from a pond in the Tuileries Garden. It was against the rules, but, after all, said one of them later, they were only twenty years old—and really hungry. One of the men supplemented his diet by becoming an expert at trapping the pigeons that were forever roosting on the façades, windowsills and roofs of the museum.

B y 1943, as Parisians were resigned to going hungry, they were also resigned to fear from the sky. The Germans had briefly bombed the city in June 1940. In 1942, the Allies had conducted extensive bombing raids to target the Renault factory in the Paris suburb of Boulogne-Billancourt. The first attack, in March, caused significant damage to the factory that had already made over

25,000 trucks for the German military. Overall, the French lauded the attack as necessary, but it also killed almost 400 civilians and destroyed several hundred nearby homes. While the goal of Allied bombing in France was to hit only strategic targets, limited intelligence and technology sometimes resulted in strikes that went wide of a target and caused significant collateral damage. Moreover, German anti-aircraft defense—subject to the same weaknesses—could cause damage as serious as that of the Allied projectiles they were trying to intercept.

The French fine arts administration knew that the Allies would not target the Louvre, but they were justifiably concerned about the unpredictable vagaries of war. Just after noon on June 12, 1942, a low-flying plane of unidentified origin fired a salvo of small-caliber projectiles onto the eastern, Colonnade wing of the museum. Was it a German plane? An Allied plane mistaking the Louvre for another structure? Nobody was sure. The projectiles crashed into the roof, balustrades and several walls. One punctured a window mullion and continued inside; some windows were also broken. Several unexploded projectiles fell into the Cour Carrée and elsewhere. Luckily, all the damage was minor.

Almost exactly a year later, on the night of June 16, 1943, the Louvre was hit again as waylaid projectiles from German anti-aircraft fire hit the museum's old, flammable roof. A heavy explosive shell crashed through the glass roof of the Cour du Sphinx, landing next to the priceless Roman third-century Four Seasons floor mosaic. Miraculously, the shell did not explode.

Throughout that summer, as the ERR was bringing seized items to its rooms in the Louvre's Cour Carrée, Jaujard met with Louvre curators and the building's chief architect to identify additional protective measures for the building and for the limited number of objects still on display.

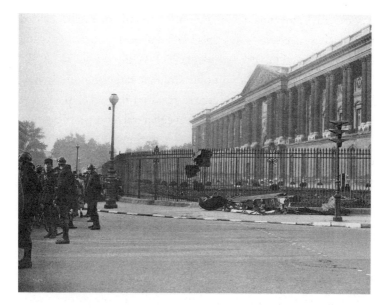

PLANE FRAGMENTS NEAR THE COLONNADE WING OF THE LOUVRE

J ust three months after the June attack, something more tragic fell
from the sky. Not long after midnight on September 24, 1943,
a British bomber returning from a raid on Mannheim, Germany
was hit by German anti-aircraft fire as it crossed over the skies of
Paris. Broken apart, parts of the plane crashed into the Magasins du
Louvre, a department store only a block from the museum. Flaming
debris set the roof and upper floors of the store aflame. Six bodies
were found, though the pilot's was not. Just after the plane crashed,
two firemen on regular patrol along the Louvre's roofs quickly veri-
fied that some debris had fallen onto the museum but no damage
had been done.

The following morning, crowds peered over police cordons at
the chunks of debris scattered across the rue Saint-Honoré, the

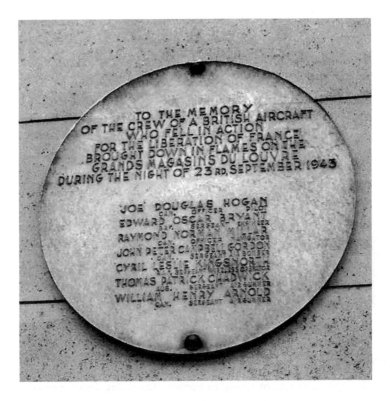

MEMORIAL PLAQUE, RUE SAINT-HONORÉ, PARIS

lawns of the Louvre and against the museum's fences. In the Cour
Carrée, museum staff found something else that morning: the body
of the plane's Canadian pilot, 24-year-old Joe Douglas Hogan, who
had attempted to parachute to safety. Before the Germans came to
remove him, the museum's guards, former military men themselves,
formed an honor guard around the young pilot's body while other
members of the Louvre staff filed by to pay their respects. The following year, the Musées Nationaux staff would gather at the Louvre
again to pay their respects, this time to one of their own.

# TWENTY-FIVE

# FRIENDS
# AND ENEMIES

T HE "EXCHANGE" PROPOSAL that the Germans had put
on the table at the end of the previous year went back
and forth throughout 1943. The French dragged their
feet about what might be acceptable in exchange; Bunjes, acting on
Göring's behalf, kept trying to press forward. He also repeatedly
indicated that the Germans wished to arrange an exchange for the
Basel Antependium but the French continued to counter that it
was too valuable to exchange. As 1943 wound down, the war was
looking grimmer for the Germans and Göring wanted closure. In
early December, he requested another viewing of two items still in
discussion for trade: the *Belle Allemande* and the *Presentation in the Temple*
altarpiece panel. He also wanted to see the Basel altar.

In July 1943, Bonnard had ordered Jaujard to return the altar
from Chambord to the Louvre for an anticipated viewing by Göring
that ultimately did not take place. Several weeks after the September
1943 plane crash, Jaujard quietly sent the altar back to Chambord
without notifying Bonnard. Was it to create distance between the

altar and bombing danger, as he officially explained, or to get it further away from Göring? In December, when Göring requested the new viewing, Bonnard called the Louvre to advise museum officials of the visit. When he learned that Jaujard had sent the altar back to Chambord, his already simmering rage at Jaujard began to boil. Bonnard called Hautecœur, Jaujard's superior, and said he was going to fire Jaujard, but Hautecœur calmed him down. The altar once again traveled back from the Loire to the Louvre.

The French and the Germans then began a tense, high-tempered debate over the arrangements for Göring's viewing of the three pieces. First, they debated over the place. Initially it was to be the Musée de Cluny, then the Louvre. After the French believed the location issue had been resolved, Göring expressed concern for his personal security and demanded that the items be moved instead to his residence just across the Seine on the quai d'Orsay in the former French foreign ministry building. The French worried what might happen when the items left the safety of the French museums and whether the ministry building might be considered German territory. After they finally agreed to Göring's stipulation, a new debate ensued as to whether French or German trucks would transport the items from the Louvre.

Finally, on December 11, the artworks were taken to the ministry building. The curators waited for two hours in an antechamber as Bonnard met with Göring and other German officials behind closed doors. Inside, Bonnard agreed to exchange the *Belle Allemande* and the *Presentation in the Temple* altarpiece panel, an arrangement that the curators had agreed to in principle. Some of them had done so for artistic reasons—pending appropriate items in return—since each item would complete an ensemble whose related works were already in Germany. Others may have hoped it would head off further German initiatives.

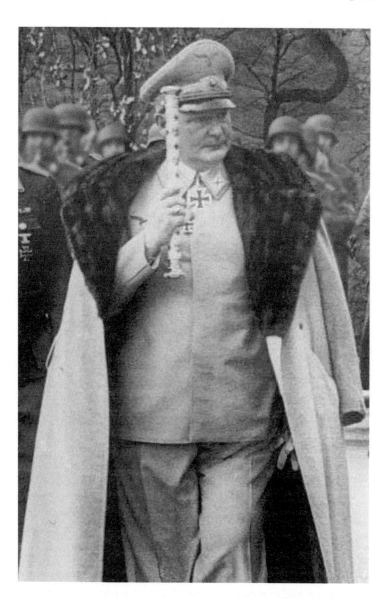

HERMANN GÖRING IN DRESS UNIFORM WITH JEWELED BATON
(BUNDESARCHIV, BILD 146-1979-089-22/O.ANG.)

Inside the meeting room, Bonnard also told Göring that the Basel Antependium could not be exchanged because its value was too great. However, he suggested, Pétain could theoretically offer it to Göring as a gift. This was the last thing Göring wanted since it would remove the thin veneer of propriety from his scheme. The curators could hear his enraged shouting through the walls. Eventually, the doors flew open and Göring, in his white dress uniform and jewel-encrusted baton in hand, marched swiftly past the waiting curators without a glance at them. The other Germans followed, then finally Bonnard, who stopped and simply told the curators to pack up the three items and bring them back to the Louvre.

After Göring calmed down, he agreed to accept the other two pieces, but added a new stipulation: that several Louvre curators would personally bring the *Belle Allemande* and the altarpiece panel to Germany, where they could choose the objects they wished in exchange. This was not so much a gesture of generosity as it was a publicity stunt intended to suggest to the world that the French had freely agreed to the exchange, and thus avoid an international media storm like the one that had followed the theft of the *Adoration of the Mystic Lamb*. The Germans, thinking somehow that it would encourage the curators, said they would travel in a private, armored rail car armed with an anti-aircraft gun and escorted by fighter planes.

Bonnard agreed to the bizarre arrangement, designating René Huyghe as the representative who would travel to Germany. When Huyghe found out, he was horrified. Not only did he want no part of such a trip, he suspected, like the other curators, that the works from which they would be allowed to "choose" would be from pillaged collections. Moreover, if the French could not identify any acceptable works to take in exchange, there was no guarantee the Nazis would allow the French-owned works back out of Germany.

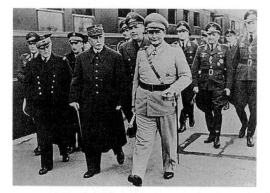

HERMANN GÖRING WITH PHILIPPE PÉTAIN

During the tumult, Jaujard had been away on sick leave and his deputy Joseph Billiet had handled the situation. Billiet had let it be known to their superiors that any "exchange" would be illegal unless the Curators Committee met and approved it, which infuriated Bonnard, who wanted to placate the Germans. Bonnard forbade the committee to meet and told the curators they could not negotiate further with Bunjes. On the urgent request of the curators, Jaujard cut short his convalescence and returned on December 29, when he reiterated to Bonnard that it was illegal to go forward with an exchange without approval by the Curators Committee. "I'll take you by the throat and make you pay personally," Bonnard threatened, adding that he would smash any resistance.

Then suddenly, in an attempt to save face, Bonnard ordered the committee to meet. However, he said, they were to consider only two specific questions relating to transportation of the exchanged works to Germany. The committee met the following day in an emergency session. They agreed that the Bonnard–Göring arrangement smacked of relinquishment of the items, not a freely negotiated

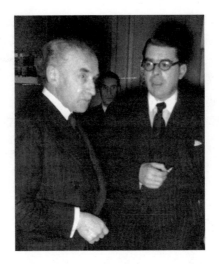

ABEL BONNARD (LEFT) IN WEIMAR, GERMANY 1941
(BUNDESARCHIV, BILD 183-B05235/HOFFMAN)

exchange. Then, instead of addressing Bonnard's transportation questions, the committee voted that they would finalize their approval of the exchange only after approving the items to be offered by the Germans. They also agreed that neither the *Belle Allemande* nor the altarpiece panel could leave the Louvre until Jaujard negotiated with Bunjes as to the process for the exchange, clearly referring in part to Göring's demand for the curators' trip to Germany.

When Bonnard learned of the committee's vote, he called Jaujard to his office and bellowed that he would not be black-mailed. "You're a little despot," he screamed at Jaujard. "I'll break you and the gang of undisciplined functionaries that support you." But having no choice, Bonnard allowed Jaujard and the curators to meet with Bunjes the following day to discuss the substance of the exchange proposal and the question of the curators traveling to Germany.

Jaujard began the meeting with Bunjes by commenting on a photograph on the wall of Bunjes' predecessor, whom he knew had been sent to the Russian front after failing in negotiations with the French. What happened to him? Jaujard innocently asked. Jaujard listened with empathy to Bunjes' explanation and then announced that the curators were ready to collectively resign over the exchange matter. Moreover, he said, the British would find out and would quickly use it for propaganda against Germany. The French wanted the Basel altar dropped from consideration, Jaujard said, and they did not want the curators to have to bring the other two works to Germany. Bunjes would utter no further word on either issue.

Bonnard ordered the Curators Committee to meet again on January 3 to address only the question of whether the two items would go to Germany or stay in Paris—with a Vichy official, not the Musées Nationaux—until the exchange was resolved. The committee again disregarded Bonnard's order and instead voted that (1) negotiations for items to be received in exchange would continue; (2) the *Belle Allemande* and the altarpiece panel would be given to Bunjes for transport to Germany, thus negating a need for the curators to travel to Germany; (3) a list, newly provided by Germany, detailing artworks for the exchange would be brought immediately to Paris to be examined; (4) any negotiations must be ratified by the curators; and (5) if no agreement was finalized, the French works would be returned.

Bonnard, his authority once again undermined, was apoplectic. He again threatened to fire Jaujard and said he would put curator René Huyghe "below ground." When Hautecœur expressed support for the curators, Bonnard replied, "You always take the side of your former colleagues. If that's the case, you'll be the one to take the hit." He would keep his promise.

J aujard once again feared for both his job and his safety. He had discussed his concerns with his close friends, the Chamsons, who were fearful that if Jaujard were arrested, not only would the entire system's artworks be at risk but the curators might also be taken into custody. Chamson arranged a contingency plan: if Jaujard or the Chamsons needed to flee, they would go to a remote Resistance safe house in the mountains, where an already-agreed password would give them access. However, the danger of Vichy action against them receded when Jaujard's staff again threatened to resign en masse if he were dismissed. Bonnard was cornered. As much as he would have liked to fire them all, he knew he could not possibly replace all of them with qualified people or without disastrous publicity. But several months later, he would get rid of Hautecœur.

The *Belle Allemande* and the altarpiece panel were tendered to the Germans on January 4, 1944, the official document removing them from the French collections signed by Bonnard. As the French had suspected, the two pieces did not go to any museum, but rather to Göring's lavish Norse-style country palace, Carinhall, which already overflowed with art that he was proud to show to guests, receiving them while dressed as an Indian maharaja complete with turban, in Roman togas and in mock-medieval hunting costumes. Not surprisingly, the items that had been promised in exchange for the *Belle Allemande* and the panel did not arrive. Eventually, five other pieces appeared instead, one of which had been confiscated from French Jews and displayed in the Jeu de Paume, proving the French suspicions correct. Göring continued to press for the Basel altar, indicating that he would accept it as a gift in appreciation for German authorities having protected French monuments and artwork during and after the 1940 invasion, a particularly ironic claim given the large number of provincial museums that had been destroyed by the Germans in the spring of 1940.

In mid-1942, Hitler might well have felt that the complete domination of Europe was within reach. But much had changed by the end of 1943. Germany was slowly being pushed westward out of Russia and Italy had surrendered to the Allies, who were making progress against the German forces still fighting there. The Allies had developed increasingly effective countermeasures against the feared German U-boats and German air superiority in Europe was no longer assured. The Germans knew their chances of a wholesale victory were looking increasingly slim. Hitler had said years before that he would get the Louvre's art upon his final victory. As 1943 drew to a close, the Germans once again began to stretch their tentacles towards the art, knowing that the opportunities to grab it were getting slimmer as well.

On January 4, 1944, the same day the *Belle Allemande* and the *Presentation in the Temple* altarpiece panel were handed over to Bunjes, Felix Kuetgens of the Kunstschutz met with a representative of Bonnard. Given current conditions, Kuetgens said, the Germans felt that the best way to protect the Louvre's treasures was to return them all to Paris. By any measure, the suggestion was absurd, given the ongoing Allied bombing and road conditions. Its only result would be to gather the artworks in a single location almost across the street from the German military headquarters in Paris, where they could most easily and quickly seize them. Kuetgens went on, saying that since there were not enough trucks or fuel for such a measure, the move could be limited to some of the "masterpieces of universal value." The German military, he said, would be happy to provide the trucks. They needed only Bonnard's approval. The next day, his approval obtained, Kuetgens relayed the message to Jaujard. Some of the biggest dangers for the treasures of the Louvre lay just ahead.

# PART V

DANGER, HOPE
AND FREEDOM

*January 1944 to August 1944*

## TWENTY-SIX

---

# CAT AND MOUSE

F ROM THE BEGINNING of the German occupation, the enemy was wary of weapon ownership by the French. While the Germans would have liked to forbid it altogether, they acknowledged the necessity for French law enforcement officials, at least until the last weeks of the occupation of Paris in 1944. However, they had confiscated most weapons at the art depots in 1940, although a few depots were allowed to retain a minimal number of pistols. By the fall of 1943, Germans had become increasingly suspicious that Resistance weapons were being stashed at the depots. In October, Kunstschutz head Tieschowitz had warned Jaujard that local German military authorities now had the authority to search any depot for clandestine supplies, including weapons. Tieschowitz was clear to specify that if they discovered any such items—even one—there would be serious ramifications for the art at every depot. Soon thereafter, Tieschowitz warned Jaujard that the searches would soon begin, at any time and without warning. Jaujard, knowing the depots often harbored Resistance activity, told the depot heads in no uncertain terms to make quite sure there were no problematic materials on the premises.

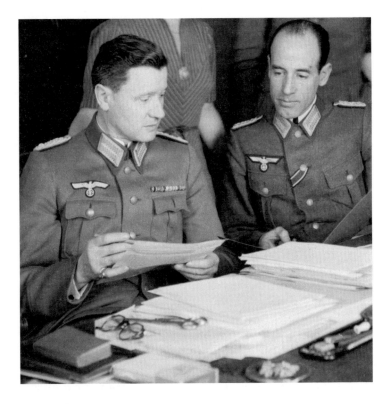

KUNSTSCHUTZ HEAD BERNHARD VON TIESCHOWITZ (LEFT)
AND FELIX KUETGENS

The German military carried out the threat of inspections, but only tentatively, demanding crates be opened at only one provincial depot. Soldiers armed with submachine guns demanded entrance to several other depots and then simply looked over the unopened crates. By December the Germans had upped the ante, announcing that searches would include not only rooms where artwork was stored but also entire châteaux in which they were located, plus any outbuildings and any lodgings of personnel. And, they said, each depot head would be held personally responsible for any infraction of the rules. This led to a flood of protest by the curators and Jaujard, who, in turn, pointed out to Hautecœur that the curators had no way of knowing what was in the crates from provincial collections, nor did they have any control over what might be stored in areas of a château under the control of its owners. And, he said, artworks could be easily damaged if unqualified individuals opened the crates for inspection. Jaujard pressed the Kunstschutz's Felix Kuetgens for a formalized and less onerous arrangement and for more weapons for the depots.

On January 5, 1944, a day after Kuetgens met with Bonnard's representative, he met with Jaujard and Billiet. First they discussed the matter of inspections. Jaujard prevailed somewhat in his push for a more reasonable and enforceable inspection protocol. Kuetgens said he had obtained official military approval for a new arrangement by which, among other measures, only qualified French personnel would open crates and any inspections would be conducted in the presence of both a Kunstschutz representative and the depot head. The new arrangement would not prevent inspections, but it would at least mean they would not be conducted by unpredictable German troops; as importantly, they would no longer be spontaneous because, to have all required parties on hand, advance notice would be required.

Kuetgens and Jaujard also discussed the issue of weapons for protection of the depots. The previous day, Kuetgens had told Bonnard's representative that, after consultation with German military, he had concluded that the few weapons in the hands of the depot guards were not powerful enough for adequate defense. Only heavy arms would do, he said, and these would not only be impossible to provide; they would also present a danger to the depots. He told Bonnard's representative that the guards should not be armed.

But in his meeting with Jaujard, Kuetgens inexplicably relayed a different message, saying that military authorities had favorably considered Jaujard's request for additional weapons but that the type of any permissible weapons had not yet been determined.

During the meeting, Kuetgens also raised the issue of returning the Louvre's principal masterpieces back to Paris. It would reduce attempts at theft, he said, if they were sheltered in a "specially chosen location such as the basements of the Banque de France." Jaujard knew there had never been any attempts at theft, except, arguably, by Abetz, Ribbentrop and Göring. And Paris was surely not a safe place for the art; it was perhaps one of the most significant potential targets for military action in all of France. Moreover, the proposal sounded quite familiar; it was the same one Abetz had made in June 1940. It was apparent that Kuetgens had been instructed to relay a message from higher in the German hierarchy and that there was a far more worrisome motivation behind the new proposal: the Germans knew they were losing their grip on France and simply wanted the artwork closer at hand where they might more easily grab it.

Jaujard replied by pointing out the risk of Paris bombing. He also said that while locations such as the basement vaults of the Banque de France might protect against bombing, they were not safe places for the art. He reminded Kuetgens that when the Louvre's pastels were sheltered in the Banque de France in 1940, they had to be removed due to detrimental conditions. Moreover, Jaujard added, such an arrangement would undermine their ability to monitor the artwork. He also pointed out that the arrangement would violate the agreement about control over the treasures that had been made with the Kunstschutz long before.

After agreeing with Jaujard's arguments, Kuetgens suggested that, instead, perhaps the principal masterpieces could be gathered together at one of the existing depots. Jaujard responded that this would create an unacceptable concentration of risk. But he knew that Kuetgens had to bring some kind of concession back to German higher-ups. The two men agreed on a two-point proposal to enhance the security of the depots. Special contingents of government police would do exterior monitoring and the large number of provincial depots would be reduced, which would also allow surveillance efforts to be concentrated.

If Jaujard felt that he had dodged another German bullet, he was wrong. On January 12, Hautecœur came to see Jaujard at the Louvre to inform him that French Minister of Education Bonnard had approved the German measure to return the masterpieces to Paris and would be sending a written order to Hautecœur to that effect.

Jaujard wanted to know what happened to the agreement he and Kuetgens had made. Had Kuetgens' superior, Tieschowitz, overruled the Jaujard–Kuetgens proposal or was the decision the work of Bonnard? Late the following afternoon, he headed over to the German offices of the Kunstschutz in the Hôtel Majestic to speak directly with Tieschowitz. Tieschowitz, who had always before proven to be both reasonable and inclined to support the French, told Jaujard he had agreed with the plan Kuetgens and Jaujard had made. Thus its undoing had been strictly the work of Bonnard and further evidence that the proposal to return the works had been floated from the top of the German hierarchy. Curator René Huyghe later said Bonnard "adhered without hesitation to German decisions;" his quick support of the German desire to return the artworks to Paris was yet another example.

The same day, Hautecœur relayed a message to Jaujard from Bonnard, who wanted, as soon as possible, a report on where and how the artworks might be sheltered in Paris. In his reply, Jaujard described his concerns in detail. He noted that given the risk of heavy bombing of Paris, the only safe shelters for art would be deep ones, such as the vaults of the Banque de France. But, again citing the damaging 1940 experience with the pastels at the bank, he added that the air-conditioning problems and resulting humidity at the bank had only gotten worse. He warned that the humidity would be damaging not only to the paintings, but also to wooden objects and ancient objects of stone or bronze. And, he noted, all the antiquities required constant monitoring and many of them needed regular care, neither of which would occur under the proposed arrangement. Jaujard also said it was a contradiction to suggest the return of the artworks to a city with a serious bombing risk since the Germans themselves had supported the evacuation of the works from Montauban when that city became a bombing risk near the end of 1942.

Jaujard also included an analysis by the head architect of the Louvre. The report supported Jaujard's argument that only a deep shelter could provide safety from all bombs, but noted that an appropriate shelter for the artworks would also need to provide heating, aeration and the ability to humidify or dry the air according to the specific needs of the artwork. Storage at the Banque of France would be irresponsible, he said. Likewise, he added, the basements of the Louvre would not be an adequate shelter. Some areas were not strong enough to protect against bombs and other had dangerous fluctuations in humidity levels. Still others had gas, water, electric and steam pipes weaving through them that could rupture upon a bomb hit and cause damage to the artworks worse than from a bomb itself.

Jaujard sent the report to Hautecœur who, in turn, passed it along to Bonnard along with additional concerns. If the artworks were too concentrated in one location, he noted, "it is up to the Government to decide" whether protection by local authorities would be adequate in case of an invasion by a foreign force or removal by force for political reasons or in the case of other disruptions. And, he said, there were additional reasons to be concerned about bombing in Paris. Strong exterior security around the Louvre could be assured, he acknowledged, but such security could not protect the museum from bombing. He reminded Bonnard of the plane that had crashed near the Louvre and of the shell that had passed through the museum roof and just missed the Antioch mosaic. And he wrote of bombs that had hit artists' ateliers near Montparnasse, just moments away from the Louvre by air. He said the only feasible solution would be to construct a special bomb shelter that would cost far beyond the current budget for the protection of the artworks. In conclusion, he said, he was perplexed, asking whether it made sense to expose the art to almost certain damage in Paris. The decision, he said, was up to Bonnard.

No immediate word came from Bonnard and for the next several weeks, Jaujard and Kunstschutz representatives finalized details of the plan to reduce the number of provincial depots and add additional guards. On February 3, Jaujard notified Hautecœur that he had reached an agreement with the Kunstschutz and that the Kunstschutz had dismissed the German proposal to return the masterpieces to Paris. Several days later, Hautecœur relayed the update to Bonnard.

On February 12, Bonnard broke his silence. He could no longer refute the logic of Jaujard and the Louvre's architect, but he was still determined to support the German wish to bring the artwork closer so he offered a new counterproposal: why not move the depots to the east of France? Though there were no depots there, he said, it appeared to be the most favorable location. But favorable for whom? Certainly not for the French, who throughout the war had kept the artworks as far as possible from the German border. But certainly more favorable for the Germans, who would be well-poised to launch a mass kidnapping of the art across that border when the timing was right. In Montal, René Huyghe and the maquis developed a detailed contingency plan to re-kidnap the Louvre's paintings from German trucks and hide them in the high limestone plateaus of France's Massif Central.

On February 15, Jaujard provided five pages full of objections to Hautecœur, knowing that they would be relayed to Bonnard. He argued that the identification of acceptable areas for depot locations had always been made by military specialists before the Occupation and that subsequent locations had required the approval of the Kunstschutz. In addition, depots had to meet specific criteria, such as having large, secure rooms, easy access for the artworks and a ready water source; certain regions no longer had any available buildings meeting these requirements. Further, there were insufficient quantities of trucks and fuel to move it all. Moreover, he said, even if these resources could be found, it would not be in the interest of the artworks to move them over long distances or close to industrial areas, both of which had always been a factor in evacuation decisions. He pointed out that eastern France was a great distance from the current depots and was home to much industry, making the area a military target. Jaujard continued to pursue the consolidation of the provincial depots to which he and the Kunstschutz had agreed but on March 7, he received a memo from one of Bonnard's staff members, once again pushing to evacuate the collections towards the east.

Perhaps the Germans were wearying of Bonnard's ineffectiveness in getting the works within reach. And they knew their window of opportunity to get the art within reach was beginning to close as Allied bombing became more intense and it was evident an Allied landing was only a matter of time. A week later, they showed their hand as Bunjes himself entered the discussion. Bunjes tried to convince Jaujard that, due to the risk of an Allied coastal landing, the depots should be moved away from the Atlantic and the Mediterranean: in other words, east. Bunjes also wanted to know the quantity of trucks, fuel and workers that would be needed to move the art. Bonnard quickly followed up on Bunjes' initiative with a request for the precise volume of items at the depots. Jaujard sent official word to each depot requesting the information. Unofficial word also went to each depot: exaggerate the volume so much that the move will seem impossible.

While the depot heads made their "calculations," Jaujard decided it was time to present a last-ditch argument he had held in reserve, turning the German and Vichy logic against them. If the art and antiquities were to be moved, then, fine, move them east. But even farther east than had been suggested. They could be moved to the extreme eastern Jura region, which did not abut the German border. In case of danger, the artworks could be moved out of France altogether. To Switzerland. On May 10, he made his case. "The high standards of hospitality of the Swiss nation are a sure guarantee that they would do everything to effectively protect our patrimony," he wrote. He was personally aware of those standards from his 1939 assistance to the Spanish in their evacuation of works from the Prado Museum to Switzerland and both Bonnard and the Germans knew it. The ploy bought a precious month of silence from Bunjes and Bonnard. The Allies were coming soon, Jaujard knew; he just needed to keep buying time.

# TWENTY-SEVEN

# ROUGH ROAD
# TOWARD FREEDOM

P REPARATION FOR D-DAY had begun long before June 1944. The previous year, Allies began concentrated attacks on German aircraft factories and airfields across Europe to begin weakening the enemy's long-term air defense capabilities. As the winter of 1943–1944 waned, the Allies began final preparations for the Normandy invasion. France's museums, knowing the invasion was only a matter of time, began to prepare as well.

On March 8, Sourches depot head Germain Bazin wrote to Jaujard that he was prioritizing the order of works to be brought to the basements and was arranging the construction of new crates since, after five years, the old ones were falling apart. He was examining how the *Raft of the Medusa* might be crated and worried about how, in an evacuation, they could move the very large paintings that could not be rolled, since the scenery trailers were no longer available. He had good reason to worry about the safety of the artwork: just a day earlier, an Allied bombing raid had hit Le Mans, just minutes by air from the château.

On March 31, Bonnard issued instructions for the protection of museums, "in the event that French territory becomes the theater of active military operations." He ordered, among other things, that the artworks were in no case to be abandoned; if personnel left the depots, they were to take the art with them. Bonnard further stated that depot heads had the authority to move the artworks under their care if a region became dangerous and they could request the aid of local police. He also authorized any necessary actions to assure that troops respected the depots, whether German troops or those of invasion forces.

In April, the Allies began concentrated bombing to soften up the enemy for the impending assault, targeting railroad tracks and marshaling yards to sap the Germans' ability to move troops and supplies. They also hit ammunition depots as well as bridges and roads serving as supply routes. On the ground, the Resistance intensified its sabotage of railroads, bridges, telephone and telegraph lines and factories churning out German war equipment.

On April 10, Allied bombers hit the railway network running through Saint-Pierre-des-Corps. Though the town lay fifty miles from Chambord, the force of the bombs was so great that it shattered windows in the château's chapel. Depot head Pierre Schommer also saw a large formation of Allied planes fly over the château; two months later he would watch one heading straight for it.

At 2:20 a.m. on June 4, the staff members at Vayrac, one of the small depots supplementing Montal, were woken by the sound of a loud truck. Then they heard men outside, followed by loud banging on the door. French voices threatened to launch grenades if they were not allowed in. However, the depot head had orders not to open the door under any circumstances so he asked them what they wanted. Through the door, the voices said, "We don't want Mona Lisa, and we won't harm the paintings. We want gasoline."

After they threatened again to launch their explosive devices and to knock down the door, the depot head decided the artworks were at risk in any event and opened the door to six non-uniformed young men with no idea that the *Mona Lisa* was tucked thirteen miles away at Montal. After much intimidation by the men, the depot staff told them where to find the gasoline and off they went, having revealed nothing of their identities or affiliation.

June 6, 1944. D-Day. For the staff of the Musées Nationaux, as for everyone in France, there was great joy, but that joy quickly shifted to the certain knowledge that a long, dangerous road still lay ahead as intensive Allied bombing continued and retreating German forces became even more violent. On June 10, Jaujard, worried that phone or mail communications might be cut at any time, issued detailed procedures for guards, fuel and fire protection, including instructions for evacuation and coordination with fire departments in case electric power went out. On June 19, he issued another directive to depot heads that if military events threatened the area of the depot, artworks were to be taken down to the basements, if considered adequate, and raised off the floor on planks. If there was inadequate room for all of artwork, priority was to be given to the most precious items, with the others taken to areas deemed strongest, such as vaulted ground-floor rooms or between the thickest walls.

Jaujard was particularly concerned about the depots close to Paris. In 1940, when as many artworks and antiquities as possible were moved south from the Loire, it had simply not been practical to abandon Chambord, Cheverny or Courtalain. While earlier in the war these locations had seemed adequately far from bombing targets such as major road and rail lines, it had not been possible to anticipate the intensity of the Allied bombings, nor the fact that in mid-1944 the Allies would target secondary roads and rail lines that might act as supply routes to Normandy. There had also been no way to anticipate that the Germans would commandeer industrial sites in Le Mans, in so doing turning the area—including the nearby Sourches depot—into an Allied target.

The depot at Courtalain still held a portion of the Louvre's antiquities plus evacuated items from other museums. Only half a mile from a railway junction station and just alongside a national road, it was a ripe Allied target. On June 8, bombs fell near the depot and two evenings later, in a violent attack on the local rail lines, three bombs landed only 600 feet from the château. Additional bombing raids took place nearby on June 17, 20 and yet again on June 26, targeting the railway, the nearby road and viaducts. Miraculously, not a single bomb hit the château.

By June 1944, the depot at Chambord—by far the largest of the art depots—was holding over 140,000 cubic feet of art. On June 12, depot head Pierre Schommer wrote to Jaujard that all was calm, though he worried that departmental roads—a possible target—were close by, that area bombings continued and that fighter planes were regularly flying overhead. His concern soon proved justified. On June 21, a squadron of American military planes left a British airbase on a mission to hit a French airfield. The following day, one of the planes was hit by German fire, disabling three of the engines. The pilot briefly hoped that the fourth engine would keep going long enough to get them to Spain or Switzerland but the plane kept losing altitude and he ordered the crew of seven to evacuate. He and his copilot decided to stay aboard until the last possible minute, hoping to divert the plane from any inhabited area. The plane continued to lose altitude as it crossed just above a forest. Just beyond, the huge mass of Chambord appeared in front of them.

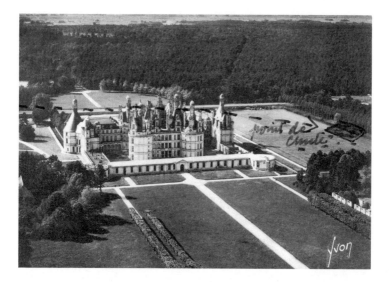

PIERRE SCHOMMER'S HANDWRITTEN INDICATION OF PLANE'S
TRAJECTORY OVER THE CHÂTEAU DE CHAMBORD

The plane continued to drop, heading straight towards the château
and the pilot was sure they would crash into the roof. Miraculously,
the plane just missed the chimneys and crashed some 200 yards
from the château, exploding with such force that pieces of metal
shot through the windows. The ground was covered with debris.
The plane's fuel set off an inferno that blazed for hours as the shaken
depot staff looked on in horror.

The pilot and copilot had safely ejected just moments before
the impact, although when the pilot, William Kalan, had pulled on
his parachute's ripcord, nothing happened. At the last second, he
had successfully yanked out the silk by hand. Once on the ground,
the copilot escaped into the woods; Kalan hid in a tree for two days
before setting off at night through the forest. The men were separately rescued by Resistance members and sheltered with families

in nearby villages, where they remained for several months. While in hiding, Kalan helped his host with Allied arms drops and other Resistance activities. Eventually, both men were able to cross the Loire, where they joined approaching U.S. troops.

By mid-June, bombs were landing within two or three miles of the depot at Sourches. Bazin had made arrangements to bring works to the basement and enhanced protective measures there, lining certain areas with fire-resistant paper and others with fabric that could absorb dampness. He also separated part of the basement into individual compartments to meet the needs of specific works.

D-Day had not diverted German interest in the art of France. In early May, Bonnard had requested the specifics of the volume of art at each depot. The curators responded to Jaujard within days, but Jaujard conveniently failed to pass on the information to Bonnard. On June 15, after a month of silence, Bonnard called Jaujard requesting the information as well as the quantity of trucks and gas needed to move the collections east and a list of potential depots. The next day, Jaujard provided the overblown volume information and indicated that he had not had either the time or available personnel to do any research on potential new depots. And, he said, his deputy Joseph Billiet was charged with this responsibility and had been away until June 7. But in any regard, he continued, it was first necessary to address the very principle of moving the art. The question should be asked, he said, if moving it along roads being bombed would constitute a more significant and certain danger than keeping it in place. Moreover, he added, it would be utterly impossible at this point to obtain enough trucks from French transport firms. It would be necessary to request German ones, which would expose the artworks to even greater bombing risks. Later that day, at an emergency meeting of the Louvre's curators, Jaujard read his letter into the minutes and asked if the curators wished to take a different position. They voted their unanimous agreement.

B onnard knew the curators would again threaten a mass resignation if he attempted to overrule them; Jaujard had won. There would be no further request to move the art and antiquities to new depots. Jaujard's almost six months of delaying tactics had succeeded in preventing the last German attempt at a wholesale seizure of the Louvre's top masterpieces. But two of Hitler's henchmen—Göring and Himmler—were still not ready to give up their dreams of claiming their very favorite pieces, though they still needed a way to wrap their desires in a veneer, however thin, of propriety.

With respect to the Basel altar, Göring had unsuccessfully tried to pressure the French curators into an exchange. At the end of March, Bonnard told Bunjes, still acting on Göring's behalf, that the head of the French government had authorized him to personally conduct exchange negotiations. Bonnard and Bunjes began to envision an arrangement of "reciprocal gifts" instead of an exchange. But those negotiations were eventually stymied when Bonnard was informed that works in the French national collections could not be used as gifts for foreign leaders in the absence of specific legislation. The clock would run out on the scheme.

H einrich Himmler's desire for the Bayeux tapestry was another matter. He had patiently waited throughout the entire Occupation and he was determined that time would not run out. In 1941, Himmler had sent an artist to begin making a painting of it. In 1942, he had sent a photographer to Sources to photograph it. The Ahnenerbe continued to conduct research off-site until mid-1943, when the artist was given permission to return to Sourches to continue his painting. In November 1943, Bazin had noted in a letter to the mayor of Bayeux that all was well with the tapestry but unbeknownst to Bazin, nothing was further from the truth.

By then, Hermann Bunjes was helping not only Göring, but also Himmler, who had promoted him to SS lieutenant in 1942. Himmler's Ahnenerbe research group had not been able to prove the Germanic origin necessary to take the Bayeux tapestry, so Himmler and Bunjes developed a secret, two-part plan with the code name *Sonderauftrag Bretagne* ("Special Project Brittany"). First, they would pressure the French to move the tapestry to Paris for "safety reasons," and then, once it was in Paris—and more accessible—the SS would take the tapestry by force and send it to Berlin. In both October and November 1943, the manager of the Ahnenerbe wrote letters to Bunjes telling of the group's intent to appropriate the tapestry. Then they simply waited for an opportune moment. The intensive bombings of spring 1944 provided a perfect excuse.

First, Himmler and Bunjes had to find a way to overcome the long-established protocol that no artwork at the depots could be moved without written authorization of both Jaujard and the head of the Kunstschutz. But they knew that the Kunstschutz was likely to oppose such a move and that Jaujard would most certainly object. To get Kunstschutz approval, they had the SS send a telegram to Tieschowitz, ordering him to authorize the tapestry's return to Paris. Then they bypassed Jaujard by getting the approval of his superior, Nazi collaborator Georges Hilaire, who had replaced Hautecœur two months earlier. Before giving the go-ahead to the Ahnenerbe, Hilaire had obtained Bonnard's approval.

While Bunjes and the Ahnenerbe manager schemed to move the tapestry, Bazin and Jaujard had concluded after careful

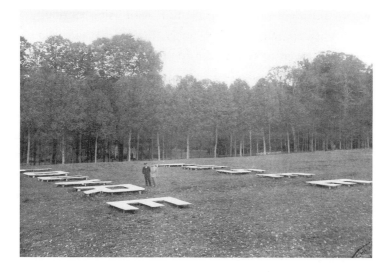

GERMAIN BAZIN INSPECTING LETTERS ON
THE GROUNDS OF THE CHÂTEAU DE SOURCES

consideration that the tapestry and the other artworks at Sourches should remain in place. Bazin said that while Allied bombing was sometimes quite close, evacuation posed even greater risks. Trucks were targets for Allied bombs and roads were subject to unpredictable barrages of machine gun fire and the work of Resistance saboteurs. Bazin and Jaujard agreed that the basements of Sourches could safely sustain bombing, particularly given the special measures Bazin had taken to ready the basements. Bazin made special provisions for the tapestry. It would go, still in its custom lead box, into a special blockhouse he had built for it in a particularly well-protected area of the basement. To further protect the depot, he had also arranged for the construction of giant letters spelling out "Musée du Louvre" to set out on the huge expanse of lawn in the hope that Allied planes would see it.

On June 26, Bazin wrote Jaujard a six-page letter describing the protective measures he had taken for the depot and others he planned. He went to sleep that night thinking all was still well. Just before 1 a.m., from his upstairs bedroom, Bazin heard an altercation below, but could not easily go downstairs to learn what it was since he had injured a tendon in his leg the previous day. Several minutes later, the bedroom door swung open and in marched SS troops with submachine guns and an order mandating him to hand over the tapestry. The men were accompanied by Jacques Dupont, the French Inspector of Historic Monuments, who arguably had jurisdiction over the tapestry. As Bazin looked over the paperwork, he noticed that, while it had Hilaire's signature, it lacked Jaujard's. Because the phones were not working, Bazin could not call Jaujard for guidance and initially refused to turn over the tapestry, even though Dupont said that his own presence constituted approval. After ten long minutes, the depot's head guard convinced Bazin to hand over the tapestry for fear the SS men would otherwise destroy the entire château.

The tapestry traveled through the night to the Louvre on a truck accompanied by a German military escort. The 150-mile journey took eleven hours; the tapestry did not arrive in Paris until noon.

Two days later, Bazin wrote a scalding letter to Jaujard describing the appalling disregard for the security of the tapestry during its transport. He pointed out that movement of the strong nighttime vehicle lights made the depot itself a bombing target. Further, he noted, because of the rolled tapestry's small size, it could have been easily transported in a car rather than a more visible truck with a military escort. And, he said, the presence of a convoy slowed the journey, exposing the tapestry to even greater risk. He also noted that during the entire voyage the tapestry was sitting next to a barrel filled with more than fifty gallons of gasoline. If there had been machine gun fire along the dangerous roads, even a single bullet would have turned the entire truck into a fireball.

On July 5, Hilaire asked the Louvre's Director of Architectural Services to verify the state of the tapestry and then bring it to the museum basements where it would be more secure. Several days later, in front of seven witnesses, the tapestry was examined, new moth powder was applied and the tapestry was tucked into a basement niche considered particularly safe.

There was a sad irony in the fact that the tapestry was in Paris. The Allies had liberated the town of Bayeux three weeks before the Germans took the tapestry from Sourches; it was the first major French town to be liberated, just a single day after the D-Day landing. Had the tapestry remained in Bayeux, it would now be safe. Instead, it was now in still-occupied Paris and Himmler had stage two of "Special Project Brittany" waiting in the wings.

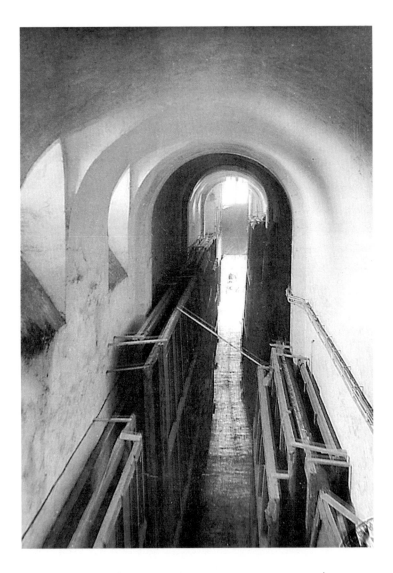

PAINTINGS IN SOURCHES BASEMENT, WAITING FOR WAR'S END

# TWENTY-EIGHT

# INSURRECTION

B Y JUNE 1944, four years of occupation had taken a terrible toll on the inhabitants of Paris. Basic goods had become almost impossible to obtain due to infrastructure damage, export of goods to Germany and other problems. Already worn out from four cold winters with hardly any heat, residents of the City of Light literally had no light by the summer of 1944. There was no electricity until 10:30 p.m. and even then it was brief and unreliable. Fuel for cooking was likewise almost non-existent; gas was provided for only a half-hour at lunchtime and dinnertime and its poor quality made it hardly usable.

The worst shortage, however, was food itself. Earlier in the war, French women had been heard to mutter, "What good are potatoes, with no hot stoves to prepare them?" By now, however, the potatoes themselves had disappeared. But potatoes were the least of it. The food shortages were so severe that the average adult had only half the necessary calories. For children the situation was even worse; a Red Cross report said the city had 25,000 malnourished babies and that deaths from tuberculosis were increasing at an alarming rate, especially among the young. In mid-August, someone from the Academy of Science helpfully suggested that "in a crisis, Paris could eat the leaves of the trees in the Bois." Ernest Hemingway reported to a friend that he had been eating pigeons caught in the Jardin du Luxembourg.

Parisians were also hungry for a sign that the Allies were on their way, listening to the radio and asking anyone heading into the city if they had news. But there was no hint to be found that Allied forces were heading to Paris anytime soon. And for good reason: Supreme Allied Commander General Dwight Eisenhower had no such plan in mind. He believed a battle for Paris would become a bloody street war that could destroy the city altogether and that it would present great risk for Allied soldiers untrained in urban warfare and unable to use two of their most important advantages: their airplanes and their tanks. Eisenhower also believed an immediate liberation of Paris would divert resources from an Allied advance to Berlin and the planned invasion of southern France to gain control over the Mediterranean.

Resistance groups in Paris were also tiring of waiting for the Allies and wanted to take matters into their own hands. The largest group in France, the *Forces Françaises de l'Intérieur* (FFI), supported de Gaulle, but other Resistance groups, most notably the Communists, had other agendas. For a time, de Gaulle asked the FFI to be patient, worried that if an uprising in Paris took place before Allied troops were close enough to control the situation, any one of these other groups might be able to take power. But by the end of June, the multiple Resistance groups in Paris, though disparate in their political beliefs, leaders and methods, agreed about one thing: they were no longer going to wait passively for their liberation. Each group in its own way was making plans to liberate the city, sooner rather than later and with or without the help of Allied forces.

Given Jaujard's ties to the Resistance, he was surely aware of plans for insurrection, and even before those plans were in the air, it was clear that with the Allies in mainland France, liberation would come soon one way or another. It was equally clear that the Louvre, just yards away from the epicenter of the German military command, would be particularly vulnerable. A number of protective measures were still in place from the 1943 response to the German anti-aircraft projectiles. At that time, steps had been taken to secure some of the artwork and the palace itself. Electrical equipment had been covered, many ground floor windows boarded up and a number of other windows stacked with sandbags. On June 14 the Curators Committee met in an emergency session to consider additional measures since they knew an even higher level of protection would be needed in case of a battle around the palace. Personnel providing essential services might need to remain at the museum for an extended period of time, perhaps cut off from outside communication and support. On June 30, the museum administration requested and obtained an advance of twenty thousand francs from the Société des Amis du Louvre to fund a canteen for that purpose. Having thus planned to the best of their ability, they waited for the battle for Paris to begin, not knowing when it would happen or whether liberation would come by insurrection or Allies. In the end, it would be both.

The unraveling began on July 14 with demonstrations. The Fête Nationale demonstrations were not the first ones of the Occupation but they were by far the largest. Though Parisians had been ordered not to gather, an estimated 100,000 people marched in the streets of the city and its environs. The day was also notable because it marked a shift in the position of the French police, who had been ordered to forbid any July 14 celebrations and to augment their forces to suppress any demonstrations. Now, for the first time during the Occupation, they disobeyed German orders, refusing to act against a huge mass of demonstrators in the working class Belleville neighborhood. The police support, in turn, further galvanized the Resistance, who stepped up their sabotage actions and encouraged additional strikes. On August 9, a thousand rail repair workers briefly stopped work. The following day, much of the rail force in the greater Paris area went on indefinite strike. On August 13, the 3,000 agents of the Paris Métro stopped working. Other strikes and acts of sabotage undermined German industrial production in Paris factories.

Then came the August 15 Assumption Day religious holiday, normally a quiet day. This year, the streets were quiet in a different way: 15,000 members of the Paris police force went on strike in response to concern that the Germans were about to confiscate their weapons. The strike left the streets virtually devoid of the police presence that the Nazis had used throughout the Occupation to enforce their regulations. This was no small development; it was the Paris police who had been sent to arrest almost forty percent of the 76,000 Jews deported from France to German death camps during the war, of whom only 2,500 survived.

The same day, Dietrich von Choltitz, whom Hitler had appointed as the city's German military commander just eight days earlier, started his morning in his office in the Hôtel Meurice on rue de Rivoli. Hitler had chosen Choltitz in part because, with a reputation for never questioning an order, he was one of the few German generals the Führer felt he could still trust. That trust would be betrayed from the start, since even as Choltitz headed towards Paris after his first and only meeting with Hitler on August 7, he felt that he had been in the presence of a madman. Any doubt was erased during his difficult day on August 15. First he headed to a German bunker nearby Saint-Germain-en-Laye, where he received orders to destroy the electric power and other utilities of Paris, including most of the aqueducts supplying the city's water. When he returned to his office, four men were waiting to transmit an order to destroy the city's industrial plants. In spite of his reputation for ruthless ferocity in urban warfare, even by Nazi standards, Choltitz believed there was still opportunity to save the city and ignored the orders for days. Before August 15 was over, he also made a visit to Jaujard at the Louvre, on yet another order from Berlin, this one likely from Himmler, to verify that the Bayeux tapestry was still there.

The August 15 police strike spurred even more Parisians to act. Two days later, 1,500 civil servants demonstrated in front of the Hôtel de Ville, singing the Marseillaise. By the end of the day, Prime Minister Pierre Laval had left town, followed by droves of other senior collaborators. Virtually all German noncombat personnel had already fled. German workers had brought the remaining looted items at the Jeu de Paume to the sequestered rooms at the Louvre, where they would remain.

On August 18, postal workers and nurses joined the strikes. Radio announcements by the BBC encouraged people to act and notices were posted throughout the city calling for a full-scale revolt. The insurrection began the next day. By then, Jaujard had already put the Louvre's plan into operation, calling in a wide group of individuals to protect the Louvre for an unknown period of time and under circumstances that were likely to become dangerous. Each of them was happy to come. In addition to dozens of guards, all curators not at the storage depots also came to take up posts day and night throughout the colossal building.

Jaujard's assistant Jacqueline Bouchot-Saupique was there, along with her husband Georges Saupique, a sculptor and former World

War I officer who brought along volunteers recruited from among his fellow sculptors. Jaujard's wife was there as well. During the planning, she had been asked to stock enough food for them all, an almost impossible task given the food shortages. Christiane Desroches Noblecourt, the Egyptian Antiquities staff member, was also on hand. She later said that Madame Jaujard had gathered so much food for the entire staff that she had performed a miracle. Not only food was stockpiled; when the staff arrived, Jaujard instructed them to retrieve illegal weapons that "we may have hidden in the depths of the palace."

Also on hand was the head of security, whose staff and volunteers tested the fire protection systems and patrolled the palace's ancient roofs still as vulnerable to fire as they had been in 1870—the old wooden framework could ignite almost instantly from the heat and spark of projectiles.

From the beginning of the revolt, there was plenty of heat and spark around the Louvre, dangerously poised next to the German military nerve center. German soldiers and weaponry were heavily guarding place de la Concorde, parts of rue de Rivoli and the Tuileries Garden. German troops had dug bunkers in the Garden along rue de Rivoli and another on the place de la Concorde; a German watchtower sat opposite the main entrance to the Jeu de Paume. Resistance fighters fired on them from the quais of the Seine and from rue de Rivoli. The Louvre—bordered on three sides by the Seine, the Tuileries Garden and rue de Rivoli—sat in the middle of the heated action. Skirmishes also occurred between the Germans and the FFI along the museum's fourth side, the eastern Colonnade wing, as the FFI fought for control of the first arrondissement's town hall, just across the street.

Several Louvre staff members were almost caught in the crossfire. The first morning of the revolt, Jaujard called Rose Valland to his office in the Louvre. At 11 a.m. she was crossing the Tuileries when she witnessed volleys of shots at the place de la Concorde and on the pont du Carrousel, a bridge across the Seine facing the Louvre's Grande Galerie. Christiane Desroches Noblecourt arrived at the museum on her old bicycle amidst street combat just as the museum blocked all its exits.

The vast galleries of the Louvre echoed with gun- and shell-fire from the surrounding streets and the crackle of missed shots against the windows and walls. In an attempt to avoid stray shots that might come through windows, the staff tried to move about the building using the basement level. During street fighting on the quais of the Seine, a bullet just missed Jaujard when it burst through a window.

Unexplained shots caused another problem for Jaujard. The French Ministry of Finance occupied the Pavillon de Flore, located in the far southwestern corner of the Louvre adjacent to the Seine and the Pont Royal, both strategically important points for the Germans. On August 20, the Germans complained that in spite of a temporary truce, someone was firing shots from the roof of the Ministry into the Tuileries Garden, where Germans were stationed in tanks and bunkers. They threatened that if the problem continued, they would take fifty hostages from the Ministry. Jaujard sent three men to inspect the roofs of both the Pavillon de Flore and the adjacent Grande Galerie; they reported no evidence of any shooters.

Just minutes later, Jaujard learned of another presumed shooting incident. Members of the FFI, convinced that a German or collaborationist sniper was shooting at the French from a window in the museum's Colonnade wing, were trying to force their way into the Cour Carrée to look for the sniper. Jaujard sent several of his staff with the FFI men to the window in question, which could not have been the origin of any shots since it was entirely blocked from the inside. He then sent a patrol on a fruitless search of the roofs and attics of the four wings surrounding the Cour Carrée.

Several days later, a German bullet fired from the Tuileries Garden hit a roof of the Cour Carrée while Jaujard was making yet another patrol of the area, accompanied by four guards, leading Jaujard to believe that what the FFI had heard days before could have been just a reverberated sound. "Echo phenomena happen constantly," he wrote, "enhanced by the layout of the buildings of the Louvre, which form large square wells on the inside and large stone cliffs on the outside, reflecting and amplifying sound. In addition, the crack of bullets against these surfaces sometimes produces sparks when the bullets hit bits of silica as well as a small cloud of pulverized rock. This phenomenon could in many cases be mistaken for the shooting of a projectile rather than its impact."

While Jaujard's conclusion might explain the FFI's accusation, it could not rule out the German claim that there were snipers on the roof of the Pavillon de Flore. In the hope of avoiding further gunshots from the roof—and preventing the Germans from taking hostages—he arranged a permanent guard patrol on the roofs near the point where the Ministry's roofs met those of the rest of the Louvre.

Throughout the week of insurrection, the firemen stationed in the Louvre had a bird's eye view of the action. On the roof above the Salon Carré stood a sentry booth overlooking the entire expanse. From here and other access points on the roof, some accessible by spiral staircases and others by metal ladders bolted to the stone walls, the firemen had a unique view of German tank movements on the surrounding streets. Men on the roof signaled tank movements to a man in the sentry booth, which was equipped with a telephone linked to the firefighters' quarters in the Cour Visconti on the ground floor. The information was relayed downstairs and passed along to Resistance members using the station's landline.

Heinrich Himmler had been monitoring events from Berlin, still intent on grabbing the Bayeux tapestry before Paris was lost. On August 17, he had sent a coded message to Carl Oberg, the commander of the SS and Gestapo in France, reminding him not to forget to bring the Bayeux tapestry to a place of safety. On August 21 Himmler finally made his move, sending two SS commandants to see Dietrich von Choltitz. They came to his offices in the Hôtel Meurice on rue de Rivoli. When Choltitz learned of their arrival, his first thought was that they were there to arrest him, since he had just sent word via the Swedish consul to advise the Allies to head to Paris as fast as they could. But after exchanging Heil Hitlers, the SS men explained they had orders to obtain the tapestry. Choltitz, who had ignored so many orders in recent days, decided to undermine yet another, replying, "What luck! You want to take it out of harm's way?"

"Ja, Herr General."

"That would make me very happy," replied Choltitz. "Would you follow me out to the balcony?"

From the balcony, the three men looked left and across to the Louvre, where projectiles were raining down.

"You see," said Choltitz, "the tapestry is over there, in the basements of the Louvre."

"But, Herr General, the Louvre is occupied by the enemy," replied one of the SS men.

"Of course it is occupied, and considerably well," he replied.

"But under these conditions, Herr General, how can we get hold of the tapestry?"

"Gentlemen, you are the leaders of the best soldiers in the world. I will provide you with five or six of my best men and with cover fire as you cross the rue de Rivoli. You will only need to break open one door and then take the tapestry by force."

The two SS men hesitated, then one of them asked, "Herr General, did the French government not evacuate the tapestry a long time ago?"

"Not at all," replied Choltitz. "The tapestry is there, but you will have to take it by force."

Choltitz called in his art expert, who confirmed that the tapestry was still there.

"So, gentlemen," continued Choltitz, "this afternoon the Bayeux tapestry will be rescued under your command."

One of the men told Choltitz he would radio Berlin for further instructions and that they would report back in an hour. Choltitz never saw them again.

Throughout the first three weeks of August, as insurrection in Paris brewed and then burst forth, Eisenhower refused to send Allied troops to Paris. De Gaulle began pressing for the Allies to march on the city, warning of a possible repeat of the destructive Paris Commune of 1871. He was not the only one committed to action. As early as 1943, the Allied command had promised that French troops would be present at the liberation of Paris, and, specifically that it would be the 2nd French Armored Division, headed by General Jacques-Philippe Leclerc.

On August 14, General Leclerc had asked General Patton when his 2nd Armored Division might head to Paris; he was told to stay where he was. The next day, he asked Patton again and threatened to resign if he could not go. Patton recounted his reply in his journal: "I told him in my best French that he was a baby, and I would not have division commanders telling me where they would fight." On August 19 Leclerc asked again, aware of the revolt brewing in Paris and arguing it was time to march. Allied leaders simply assured him that his troops would be present at any liberation. Furious at being ignored, he stopped reporting vehicles lost in battle elsewhere but continued to requisition gasoline for them and hoard it in preparation. On August 20, with Paris in full revolt, Leclerc again argued his case, again without success. The following day, he decided to act on his own, sending 150 men and 30 military vehicles towards Paris, purportedly to conduct reconnaissance but also to ensure that when the Allies finally were sent to Paris, which was inevitable, French troops would be there as they had been promised long before. The following morning, he was ordered to bring his men back but refused. Instead, he went to see Eisenhower and Patton.

War correspondents and the BBC were partially aware of Leclerc's efforts and began announcing—incorrectly—that a part of his 2nd Armored Division was marching on Paris, which stirred up even more frenzy amidst Resistance members and the other citizens of Paris. The Resistance brought increasingly urgent messages to the Allied command that they had weakened the Germans enough that the Allies could easily take the city but that the effort was running thin and the window of opportunity would soon close. On August 22, the Swedish consul handed the Allies a message from Choltitz: "Twenty-four, forty-eight hours are all you have. After that I cannot promise you what will happen here." Pressure from all sides had converged. Eisenhower turned to General Bradley and said, "Well, what the hell, Brad. I guess we'll have to go in."

At 7:15 p.m. on August 22—the same day Leclerc was told to turn back—he at long last received the go-ahead from Bradley. He returned to his command post and shouted to his chief of staff, "*Gribius, mouvement immédiat sur Paris!*" Paris was finally about to be liberated.

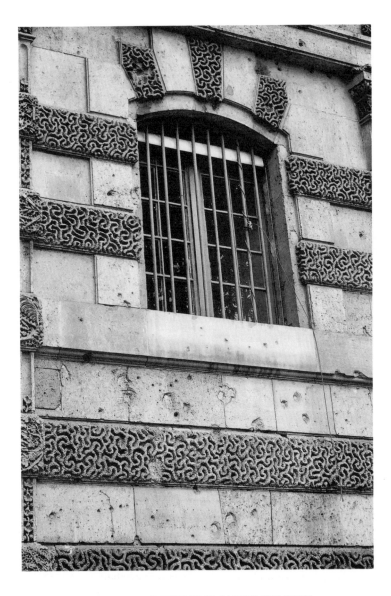

DAMAGE TO LOUVRE WALL FACING THE SEINE

# TWENTY-NINE

# RETREAT AND RETRIBUTION

FTER D-DAY, GERMAN troops in the south and south-west of France were on the move after receiving orders to head north towards the front in Normandy. Later, they would head in retreat towards Germany. As the endless columns of troops passed through the villages and towns of France, they left a trail of violence in their wake.

On June 8, the dreaded "Das Reich" division of the SS started north from Montauban. A day later, in Tulle, they took hostages and hanged 120 of them, three for each German soldier recently killed by the Resistance. The following day, they killed 642 men, women and children in Oradour-sur-Glane, almost its entire population, in a horrific manner and for no reason. The massacres continued through July and August. The withdrawing troops also executed Resistance members more frequently. Sometimes the murders were retribution for killing their comrades or even the suspicion they may have been responsible; other times, the executions were simply punishment for engaging in Resistance activity, whether actual or suspected.

And when they suspected someone at one of the Louvre's art depots, they did not hesitate to threaten to destroy the art as well.

Two days after the Normandy landing, a German division passed through the village of Saint-Céré. A mile away at the château de Montal, the depot staff heard several hours of combat and machine gun fire. Later they learned that part of the gunfire had been the execution of three maquis members captured and taken to the village square to be shot in public view. Montal depot head René Huyghe became further concerned when a group of ninety maquis fighters passed within a hundred feet of the depot, knowing the havoc that could result for the depot and the art if Germans spotted the men; he asked them to move further away. Inside the château, Huyghe took precautions nevertheless, closing the window shutters and blocking all openings from the inside with mattresses and other materials to prevent stray bullets from getting in and starting a fire. Later, there was a brief exchange of gunfire between the Germans and the maquis along the road in front of the château and several wayward bullets hit the walls but no other damage was done. When the electricity went off around 10 p.m., they lit the emergency gas lamps and heard shots throughout a sleepless night.

On August 13, as German troops were evacuating areas south of the Loire, the German commander of nearby Blois arrived at Cheverny with three men "armed to the teeth," intent on taking possession of the château and the outbuildings. As at the other depots, curator Hans Haug had documents from the senior German military command indicating that the depots were off limits to German troops, but the men were not impressed. They moved off only after concluding there was not enough room for their needs. Two days later, several young men in the maquis managed to get onto the grounds of the château, then shot at a German vehicle that had broken down on the road alongside the property. In return, several of the Germans began shooting at the walls surrounding the château's grounds. The noise roused nearby inhabitants and a number of panicked men in a nearby inn fled onto the grounds of the château, leading the Germans to believe that the property was full of "terrorists." They marched onto the grounds and began firing bullets and grenades at the windows of the outbuildings. Haug tried his best in his halting German to calm the enemy. After a solid half-hour of discussion and an inspection of the buildings, Haug convinced them to leave. The gunfire had just missed some frightened children who had run across the esplanade of the château. The only damage to the château itself was a bullet hole in the front door that had also pierced the Kunstschutz notice of protection that had been posted long before.

In early 1943, the Vichy government, with German assistance, had created the Milice, a secret paramilitary force of extremist Frenchmen. Each of its 30,000-plus members swore a 21-point pledge to fight, among other things, democracy and "Jewish leprosy." The Milice conducted political assassinations and helped track down Jews and others, but their primary target was the Resistance. They used brutal torture methods, first just against captured Resistance members, but later, like the Germans, even against local populations suspected of offering aid to them.

By mid-August, 1944, as German convoys passed through Valençay in retreat, an explosive tension hung in the air between the Resistance on one hand and the Milice and Germans on the other. On August 10, a Milice regiment assembled on the road in front of the château. Curator André Leroi-Gourhan came out and asked them to move elsewhere. After a half hour with no movement, Gérald Van der Kemp renewed the request. The Milice group agreed to disperse, but before they had moved on, they engaged in combat with FFI forces that had come along. Leroi-Gourhan again tried to convince the Milice to leave. Instead, they came onto the grounds and unsuccessfully tried to shoot him, claiming that he had been firing on them from inside the château. The Milice force then threatened to shoot both Van der Kemp and the duke's driver. Van der Kemp finally managed to convince them to leave without doing any harm.

On the afternoon of August 12, another skirmish broke out in front of the château, this time between armored German convoys and the FFI. It ended quickly, but started up again in the early evening and lasted three hours. During the fighting, a German shell set fire to the stables and spread to nearby outbuildings. The fire did not threaten the Venus de Milo and other works sheltered with her only because, unlike some of the other outbuildings, the one housing the large statues was freestanding and its roof had no flammable material.

At all the museum depots, one of the biggest risks to the art was fire, which could quickly destroy everything. Each depot had a carefully arranged protocol for contacting the local fire department, but that day, the phones had been knocked out. The depots also had their own fire-fighting equipment. Originally, the Valençay depot had only one large water pump that was constantly breaking down, but Van der Kemp had managed to secure another. He had also managed to assemble a secret stockpile of fuel for it that he kept hidden in a nearby ditch. That evening, the depot employees—dodging bullets—used the two pumps to battle the fire. At 10 p.m., the firefighters of the town of Valençay joined the effort and together they extinguished the fire, which had injured Leroi-Gourhan's arm.

Four days later, the town and the château would face far worse problems. In reprisal for German and Milice troops killed in the fighting of the previous days, the local German military commander took action. During the afternoon of August 16, an armored division of 300 SS troops circled the town and pillaged it, setting fire to forty-two buildings and killing eight people. They also went in search of several injured maquis members who were being treated at the local hospital, which was run by nuns. The maquisards and the hospital were only spared due to the courage of three of the nuns who held out a baby and said the building was a maternity hospital.

The Germans also had the château de Valençay in their sights due to rumors that a maquis head was at the château and that the bodies of three Germans had been buried on the grounds. The Germans were right on one count; a maquis member—Leroi-Gourhan—was indeed at the château. And they may have been partially right on the second count. A German captain had been injured in a skirmish with the FFI and taken prisoner, followed by a maquis war council decision to shoot him to avenge comrades who had been recently killed under terrible conditions; they also had no prison in which to keep him, a Resistance fighter later said. No mention was made of where he was buried, but the endless château grounds and surrounding forests that were hiding so many maquis would have been a logical location.

In the afternoon of August 16, Van der Kemp and his wife were finishing a late, leisurely lunch with the duke when they heard detonations outside: fifty SS troops had arrived with tanks. As several of them marched with their heavy footsteps into the château, one of the employees crouched in a corner of her quarters, convinced her last moments had come. But the men were in search of someone else: the rumored maquis head. Van der Kemp, in his elegant haberdashery with flower in his lapel and cane in hand, was marched by four armed men to the forecourt of the château, where the depot employees and the duke's wife and stepson had already been ordered face down on the lawns, rifles pointed at them. Van der Kemp was pushed against a wall, where officers accused him of being the FFI head, of giving assistance to the maquis and of allowing them to set ambushes from the château's grounds. In fact, they were mistaking him for Leroi-Gourhan, who was face down on the lawn with the others.

As at Cheverny, the German troops were not impressed with Valençay's Kunstschutz off-limits sign and told Van der Kemp they were going to shoot him and then burn down the château. With the duke's cowhand acting as interpreter, Van der Kemp told the Germans he was the keeper of the treasures of the Louvre, including the Venus de Milo and the Winged Victory of Samothrace and that he had engaged in contact with the FFI solely to keep the artwork safe. He said the surrounding miles of forests were filled with Resistance members and that if the château and its artwork were destroyed, the men, by the next day, would "reveal to the entire world a catastrophe equal to the burning of the library at Alexandria by Julius Caesar." One of the Germans, nonplussed, replied that they were there to make war, not art history.

While Van der Kemp, still pushed against the wall, continued to seek an effective argument to diffuse the situation, his wife approached and said she wanted to die with him. He answered with one whispered word, "drapeau." She quickly went upstairs to their room and tossed into a stove the French flag her husband had prepared out of bits of parachute fabric in anticipation of the town's liberation. She did it just in time; the Germans had begun a thorough search of the living quarters, including the Van der Kemps' room. The SS men took all their money, including cash Van der Kemp had been holding for Carle Dreyfus, still in hiding.

In the meantime, German gunfire had set one of the outbuildings ablaze. As the fire began spreading to other structures,

Van der Kemp still kept calmly trying to convince the Germans to stand down. After several hours, running out of options, he tried a more personal touch, telling the two SS captains they could certainly kill him, but if they burned down the château and in so doing destroyed the art treasures, they would be shot as soon as Göring heard the news. This last tactic resonated: the Germans released Van der Kemp and the staff and authorized the guards to put out the fire, with a promise that the guards would be safe as they did so.

Two museum guards were sent less than one hundred feet from the château's front door to open the valves that would allow the water to flow. A moment later, a burst of German machine gun fire hit guard Lucien Nervet at close range, killing him instantly. While the remaining soldiers were distracted by the noise, Leroi-Gourhan— knowing he was the man the SS were looking for—made a run for it. He sped off, jumped over a wall and headed towards the Gâtines Forest and his fellow freedom fighters.

Once the fire was out, Van der Kemp lent the depot's pumps to the town to combat the flames still raging there; both the château and the town benefitted from the almost eight hundred gallons of fuel he had so carefully accumulated to power the water pumps and hidden for four years. When it was all over, Van der Kemp returned to his quarters, his arms and legs shaking violently. His day had started like that of a seventeenth-century lord; it ended as that of a twentieth-century hero.

Events at Chambord several days later had an even more tragic outcome. On August 20, the village of Chambord was liberated by local Resistance troops, who then posted sentinels in the area in case of further German activity. The following morning, when a convoy of retreating German vehicles entered the grounds of the château, FFI troops engaged them in battle for several hours, causing residents of the hotel on the edge of the property to flee to the safety of the château. Depot head Pierre Schommer squeezed the refugees from the hotel between the crates of the artwork and told them to be silent and closed all the window shutters. In the course of the battle, a German soldier was killed and the German troops set fire to the hotel and half of the buildings in the village.

One of the depot guards slipped out of the château to hang the Kunstschutz off-limits sign, only to have shots ring out and a bullet fly directly over his head. The sign had no effect: three helmeted Germans with grenades on their belts demanded entry into the château. Schommer and Monsieur Foeller, the head guard, both of whom spoke German, opened the door. One of the German soldiers pointed an automatic rifle at them; the other two pushed their batons against the throats of Schommer and Foeller. Schommer explained to the senior officer, a major Leye, that the building sheltered the art of the French national museums. Leye responded that he did not care about aesthetics and that he would destroy the depot if he found that the building housed any "terrorists," or found proof that any of them had fired on his troops from the château, as he was convinced, or even if he found anyone not in service to the château on the premises.

Schommer explained that innocent people were there from the hotel, to which Leye responded that he had never made war against women or children, but that any men in the château were to be held accountable. One of his men had been injured and another killed and they would be avenged.

Schommer's wife guided the soldiers to the refugees from the hotel. The terrified children had their arms up and the soldiers saw a several-month-old infant in the arms of its mother. Leye made a sign to the children to lower their arms and ordered the women and children to move to the guardhouse; the men were taken to the courtyard to be kept under guard by German soldiers. The Germans interrogated every woman, eventually allowing several of them to leave, then began interrogating the depot guards, examining their clothing, shoes, hands and papers.

Leye, still convinced the Resistance had fired from the towers of the château, ordered Schommer and Foeller to show them the towers, edging them up the stairs with a machine gun at their backs. The many cobwebs and dust on the floors with no footprints were proof that no snipers had been there, but these findings did not placate the Germans, who took even more male hostages. For six hours, Leye and another German soldier examined the château accompanied by Schommer and Foeller. In spite of the hours of terror, the two Frenchmen, like Van der Kemp at Valençay, remained calm and Schommer kept trying to think of some way to regain control of the situation. In response to Leye's endless questions about his role at the château and the contents of the crates and his obvious suspicion that they contained weapons, ammunition or other Resistance supplies. Schommer replied that his responsibility forbade any such activity. He added that the artwork had an immense value to the culture of all civilized people and that he had kept it safe throughout the war in spite of difficult circumstances. He appealed to Leye's honor as a German officer, saying that the crates included important representations of German civilization, including works by Dürer, Cranach and others. Leye was silent for some time and then with a single word, "Fine," he stopped interrogating Schommer.

As the sun went down, the German soldier who had been killed was buried just outside the château. The flames and thick smoke from the burning village were still visible, the burning trees still crackled and explosions rang out as the Germans destroyed Resistance ammunition they had found on the grounds. Schommer, Foeller, the local priest and another man convinced the Germans to release most of the hostages. As night fell, five remaining prisoners were lined up on the château's lawn with their hands behind their necks and five Germans readied their weapons. One of the hostages, a member of the local Resistance, took advantage of the darkness and the momentary German attention to their weapons to escape into the woods. The other four men were shot dead, their bodies then mutilated and dumped in a nearby manure shed. The Germans left late the following afternoon. As they made their way out of the village, they set yet another building on fire.

It could have been worse. Three days later and ninety miles north of Chambord, at the same time Leclerc and his men were heading towards Paris, a division of retreating German troops entered the village of Maillé. As a reprisal for a minor skirmish nearby the previous day between a small group of Resistance members and two German vehicles, the German troops torched almost every building in the village and killed 124 of its 500 inhabitants, including a semi-paralyzed 89-year-old man and forty-eight children, half of them under age five. It would be the last German massacre in France.

At Sourches, the last days of the German occupation of the area were less traumatic. Several days before the Allies arrived, a German officer who served as a liaison between the depot and the regional German command in Le Mans came to say goodbye to depot head Germain Bazin. "Do me a favor," he said to Bazin, "could I see her?" Bazin asked whom he meant. "Mona Lisa," said the German. "But you know better than anyone that she's not here," replied Bazin. The German replied: "Everyone knows that her residence is secret and that it's changed often. But I tried my luck, so I wouldn't have gone to war for nothing."

# THIRTY

## LIBERATION

L ECLERC RECEIVED THE green light to march on Paris in the early evening of August 22. He and his sixteen thousand men and four thousand vehicles of the French 2nd Armored Division set off the following morning. The Allied command hoped Leclerc's troops could reach Paris the same day, to be quickly joined by other Allied divisions, but German resistance was heavy and progress was slow. By noon, Leclerc and a small detachment of his men had only reached Rambouillet, thirty miles from Paris. A half hour later, the BBC began to erroneously announce that Paris had already been liberated, setting off premature celebrations as far away as New York City. At Rambouillet, Leclerc received reports that German defenses just outside Paris were stronger than previously believed, meaning that the city would have to wait yet another day to be liberated.

Days before, on August 19, Resistance members had hoisted the French flag over the main building of the Préfecture de Police on the Ile de la Cité, the first time the tricolore had flown in Paris since the Germans forbade its display in 1940. Some of the museum's staff had wanted to do the same, but Jaujard convinced them it was in the

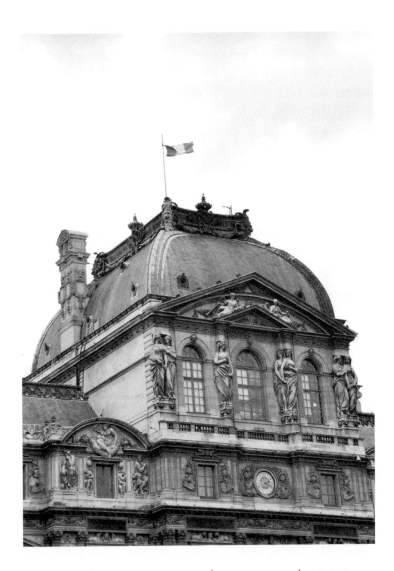

FLAG RAISED ATOP THE LOUVRE'S PAVILLON DE L'HORLOGE

best interest of the safety of the museum to wait. His call was right: the firemen stationed in the Louvre's Cour Visconti had received a phone call that day telling them about the prefecture's flag and asking them to raise a flag as well. They scurried to find a flag and raised it at the corner of the eastern end of the Louvre and the Seine. Within seconds, it drew enemy fire from the dome of the Institut de France just across the river.

But several days later, with the insurrection holding up and sporadic truces taking place, Jaujard, who had been attentively listening to the news on a failing radio, heard that French troops were on their way. He decided that the time had come. In the gray dawn of August 23, the museum staff gathered in the Cour Carrée and watched the French flag rise atop the 300-year-old Pavillon de l'Horloge, a sight that curator Jean Charbonneaux later said he would never forget.

In Berlin that same day, Hitler also heard the news of the imminent arrival of the Allied troops. He responded by issuing his famous order to prepare the Seine bridges for demolition, declaring, "Paris must not fall into the hands of the enemy except as a field of ruins." At dawn the following day, Choltitz's aide Lieutenant Dankwart von Arnim handed his boss another message from Hitler: "Execute the order."

At dawn on August 24, Leclerc's men left Rambouillet in multiple columns, pushing forward through pouring rain. They were delayed by narrow, crooked roads that snaked through densely populated small stone villages as well as by artillery fire, mines, and heavy street fighting with German troops. By early evening, only one column was near the Paris line. At that point, General Bradley authorized American troops to head towards the city, violating the promise that French troops would make first landfall in Paris.

Leclerc, having learned the Resistance could not hold off the Germans much longer, had already sent a Piper Cub spotter plane to Paris to drop a message via a little parachute to the FFI at the Préfecture de Police, saying: "Hold on, we're coming." At 7:30 p.m., he ordered Captain Raymond Dronne and his small group of men to head for Paris as fast as they could. Just over an hour later Dronne and his men crossed the Porte d'Italie into the thirteenth arrondissement of Paris, becoming the first Liberation forces to enter the city as he had been promised so long before. French troops had returned to Parisian soil after more than four years.

That same day, Hitler, five hundred miles away and unaware that his orders for total destruction had been ignored, was asking, "Is Paris burning?"

As Dronne and his men made their way to the center of the city, church bells began to ring behind them. Before long, the great bells of Notre Dame began to clang and Resistance radio announcer Paul Schaeffer broadcast a call for all the priests of Paris to ring their churches' bells in celebration. Bells rang out while people sang and shouted from open windows. Where there was electricity, windows were lit, in flagrant disregard of the German nightly blackout rule to which Parisians had been subject since 1940. The people of Paris thought liberation had come. But 150 men could not liberate a city and the Germans made sure the people knew it, shooting at the illuminated windows and at the ringing towers of Notre Dame. Before long, a subdued Schaeffer announced, "It would be best to close your windows." Nevertheless, Choltitz's aide wrote that night in his journal, "I have just heard the bells of my own funeral."

By the morning of August 25, the full force of Leclerc's division had arrived, supported by the U.S. 4th Infantry Division. Some of the most intense fighting that day occurred around the Louvre as the Allies fought for control of the central bridges over the river and the German command buildings just beyond them on the north side of the Tuileries Garden. The museum, sitting between the Seine and the rue de Rivoli, was caught in the firestorm as the Allies battled fire from German bunkers and tanks in the Tuileries Garden, place de la Concorde and rue de Rivoli. Allied tanks rolled through the archways under the Grande Galerie as they headed towards battle against the Hôtel Meurice, where Choltitz would soon surrender. At one point, Jean-Jacques Haffner, the Louvre's head architect, entered the command car of one of Leclerc's detachments to give them information to reduce the risk of damage to the Louvre. But the palace was caught in the crossfire nonetheless, taking fire on all sides, including shots at the windows of the Pavillon de Flore by an ill-informed FFI member.

As the battle raged at the northwestern corner of the Tuileries at place de la Concorde, Germans fired from behind the metal shutters of the Jeu de Paume and from sandbag-blanketed statues in the museum's gardens; nine men there lost their lives.

Across from the Jeu de Paume on the Seine side of the Tuileries Garden stood the Musée de l'Orangerie and, inside, Monet's *Water Lilies* that had been housed there since a year after his death in 1926. During the battle, shells punctured the building; several of them also pierced Monet's work. Another shell exploded in a roomful of German prisoners who had surrendered to the head guard in the mistaken belief that he was a military officer, based on his cap and the gold stripes on his uniform. One of the prisoners was killed and several others seriously wounded.

By mid-afternoon, the Hôtel Meurice was surrounded. Allied forces launched smoke grenades into the lobby, then French troops and FFI members stormed into the building. Choltitz offered his surrender and was led from the building amid the still-swirling smoke. He was taken to the Préfecture de Police, where he came face to face with Leclerc. "*Maintenant, ça y est,*" Leclerc said. "It's over."

Then he introduced himself and conducted the signing of the surrender documents. Choltitz's formal surrender to Charles de Gaulle, who had arrived in Paris that afternoon, took place shortly thereafter at the gare Montparnasse.

A ceasefire had been announced as soon as Choltitz agreed to surrender, but scattered combat continued with small groups of German soldiers who, amid confusion and lack of communication, had not learned of the ceasefire and surrender. Other uncaptured Germans simply refused to observe the ceasefire. But Paris was free.

Augustus 26 dawned brilliantly sunny. Parisians had celebrated through the night and looked forward to another day of revelry; Allied troops continued to fight small pockets of Germans. That afternoon, more than a million people gathered for the Liberation parade, cramming the route from the Arc de Triomphe down the Champs Elysées to place de la Concorde, then continuing along rue to Rivoli and finishing at Notre Dame Cathedral. Generals de Gaulle and Leclerc triumphantly led the parade. But as the procession reached place de la Concorde, snipers began firing into the crowd. There was more sniper fire as the tail end of de Gaulle's procession passed the Louvre. Thousands of people along the parade route ran for cover, so many that soon they were piled on top of each other. Jean-Paul Sartre was shot at as he watched the parade from his balcony at the Hôtel du Louvre. A senior official at Ministry of Finance offices on the rue de Rivoli side of the Louvre was shot and killed at his office window.

Chaos also erupted at the Jeu de Paume Museum when the sniper fire rang out. Crowds in search of shelter forced open doors and windows of the museum. One of the guards, in violation of orders, had climbed up to the roof to get a good view of the parade. After he was mistaken for a sniper, both he and the museum drew

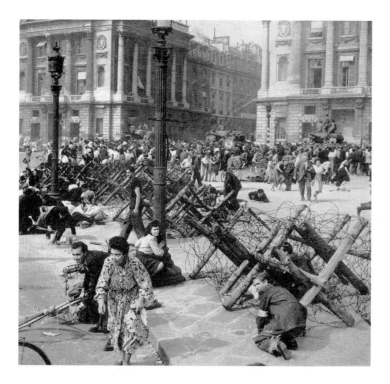

CROWDS RUNNING FOR COVER AT PLACE DE
LA CONCORDE, AUGUST 26, 1944

fire from Leclerc's men until Rose Valland protested to one of the officers. When she tried to prevent crowds from heading to the basement, where the museum's own artwork was stored, they began to accuse her of hiding Germans and, with a submachine gun to her back, she was forced to show them otherwise.

Jacques Jaujard's troubles were not yet over. The city lacked adequate facilities to hold the thousands of German prisoners and had to improvise quarters for them. Over six hundred prisoners

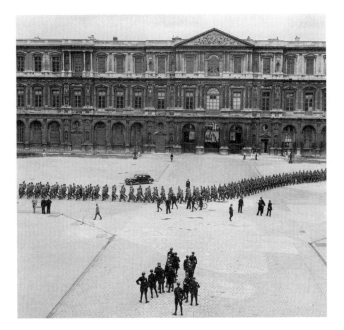

GERMAN PRISONERS IN THE LOUVRE'S COUR CARRÉE

had been brought to the Cour Carrée of the Louvre, its exits securable by iron gates. There the men would stay for three days, sleeping on the ground and eating hunks of bread thrown through openings in the gates.

During the parade melee, as shots seemed to ring out from every direction, some reached the Cour Carrée. Some observers said the shots were fired from the Ministry of Finance, others said they came from rue de Rivoli; yet others said they were from the roof of the Louvre itself. Some of the panicked German prisoners, thinking they were being fired upon, sought shelter in corners of the courtyard while several others catapulted through the ground-floor windows of the museum's Egyptian Antiquities galleries. One frantic prisoner tore a 4,500-year-old Egyptian mummy to pieces as he tried to find a hiding place. Several others hid in the ancient pink granite sarcophagus of Ramses III, where Desroches Noblecourt and some guards later found them, hands up in the air and faces covered with the burial vault's accumulated grease and dust.

The shooting and the panic in the courtyard caught the attention of a group of nearby FFI men, who surged into the Louvre to look for the prisoners. They found a staff member taking two wounded Germans to the infirmary and began to wonder why the staff were helping German prisoners. Then they asked themselves how the Louvre had escaped damage and looting throughout the entire war. They decided the museum's managers must have been collaborators, a conclusion that not could have been further from the truth. The FFI men grabbed Jaujard, Robert Rey—the Resistance member who had transmitted Jaujard's messages to London—and several others and marched them, Jaujard with a gun barrel against his back, across the street to the town hall of Paris's first arrondissement. The misunderstanding was quickly cleared up and they were free to go. With their release, the Louvre was out of danger—or so it appeared—and the old palace, though sporting bullet holes and broken windows, had survived intact.

Several days after the Liberation, several U.S. Army officers of the "Monuments Men" assigned to protect art, archives and monuments in France came to congratulate Jaujard. Smiling, they handed back to Jaujard the messages he had courageously passed to the Resistance during the war to help protect the art under his care.

# PART VI

## HOMECOMING

*August 1944 to October 1947*

Just a day later, Germans were back on the grounds but this time there were twelve hundred SS troops. A skirmish with the FFI had resulted in five German deaths and they sought reprisal. They once again stormed into the château and gathered the staff at gunpoint, warning Van der Kemp that if the French fired a single additional shot in the town while they were still there, he would also be shot and the town and the château razed to the ground. He managed to calm them and sent his sister-in-law to town in the midst of German gunfire to get word to the FFI to keep a low profile. Several hours later, eighteen of the German officers settled themselves in bedrooms of the château. During the early afternoon, a German supply truck was destroyed half a mile from the château and three men were killed, once again stirring the Germans' ire. Again Van der Kemp sent his sister-in-law into town to tell the FFI to hold their fire. In early evening, the SS troops finally prepared to leave. Before they left, Van der Kemp convinced the commander to sign a document stating that, in the event of future German visits, the inhabitants of the château should not be harmed. Shortly thereafter, they left, torching nine vehicles on their way out. Van der Kemp made good use of the SS document. Within hours of the first group's departure, a new contingent of German troops arrived, but after being shown the document provided by the previous German commandant, they quickly left. Yet another group arrived the following morning and stayed all day, but made no threats and caused no problems.

Still more problems plagued Van der Kemp in the weeks that followed. Many of the guards, still traumatized over the events of August 16, did not want to work. Then the local FFI head decided, without Van der Kemp's approval, to set up camp on the grounds with a large contingent of his own troops in order to protect the château from the Germans still holding out in town. Van der Kemp, however, believed that because the situation in town was militarily and politically unstable, the large FFI presence would just court more trouble with the Germans. He went to Paris to appeal directly to General Koenig, national commander of the FFI. It was finally agreed that all the men would leave except for ten officers in the château and thirty with quarters in the stables, set away from the château itself, from which they could guard the premises without drawing undue attention by passing German troops.

Valençay was officially liberated several days later, but a group of Resistance members remained at the château through the second half of September to wrap up loose ends. Working from the château's orangerie, Gaëtan Ravineau, the treasurer of the area's maquis group, finalized the group's financial records. Also at the château with Ravineau and others was a young woman named Pearl Witherington (later Cornioley)—code name Pauline—a prominent member of the Special Operations Executive (SOE). Cornioley was part of the SOE's F Section, which had operated in the Valençay area since 1941. She had parachuted into France in 1943 and the following spring took over a large F Section network. Under her command, 1,500 men blazed a trail across central France, sabotaging railway lines leading to Normandy more than eight hundred times in preparation for D-Day and conducting so many other successful missions that the Germans put a large bounty, said to be perhaps a million francs, on her head. Her group's territory included the Gâtines Forest, part of which belonged to the duc de Valençay.

While Cornioley was at the château, she slept in a bedroom so big, she said, it felt like a ballroom, and the six-foot-square bed so big it seemed like a battlefield. At one point, Leroi-Gourhan, curator and fellow Resistance member, told her and the other guests, "I'll show you things the public never sees," and, opening one of the crates, displayed a papal tiara and some engravings by Rembrandt.

The Resistance members may have enjoyed warm hospitality

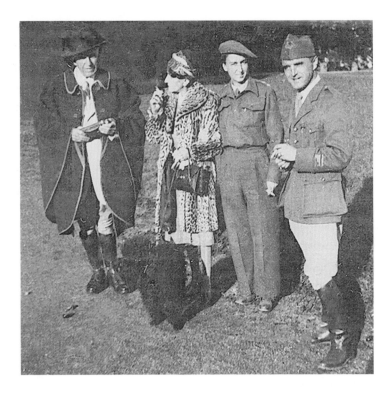

FROM LEFT: DUC DE VALENÇAY, PRINCESS RADZIWILL, PEARL
WITHERINGTON CORNIOLEY AND FRANCIS PERDRISET, LOCAL FFI HEAD

at the château, but the idyllic relationship that Van der Kemp had
long enjoyed with the duke had turned icy after August 16. Two
days later, he had told the duke, "This is the last time I will speak
to you . . . .I cannot tolerate having heard a Frenchman claim that
he is a German prince simply because his house is burning," though
the château itself had not been on fire. Van der Kemp later said bit-
terly, "the duke himself had come to the wall, saying that he could
do nothing for me since he had presented himself to the SS with his
title of German prince." The duke, on the other hand, said his title

had helped protect the château and the artwork. Early the following year, Jaujard would diplomatically remove Van der Kemp from the untenable situation by transferring him to the depot at the château de Montal while René Huyghe, the long-standing depot head at Montal, returned to Paris to focus on the ongoing renovations of the Louvre galleries and the reorganization of the collections.

I n August 1944, the Allies' Monuments, Fine Arts, and Archives program (MFAA)—the "Monuments Men"—arrived in France to assess the need for protection and recovery efforts. Several representatives visited Sourches and nearby depots even before Paris was liberated. Depot head Germain Bazin, who had successfully protected the art under his care for four years and had brought many of the artworks to the basement in the summer of 1944 as a necessary precautionary measure, was not enamored of MFAA head James Rorimer who, shortly after his arrival, yelled at Bazin, "You put all your artwork in a basement? You're crazy!" While the MFAA would provide important help throughout Europe, the Musées Nationaux had already taken care of its art.

However, the military group did lend a hand measuring humidity conditions at Sourches since the Louvre specialist who normally made monthly visits to verify conditions had not been able to come in several months due to combat conditions. The MFAA also helped ensure that Allied troops would not disturb the depots. During the war, the Kunstschutz had posted signs indicating that the depots were off limits to the German military. As the liberation approached, posters announcing Resistance protection often replaced them or were hung side-by-side with them. By September 1944, the last of the German signs had vanished, replaced by ones in English prepared by the curators. Before the end of September additional signs provided by the MFAA proclaimed "OFF LIMITS."

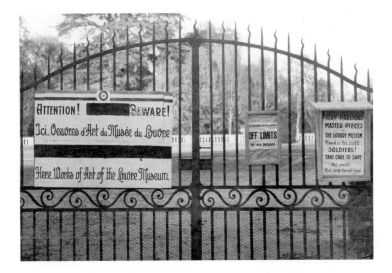

CHÂTEAU DE SOURCHES, 1944

On October 3, 1944, a very small part of the Louvre reopened, just a group of rooms displaying Egyptian, Greek and other sculptures that had never left. The evacuated art and antiquities could not yet return. Pockets of France were still at war, a large part of the museum was still undergoing renovation and there was not enough coal available to heat the hundreds of rooms—and properly protect the artwork—as cold weather approached. The museum could safely display certain sculptures without heat, but paintings were more delicate. They needed constant temperature and consistent low humidity, impossible to achieve in a building right next to the Seine. Moreover, unabated winter humidity in the unheated museum would give way to a film of moisture on the walls—and surfaces of the paintings—during the spring thaw.

Another change took place at the Louvre in October 1944. Jacques Jaujard, amid public acclaim as a national hero, handed

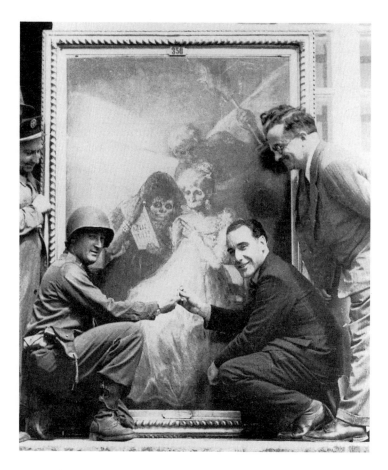

JAMES RORIMER AND GERMAIN BAZIN (KNEELING, AT RIGHT) AT THE
GRAND-LUCÉ DEPOT NEAR SOURCHES, AUGUST 1944

over the helm of the Musées Nationaux to Georges Salles, director
of the Musée Guimet and grandson of Louis Eiffel, architect of the
famous tower. Salles was also the man whose release from prison
camp Jaujard had arranged with Wolff Metternich in 1940. Jaujard,
in turn, became France's Director General of Fine Arts.

I n January 1914, the Louvre had installed plaques at an entry to the Galerie Denon to honor the courageous efforts of three Louvre staff members during the 1871 Commune, plus a soldier who had helped save the museum from destruction by the Tuileries fire. After World War I, a new plaque was hung to honor the memory of Musées Nationaux staff who had lost their lives during that war. Each subsequent November 11—the date of the World War I armistice—a commemoration ceremony was held in front of the plaques. When staff members gathered in November 1944, they saw yet another new plaque, this one honoring the staff fallen during World War II. One of the engraved names was that of Lucien Nervet, the guard killed by machine gun fire several months earlier at Valençay.

The end of 1944 also brought a new chapter for the Bayeux tapestry. Immediately after Paris was liberated, the mayor of Bayeux had wanted to retrieve the tapestry, but Jaujard asked if the Louvre could keep it just a while longer to mount an exhibition. After several weeks of reflection, the mayor agreed, in gratitude to the Fine Arts Administration for having protected it during the war. The Louvre inaugurated the exhibition on November 10, the day before Winston Churchill's visit to Paris to commemorate Armistice Day. Originally scheduled to end in mid-December, the exhibition was extended until January 1 due to its popularity. All seemed well—until the night of December 26 when three German planes dropped bombs on Paris. Two bombs landed in the Tuileries Garden, just missing the Louvre. The gardens sustained minor damage and there was blast damage to nearby shop and hotel windows but the Louvre was not harmed. The bombs were the last ones of the war to fall on Paris.

FONCTIONNAIRES ET AGENTS DES MUSÉES NATIONAUX
1914 MORTS POUR LA FRANCE 1918

ADAIN GABRIEL
BÉRÊME GEORGES
CLUSE ÉMILE
COCQUEREL LÉON
DANIEL HENRI
DAUDÉ ODILON
'ELPORTE LAURENT
'ZILES LOUIS
'OUR VINCENT
MEL GUSTAVE

GRANDAM ANDRÉ
GIGOT ÉTIENNE
JULIENNE MARCEL
JOURDA CYPRIEN
LE BORGNE LOUIS
MASPERO JEAN
MERCIER CAMILLE
MILOT GEORGES
MOCQUARD RENÉ
NAU ALFRED

PRUNIER GUSTAVE
RAULT FRANÇOIS
RIEU MARIUS
RIGAUT ALFRED
SARDA JEAN
SERON ERNEST
SORAY PROSPER
TERRIER CHARLES
UHEREK HUGO
VIGINIER MAURICE

1941
O
'ONIN     HACKIN JOSEPH
'ENT      HACKIN MARIE

1944
NERVET LUCIEN
FAUCHER JEAN-BAPTISTE

MEMORIAL PLAQUES IN GALERIE DENON, WORLD WAR II AT BOTTOM

# THIRTY-TWO

# COMING HOME

URING THE WINTER of 1944–1945, Paris was a city of light but almost no heat. The coal to warm buildings also had to serve the country's needs for electricity and rail transport and there was precious little of it to go around. Large numbers of coal miners were still prisoners or forced laborers in Germany. Mining machinery had been sabotaged or taken by the Germans, who had also destroyed bridges and railroads, making it next to impossible to transport any coal that was produced. And it was difficult to import large quantities of coal from the Allies because the Germans had systematically destroyed harbor facilities in the wake of their retreat and ensured they could not be rebuilt anytime soon. They filled the mouth of the Gironde River, for centuries a major gateway to the Atlantic Ocean, with sunken ships filled with concrete and explosives, then blew them apart to make them almost impossible to raise. They also attached mines to the hulls so divers could not safely conduct salvage operations.

Record-setting cold temperatures that winter exacerbated the suffering from lack of heat. People wore multiple layers of clothing when they could but after the many years of war and the ongoing industrial production and transport problems, it was hard to obtain enough clothing to layer. Desk workers swathed their feet in blankets; concertgoers and even performers kept their coats on. The few rooms open in the Louvre to display the unevacuated sculptures and stone antiquities were cold as well; there was no source for the huge quantities of coal needed to heat the museum.

And then came spring. On April 30, 1945 Adolf Hitler drafted his will. The only assets he mentioned in any detail were his paintings, which he noted had been intended for his Linz museum, not for personal gain. He left them all to his Party. Several hours later, the man responsible for the murder of six million Jews and millions of others that he considered "undesirable," and military and civilian casualties in the tens of millions, took his own life. On May 7, the Germans, beaten after a long winter of battle, surrendered to the Allies.

Three weeks later, the Curators Committee of the Musées Nationaux authorized the evacuated artworks to begin coming home, contingent upon the availability of trucks, the anticipated availability of heat for the forthcoming winter and the progressive completion of the massive renovations that were still underway in many of parts of the museum. During a June 14 press conference, museum officials discussed the progress of the renovations and the lack of coal, indicating that it would be a long process until the museum was completely reopened. In fact, it would take two more years.

However, the first trucks carrying the Louvre's treasures back from the countryside arrived within a week of the Curators Committee approval. The depot heads had begun to make arrangements for crates and packing materials a month earlier.

On June 1, 1940, when Christiane Desroches Noblecourt had evacuated some of the masterpieces of the Louvre's Department of Egyptian Antiquities from the Loire to Saint-Blancard, she had been moving between enemy lines and just missed a bomb. Five years and two weeks later, on June 14, 1945, she headed north on peaceful roads from La Treyne towards Paris with thirty-five crates of antiquities, many of them the same items she had taken to safety in 1940, including the Seated Scribe. The Stele of the Serpent King and the bas-relief of Goddess Hathor Welcomes Sethos I would return in September. In the five years of their absence from the Louvre, they had traveled first from the Louvre to Courtalain, then to Saint-Blancard, Montauban, Loubéjac and La Treyne and finally back to Paris.

On June 15 at 5 a.m., a convoy of artworks left the château de Montal for Paris. It was a very small convoy, just two trucks and an auto driven by the depot head, Gérald Van der Kemp. Great efforts had been made for its safety. Civil and military authorities and police prefects along the way had been notified and asked to provide protection; there was also a large motorcycle escort preceding and following the vehicles. *Mona Lisa* was heading home.

Two hours later, at Valençay, the 3.5-ton Winged Victory of Samothrace departed for Paris in an enormous truck supplied by the British army. The 150-mile trip took nine hours, in part due to the circuitous route required to bypass bridges destroyed during the war. Two weeks later, Venus de Milo and Michelangelo's *Slaves* would also return to the Louvre. All three works had been away for almost six years.

On June 16, Boucher's *Diana Leaving Her Bath* left Sourches, along with Delacroix's *Liberty Leading the People*. Since her departure for the Loire in 1939, *Diana* had subsequently gone on to Loc-Dieu, then

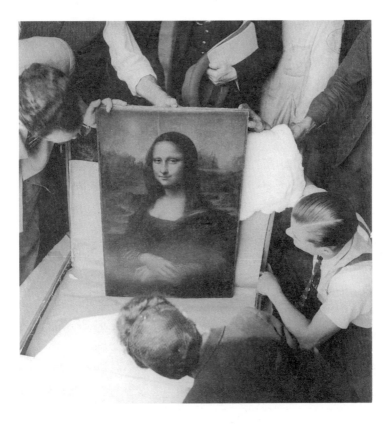

*MONA LISA* JUST UNPACKED AT THE LOUVRE, JUNE 1945

Montauban, back to Paris, to Germany, back to the Louvre, then to Sourches.

On the morning of June 21, the Winged Victory of Samothrace, wrapped in burlap and suspended via cords and cables, began to rise along a giant ramp on the soaring Daru staircase from which she had slowly descended six years earlier. When the giant sculpture was brought down in the fall of 1939, there were few witnesses. Her ascension, in contrast, was witnessed by all the Louvre curators and

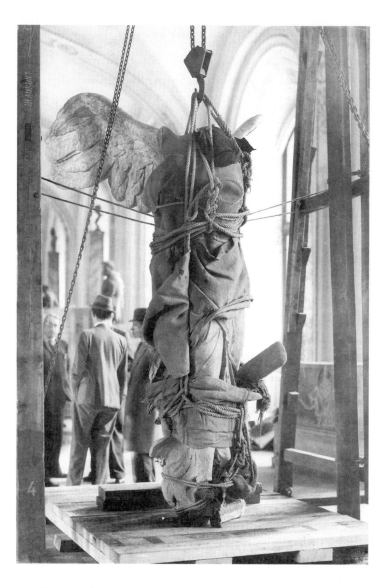

WINGED VICTORY OF SAMOTHRACE READY FOR HER ASCENT
JUNE 21, 1945

representatives of other museums and the press. It took two hours for the sculpture to reach the top. There she remained suspended during the lunch hour, after which eight workers returned and slowly lowered her onto the prow of the ship that formed her base.

At 5 a.m. on July 3, Jean Morel, the 14-year-old adopted son of the duc de Valençay, heard noise outside the château. By the time he had had breakfast, the crown jewels were gone, on their way back to the Louvre. Since the time they had arrived at Valençay in August 1939, the jewels had been hidden in a wall safe near the château's entrance, overlooked by the many German troops that had passed right in front of it the previous year.

The public had long been clamoring for the Louvre's treasures; on July 10, 1945 they could at long last see some of them during a special exhibition at the museum showcasing Venus de Milo, Winged Victory of Samothrace and Michelangelo's *Slaves*, plus eighty-three paintings, including the *Mona Lisa*. It was also an opportunity to show how some of the paintings had been restored during their exile, including the removal or thinning of old, darkened coats of varnish. The fragile *Mona Lisa*, however, had not been touched. Another exhibit displayed photographs and documents relating to the evacuations and other museum activities during the war. Among the items on view was correspondence with Ribbentrop regarding the return of Boucher's *Diana*. That fall, another temporary exhibition opened to showcase art acquired during the war.

The artwork of the Musées Nationaux was not alone in coming back; so, too, came the Jewish staff that had been forced to flee the country or go into hiding and Resistance members who had been imprisoned. All of them had been reinstated by official

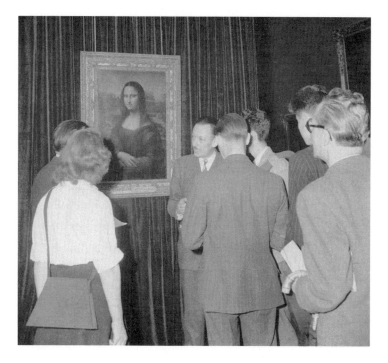

EXHIBITION AT THE LOUVRE, JULY 1945

decree. Curator Charles Sterling returned from the United States. Staff member Suzanne Kahn, who had been detained at the Drancy internment camp, became a curator. In October 1944, Agnès Humbert, art historian at the Musée National des Arts et Tradition until she was fired by Vichy in 1940, was officially reinstated to her position although she was still in a German slave labor camp. Upon her liberation in early April 1945, she chose not to return to the Musées Nationaux and instead turned to writing books on art. Jean Cassou, a Musées Nationaux curator until he was fired by Vichy in 1940, had been released from prison in 1943 and had spent the rest of the war conducting Resistance activities. In 1945, he returned to the Musée National d'Art Moderne as head curator. After the Liberation, Carle Dreyfus came out of hiding in Valençay; reinstated as a curator, he traveled to Germany in 1945 to assist in restitution efforts.

The Louvre palace of 1945 remained a work in progress. Thousands of empty frames still leaned against empty walls and workers were still in the midst of the reconstruction of the galleries that had begun before the war. A great many paintings remained at their countryside depots. That November, a small group of works still at Montal—among them Clouet's portrait of François I—went on display in a special exhibition in nearby Cahors as a means of thanking municipal authorities for their assistance during the German occupation.

During the winter of 1945–1946, coal was still in short supply and once again Parisians suffered from the cold. The special exhibition of the masterpieces remained open, which meant that those rooms had to be heated. When a visiting British officer noticed a crowd gathered near a painting and moved closer to find out what was fascinating them, he realized they were simply huddling around a hot air vent.

On February 7, 1946 a truck left Montal with three huge paintings: David's *Coronation of Napoleon* and Gros' *Napoleon Visiting the Plague Stricken at Jaffa* and *Battle of Eylau*. Since September 1939, they had been to Versailles, then to Chèreperrine, Loc-Dieu, Vayrac and Bétaille. Six days later, Veronese's *Wedding Feast at Cana* headed back to Paris.

On February 26, the two items for which Göring had forced the supposed "cultural exchange"—the *Belle Allemande* and the altarpiece panel *Presentation in the Temple*—returned to the Louvre. They had been found in May 1945 in the Unterstein, Germany bunker in which Göring had stashed them as the Allies approached. The bunker was damp and water dripped from the ceiling. When the two Louvre pieces were found, the frame of the altarpiece panel was cracked and the *Belle Allemande* was covered with grime but both were in good condition otherwise.

In mid-March, the da Vinci drawing of Isabella d'Este that had slept by the bedside of Louvre staff during the June 1940 move to Loc-Dieu returned to Paris.

The spring of 1946 brought yet more progress. Louvre artworks continued their gradual return to Paris from the countryside. On April 13, Chambord reopened its doors to visitors; it had been closed for seven years. It had also survived a July 1945 fire in one of its towers, the only fire in any Louvre depot during the war—remarkable, given the conditions they had faced. Among them: when artworks at Sourches were brought to the château's basement in the summer of 1944, open charcoal fires had been used to help control the humidity.

I n May 1946 the Louvre inaugurated a new exhibition, the largest since before the war. However, it was not housed in the Louvre palace itself, which was still not ready for a large-scale show. After a difficult search for an available location, permission was obtained to use the Petit Palais, just off the Champs Elysées. Built for the 1900 Universal Exhibition, it had served as a museum since 1902. Shelled by the Germans, then used by American troops as barracks and in the process of being restored, the structure was perfect. The new exhibition displayed over 300 of the Louvre's paintings by French artists. Among the works on display were Boucher's *Diana Leaving Her Bath*, Clouet's *François I* and Delacroix's *Liberty Leading the People*.

André Chamson curated the exhibition; the assistant curator was Suzanne Kahn, whom Jaujard and Wolff Metternich had saved from deportation to Germany. Except for the Clouet work, which had been displayed briefly in Cahors the previous fall, the paintings had been in storage for seven years. Mazauric had not dared to believe she might be one of the first to witness the return of the art to public view but on the spring day of the public opening, she and Chamson watched emotionally as crowds of all ages filed in.

On July 9, Géricault's giant *Raft of the Medusa* left Sourches on a scenery trailer along with eight other large paintings. It had survived the trolley wires at Versailles and multiple difficult moves across France during its seven-year exile from the Louvre. For the painting's return, there were to be no chances taken with wires or other obstacles. Bridges and wires along the entire route were painstakingly identified and a four-page itinerary indicated every road to be taken along the way. Once back in Paris, the painting joined the other works on display at the Petit Palais. The only evidence of its travels were several small areas of flaking and three small perforations near one edge.

Little by little, the Louvre reopened. But one part of the palace had remained a work in progress: the almost 350-year-old Grande Galerie. At long last, on October 7, 1947, the renovated wing was inaugurated, the first time it had been open to the public since August 25, 1939. Just a few finishing touches remained, including the placement of velvet on the walls. A day before the grand opening, *Mona Lisa* took her place in the center of the gallery as the Louvre turned a final page on World War II.

During World War II, Jacques Jaujard shepherded the treasures of the Louvre to safety with an almost unimaginable amount of energy and a miraculous mix of diplomacy and cunning. James Rorimer, one of the "Monuments Men" who worked with him after the liberation of Paris, said Jaujard "had fought the German demands for France's national art treasures again and again with no weapon but courage and no defense but integrity."

The Louvre, its art and its caretakers had miraculously avoided—with one tragic exception, guard Lucien Nervet—gunfire, shells, bombs, damage from a crashed plane, fire and an enemy that wanted the museum's treasures and in some cases, came close to destroying some of them without a second thought. The history-laden stone walls of the palace had survived intact except for a few chunks lost to stray shells and bullets. But by the time the Grande Galerie reopened in 1947, every single one of the many thousands of pieces of priceless art and antiquities was safely back in place except for one mummified sheep. A small army of French men and women—and one German, Franz von Wolff Metternich—had risked their jobs and their lives to keep the Louvre and its treasures safe, in service of a singular goal, as Rose Valland described: "to save a little of the beauty of the world."

# EPILOGUE

I N THE IMMEDIATE aftermath of the war, several curators, such
as Jaujard, Chamson and Van der Kemp, moved to other positions, while Bazin, Huyghe, Mazauric and others remained
at the Louvre until much later. Throughout their careers, all of the
curators were prolific contributors to the world of art, whether by
research, writing, teaching, fund-raising, lecturing, volunteer work
in the arts or, in many cases, all these areas.

André Chamson returned to his post as assistant curator at
Versailles but was soon appointed director of the Musée du Petit
Palais. In 1959, he was named Directeur Générale des Archives
de France, where he remained until 1971. For several years thereafter, he served in various arts-related capacities. Chamson
received multiple honors, among them the Grand-Croix of
the French Legion of Honor, the Croix de la Guerre, and the
Médaille de la Résistance and was named Grand Officier de
l'Ordre National de Mérite. In 1956, he was elected a member of
the Académie Française.

Until her retirement, Lucie Mazauric worked as the curator of
the library and archives of the Louvre. She also assisted her husband

André Chamson in his work. Before the war, Mazauric had written one book; afterwards, she wrote four more.

Gérald Van der Kemp was appointed assistant curator at Versailles in 1945 and its chief curator in 1953. He remained in this role until 1980, during which time he raised huge sums of money for restoration of the palace. He received the Médaille de la Reconnaissance Française and was named an officer of the French Legion of Honor.

René Huyghe left his position as chief curator of paintings at the Louvre in 1950 after being elected professor at the Collège de France. In 1974, he became director of the Musée Jacquemart-André, where he served until 1992. Huyghe was also named an officer of the Legion of Honor and received the Grand-Croix de l'Ordre National de Mérite and recognitions from other countries. In 1960, he was elected a member of the Académie Française.

When Huyghe left the Louvre, Germain Bazin took his place as head curator of paintings. He left in 1965 to create and direct the French National Museums' Service de Restauration des Musées, where he stayed until his retirement in 1971. He also served as a professor in both England and Canada. Bazin was named an officer of the French Legion of Honor and was elected in 1955 to the Académie des Beaux-Arts.

In 1944, Robert Rey was appointed Directeur des Arts Plastiques et de la Production Artistique for the Ministry of National Education. He taught at the École du Louvre until 1946 and was chair of art history at the École Nationale Supérieure des Beaux-Arts until his retirement in 1960.

Christiane Desroches-Noblecourt became the curator of the Louvre's Department of Egyptian Antiquities and a world-renowned Egyptologist. Among her numerous honors, she received the French Médaille de la Résistance and was made a Commander of the French Legion of Honor and a Grand Officier de l'Ordre de la Libération.

In November 1944, the Commission de Récupération Artistique was created to help locate and recover looted French-owned art. Rose Valland was designated its secretary. By the spring of 1945, she was also an officer in the French army and was sent to Germany to assist the Allies in the recuperation of looted art; she remained in Germany until March 1953. Upon her return, she became head of the Service de Protection des Œuvres d'Art. In 1955, at long last, she was named a curator of the Musées Nationaux. Valland was named an officer of the French Legion of Honor and a Commandeur de l'Ordre des Arts et des Lettres. She received the French Médaille de la Résistance, the U.S. Presidential Medal of Freedom and the Order of Merit of the Federal Republic of Germany.

Franz von Wolff Metternich, after being sacked by Göring, returned to Germany and his position as conservator for German monuments. For his efforts in helping to protect France's art during the war, he was named an officer of the French Legion of Honor in 1964.

In 1945, Jacques Jaujard became Directeur Général des Arts et des Lettres, a new position similar to Hautecœur's position in the Directorate of Fine Arts. In 1959, he became the Secretary General of the Ministry of State in charge of cultural affairs, where he remained until 1961, working for the reform of the French national theater system, the country's fine arts schools and other institutions and championing the rights of authors and artists. Until 1967, he was in charge of all foreign exhibitions and cultural exchanges, traveling around the world on France's behalf. He also served as a special advisor to the French cultural administration.

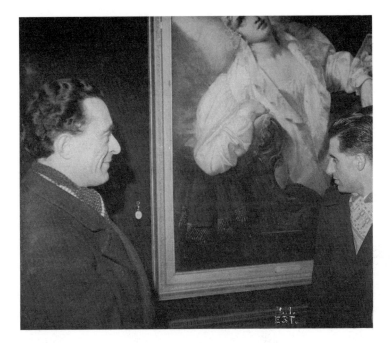

JACQUES JAUJARD AFTER WORLD WAR II

In 1955, Jaujard was elected a member of the Académie des Beaux-Arts. For his extraordinary efforts during the war, he was also named Grand Officier of the French Legion of Honor, Commandeur des Palmes Académiques, Commandeur of the Ordre des Arts et des Lettres, and Knight Commander of the Order of the British Empire. He also received the French Médaille de la Résistance and the U.S. Medal of Freedom.

An entrance to the Louvre palace was later renamed in Jaujard's memory; it is one of the entrances to the École du Louvre. The sign bearing his name is a symbol for the future art curators who pass through the doors that the conservation of art has profound levels of meaning.

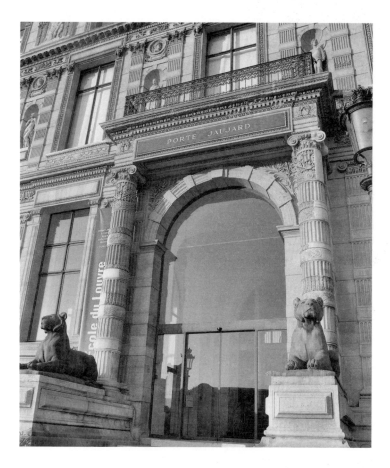

THE JAUJARD ENTRANCE AT THE ÉCOLE DU LOUVRE.

# ACKNOWLEDGMENTS

Weaving together this story was very much like assembling a puzzle of thousands of tiny pieces. I would not have obtained many of the details without the generosity of time and spirit of museum and archive curators, librarians and others on both sides of the Atlantic.

In France, a great debt of gratitude goes to Alain Prevet, director of the Archives des Musées Nationaux in Paris, for his warm welcome and for taking the time to point out additional resources and to Séverine Vaillant and Elisabeth Rey, also at the Archives, for their assistance and their patience. I would particularly like to thank Madame Rey for her repeated digging for answers to my obscure questions. Thanks also go to Guillaume Fonkenell, Louvre historian and curator in the Department of Sculptures and, at the château de Chambord, to Alexandra Fleury and to Denis Grandemenge, the château's Régisseur des Collections, for his generosity of time and information. I would also like to thank Corine Legrand at the Bibliothèque Universitaire de Saint-Quentin-en-Yvelines, Emmanuel Marguet at the Médiathèque de l'Architecture et du Patrimoine, Alexandre Cojannot at the Ministère des Affaires

Etrangères and Adélaïde Bonnetat at the municipal library of Valençay.

Multiple librarians in the U.S. went out of their way to help, including Vincenzo Rutigliano and Ryan Haley of the Art & Architecture Collection at the New York Public Library; Clint Tomlinson at the Ohio State University Library; Linda Seckelson, Dan Lipcan, and Jenny Adolfson at the Thomas J. Watson Library of New York's Metropolitan Museum of Art and Naima Sakande at Yale University's Sterling Library.

I would like to thank Yvonne Bell-Gambart, Executive Director of the Société des Amis du Louvre and Mel Yoken, Chancellor Professor Emeritus of French Language and Literature at the University of Massachusetts at Dartmouth, as well as Catherine and Nicholas Velle. A special debt of gratitude goes to author Frédérique Hébrard, daughter of André Chamson and Lucie Mazauric, not only for sharing her memories but also for her warm welcome. Elizabeth Karlsgodt and Gérard Coulon both went out of their way to answer my questions. Much appreciation goes to Hervé Larroque, co-author of *Pauline*, for all his information and for relaying my questions to two still-living witnesses of the events. Thanks also go to Doris Walsh of Paramount Market Publishing, Fred Davis, Susan Ford Collins, Pierre Bodilis and Clémence Grandaud as well as to Jordan Wannemacher for her design talent and Colleen Katz for her knowledge of art, history and France and her insightful editing.

For transcription of certain video and handwritten material, I would like to thank Nicole Michel of Translingua's Manhattan office and Thomas Ragot and for German translation assistance, Peter van Suntum and Domenico Sciurti.

Any achievement requires special people that provide wind beneath one's wings. I am grateful to have in my life, among others: Morene, Muriel, Eric, Steve, Margaret, Sam, Marc, Stephen, Robin and Aunt Ellie, all of whom sustained me with assistance, interest and encouragement. There are simply no words to adequately thank Colleen Katz and Sylvia Cassel for all their help; without them, this book would simply not exist. And to my amazing children, for everything.

# NOTES

## ABBREVIATIONS USED

AMN     Archives des Musées Nationaux, Paris
AN      Archives nationales de France, Pierrefitte-sur-Seine
CDJC    Centre de documentation juive contemporaine, Paris
MAE     Ministère des affaires etrangères, La Corneuve
NA      National Archives, Washington, D.C.
RG      Record Group
SAL     Société des Amis du Louvre

## PROLOGUE

xviii   IF IT WERE DECREED Payne, *Leonardo*, 138.

## ONE · PROTECTING PARIS, PROTECTING ART

5     NOTED CULTURAL CENTER Knecht, *Renaissance Warrior and Patron*, 449.

7     BAD WEATHER Carmona, *Le Louvre et les Tuileries*, 50, 77.

9     MORE THAN FOUR THOUSAND Quoniam, *Le Palais du Louvre*, 184

9     ONLY ONE HUNDRED Ibid., 184.

11    RESPECT THE NATIONAL PROPERTY Rozet, *Chronique de Juillet 1830*, 185.

12    NOT A SINGLE ONE Chennevières, *Souvenirs d'un directeur des beaux-arts*, 53.

15    IMPOSSIBLE TASK Chennevières, "La France méconnue: M. de Tauzia," *Nouvelle Revue*, 329.

15    IN CIVILIAN DRESS Ibid., 329.

15    ITEMS ABOARD "ML SM II, Galerie de Sept Mètres," AMN Z 2 (1870-1890).

16    123 CRATES "Résumé des caisses," AMN Z 2 (1870).

16    CRATES IN TRANSIT And other details regarding protection, Darcel, "Les Musées, les arts et les artistes pendant le siège de Paris," *Gazette des Beaux-Arts*, 287, 295, 296, 302–303.

16    LOUVRE WAS PREPARING F. Reiset, "Note concernant le retour à Paris des Tableaux du Louvre envoyés à Brest dans les premiers jours de septembre 1870," 9 juin 1870, AN F21 3967.

17  INSURGENTS ROLLED  Du Camp, Maxime, "Les Tuileries et le Louvre Pendant la Commune – II," *Revue des Deux Mondes*, 129, 142;  Carmona, *Le Louvre et les Tuileries*, 343; Ussel, "Barbet de Jouy, Son journal pendant la Commune," *Revue hebdomadaire*, X, 36–41.

18  BATTALION OF 100 MEN  Ussel, "Barbet de Jouy, Son journal pendant la Commune," *Revue hebdomadaire*, X, 42; Delambre, "5 juillet 1871," AMN Z 00 (Commune de Paris).

18  THE LOUVRE TURNED  Carmona, *Le Louvre et les Tuileries*, 346–347.

18  LAST VESTIGES  Fonkenell, *Le Palais des Tuileries*, 210.

## TWO · WORLD WAR I

19  FEWER THAN 150 GUARDS  Sassoon, *Mona Lisa*, 177.

19  COVERED WITH GLASS  "'Mona Lisa' Under Glass,'" *New York Times*, October 13, 1907, C1.

19  NOT MORE STRONGLY SECURED  Spielmann, "Picture Thefts," *Times* (London), August 30, 1911, 9.

19  THERE WERE OTHER SECURITY PROBLEMS  Scotti, *Vanished Smile*, 42 and 57–58.

20  AT 3 A.M.  "'Mona Lisa' in France," *New York Times*, December 31, 1913, 4.

21  ADVANCES IN  "Le Directeur des Musées Nationaux à Monsieur le Sous-Secretaire d'Etat des Beaux Arts," 31 juillet 1914, AN F21 3967.

21  THE NEXT DAY  And additional details, except as noted: Pottier, *Le Musée du Louvre pendant la guerre 1914–1918*.

21  FELT LIKE FILLING  Pottier, *Le Musée du Louvre pendant la guerre 1914–1918*, 7.

22  ARTWORK WAS LOADED  Hautecœur, *Histoire du Louvre*, 108.

22  "BUT IF THIS WAS DISCOVERED . . ."  Pottier, *Le Musée du Louvre pendant la guerre 1914–1918*, 17–18.

23  SOME AREAS OF THE MUSEUM  Ibid., 9–11.

23  BEHIND THE SCENES  "Reopening the Louvre," *The Living Age*, February 22, 1919, 508.

23  TWICE DURING THE WAR  Pottier, *Le Musée du Louvre pendant la guerre 1914–1918*, 11.

23  LOUVRE WAS HIT  Ibid., 12–13.

24  BOLD APPEAL  G. Bénédite, "A Monsieur le Directeur des Musées Nationaux," 6 juin 1918, AN F21 3967.

24  CANNONS AND CHURCH BELLS  Callu, *La Réunion des Musées Nationaux 1870–1940*, 267.

## THREE · DRUMS OF ANOTHER WAR

25  "THIS IS NOT PEACE . . ."  Churchill, *The Gathering Storm: The Second World War*, Vol. 1, 7.

26  FINE ARTS ADMINISTRATION  "Le Sous-Secrétaire d'Etat des Beaux-Arts à Monsieur le Préfet de la Seine (Direction des Beaux-Arts et des Musées de la Ville de Paris)," 10 février 1932, AMN Z 2 (1931–1938).

26  THE BRITISH WERE DISCUSSING  Nicholas, *Rape of Europa*, 49.

26  "AN EVENTUALITY..."  "Le Directeur des Musées Nationaux à Monsieur René Dussaud," 4 octobre 1932, AMN R I.I.

26  EVACUATION PLAN  "Le Directeur des Musées Nationaux et de l'École du Louvre à Monsieur le Ministre de l'Education Nationale," 13 juillet 1933, AMN R I.I.

26  CONSIDERING THE EFFECTS  "Directeur des Musées Nationaux et de l'École du Louvre," 21 décembre 1933 and "Lieutenant-Colonel Islert, Commandant le Régiment de Sapeurs-Pompiers de la Ville De Paris," 11 décembre 1933, AMN Z 2 (1933–1938).

26  CONSIDERING SPECIFICATIONS  "Le Ministre de l'Education Nationale à Monsieur Ferran, Architecte en Chef," 11 avril 1934, AMN R I.I.

27  PRADO MUSEUM  Domaine national de Chambord. *Otages de guerre: Chambord 1939–1945*, 16.

27  BOMBING TARGETS  For example, "Extrait de l'Instruction générale pour l'établissement du Plan d'Aménagement de la Région Parisienne," 19 octobre 1934 and le Chef du Bureau de la liquidation des dépenses des Monuments Historiques, délégué à la Défense Passive, "Note," n.d., AMN R I.10.

29  TO BE DISPERSED  "Le Sous-Sécretaire d'Etat des Beaux Arts à Monsieur le Directeur des Musées Nationaux," 5 février 1934, AMN R I.I.

29  MORE THAN EIGHTY  Domaine national de Chambord, *Otages de guerre*, 17.

29  RAILROADS WOULD BE ENCUMBERED  "Le Directeur des Musées Nationaux et de l'École du Louvre à Monsieur le Directeur Général des Beaux-Arts," 6 novembre 1934, AMN R I.I.

30  SECONDARY TRANSFER  "Le Ministre à Monsieur le Préfet de la Seine (Secrétariat Général de la Mobilisation Nationale," 28 janvier 1937, AMN R I.I.

30  FIVE OR SIX DAYS  For example, "Le Directeur des Musées Nationaux et de l'École du Louvre à Monsieur le Directeur Général des Beaux-Arts," 10 décembre 1936, AMN R I.I.

30  TRANSPORT BY TRUCK  Handwritten, unsigned report attached to business card of J. Paul Debeaux, Conservateur des hypothèques. N.D; "Rapport à Monsieur le Ministre de l'Education Nationale sur les mesures prises dans les Musées nationaux en vue de la sauvegarde des collections nationales en temps de guerre, 5 août 1939, AMN R I.I.

30  SPECIALIZED IN MOVING  "Le Ministre à Monsieur le Préfet de la Seine (Secretariat Général de la Mobilisation Nationale), 28 janvier 1937, AMN R I.I.

30  THAT WOULD NOT SUFFER  Jacques Jaujard, "Rapport à Monsieur le Ministre de l'Education Nationale sur les mesures prises dans les Musées Nationaux en vue de la sauvegarde des collections nationales en temps de guerre," 5 août 1939, 4, AMN R 2A.

31  THEY SOUGHT TRUCKS  "Eloignement des Collections nationales en cas de guerre," 20 août 1938, AMN R I.I.

31  TWO LARGE VAULTS  "Monsieur le Gouverneur," 15 septembre 1938, AMN R I.I.

31 EVACUATION ORDER "Le Conservateur du Département des Peintures à Monsieur Henri Verne, member de l'Institut, Directeur des Musées Nationaux et de l'École du Louvre." n.d., AMN Z 2 (1931-1938).

32 SOME CRATES Domaine national de Chambord, *Otages de guerre*, 12.

32 AT 6 A.M. Valland, *Le front de l'art*, 3.

32 CROWN JEWELS AND OTHER Pierre Schommer, "A Monsieur le Directeur des Musées Nationaux et de l'École du Louvre, Membre de l'Institut, " 3 novembre 1938, AMN R 2A.

32 THIS TIME Hébrard, *La Chambre de Goethe*, 42; interview with Frédérique Hebrard June 2013; Mazauric, *Le Louvre en voyage*, 34–35.

33 WITHIN A WEEK Pierre Schommer, "A Monsieur le Directeur des Musées Nationaux et de l'École du Louvre, Membre de l'Institut," 3 novembre 1938, AMN R 2A.

## FOUR · FINAL PREPARATIONS

37 HEAD ARCHITECT Fonkenell and others, *Le Louvre Pendant la Guerre*, 44–47.

38 CRATES SAT OPENLY Valland, *Le front de l'art*, 4.

38 RESISTANCE OF WALLS "Rapport de la visite du Lieutenant de Génie Vignon envoyé par le Colonel Burtaire," n.d., AMN R 5.1.

38 THE INITIALS "Annexe no. 1, "Marques et étiquettes des caisses ou colis, 15 avril 1939, AMN R 1.1.

38 ELEVATORS AND STAIRWAYS "Volume des ascenseurs," n.d., AMN R 5.1.

38 PRACTICE DRILLS Huyghe, *Une vie pour l'art*, 112.

38 ADMINISTRATION HIRED Le Directeur des Musées Nationaux et de l'École du Louvre, Membre de l'Institut, "Plan d'Evacuation et de Protection des œuvres d'art, Leçons tirées de l'Expérience de 1938," 3 février 1939, AMN R 1.1.

39 TARPS TO COVER Mazauric, *Le Louvre en voyage*, 14–15.

39 CAME ABOARD IN 1926 AN F17 27852/Jaujard.

39 INSURANCE SALESMAN Dorléac, *Art of the Defeat*, 24.

39 MAN OF LETTERS Varennes, *Un bienfaiteur de la culture: Jacques Jaujard*, 4.

39 FINELY DRESSED Interview with Frédérique Hébrard, June 2013.

39 DIRECTOR IN SEPTEMBER 1940 AN F17 27852/Jaujard.

41 HAD REPEATEDLY WARNED Letter from Georges Coulondre to Georges Bonnet, 13 July, 1939. http://avalon.law.yale.edu/wwii/ylbk164.asp, (November 29, 2013).

41 HORSE-DRAWN WAGONS Photo in *Le Matin*, 28 août 1939, AMN Z 2 (1939-1945).

41 TUILERIES GARDEN Bresc-Bautier and Pingeot, *Sculptures des jardins du Louvre, du Carrousel et des Tuileries*, 156–157.

41 PORTABLE ELECTRIC LAMPS Jacques Jaujard, "Rapport à Monsieur le Ministre de l'Education Nationale sur les mesures prises dans les Musées Nationaux en vue de la sauvegarde des collections nationales en temps de guerre," 5 août 1939, AMN R 2A.

41 THEN HE LEARNED Ibid.

43 COLORED STICKER "Depuis l'ouverture des hostilities . . . ," 5 mai 1940, AMN R 20.2.

43 FIFTY OR SO "Rapport sur l'évacuation du Département de Peintures en septembre–octobre 1939," n.d., AMN R 2A.

43 LAY A PAINTING FLAT "Consignes Générales," n.d., AMN R 1.1.

43 ARMED GUARDS Jacques Jaujard, "Rapport à Monsieur le Ministre de l'Education Nationale sur les mesures prises dans les Musées Nationaux en vue de la sauvegarde des collections nationales en temps de guerre," 5 août 1939, AMN R 2A.

## FIVE · HOW TO MOVE A MASTERPIECE

45 PORTABLE LAMPS Sérullaz, "L'exode des collections nationales," *Pillages et Restitutions*, 15.

46 CALLED BACK BY TELEGRAM "Le 5 mai 1940," 6, AMN R 20.2.

46 MOST OF WHOM Ibid., 8.

46 CIVILIAN VOLUNTEERS Karlsgodt, *Defending National Treasures*, 72.

46 GABRIEL COGNACQ Bazin, *Souvenirs*, 11.

47 LOOKED TO HER Hours, *Une vie au Louvre*, 43; Nicholas, *Rape of Europa*, 54.

47 WRAPPED FIRST Huyghe, "Le Musée du Louvre dans le Lot," *Les Etoiles du Quercy*, www.quercy.net/qhistorique/resistance/louvre.html (January 14, 2013).

48 ANONYMITY WAS INTENDED Jean Zay, "Instruction sur le repliement," 10 septembre 1939, AMN R 1.1; Fonkenell and others, *Le Louvre pendant la guerre*, 86.

48 OFFICIAL EVACUATION ORDER Jacques Jaujard, "Rapport sur l'évacuation des collections des Musées Nationaux," 30 octobre 1939, AMN R 2A.

48 JAUJARD PRESIDED Mazauric, *Le Louvre en voyage*, 24.

48 HANDWRITTEN NOTE Jacques Jaujard, "Dimanche soir," AMN R 17.1.

49 PACE HAD PICKED UP "Rapport sur l'évacuation des collections des Musées Nationaux," 30 octobre 1939, AMN R 2A.

49 SEVERAL DOZEN "Pastels du Louvre," AMN R 6.

49 UNDERGROUND VAULTS Jacques Jaujard, "Rapport sur l'évacuation des collections des Musées Nationaux," 30 octobre 1939, AMN R 2A, 12.

50 THROUGH THE NIGHT Hours, *Une vie au Louvre*, 43.

50 ROLLED ONTO "Le 5 mai 1940," 17, AMN R 20.2; Jacques Jaujard, "Rapport sur l'évacuation des collections des Musées Nationaux," 30 octobre 1939, 10, AMN R 2A.

51 PRECEDE THE CONVOY Jacques Jaujard, "Rapport sur l'évacuation des collections des Musées Nationaux," 30 octobre 1939, 10, AMN R 2A.

51 WEATHER REPORT Huyghe, "Le Musée du Louvre dans le Lot," Les Etoiles du Quercy, www.quercy.net/qhistorique/resistance/louvre.html (January 14, 2013).

51 NINETEENTH-CENTURY PAINTINGS "Evacuation & mise en securité, Etat de la situation au 1er septembre 1939, 18 heures," AMN R 1.1.

51 EARLY EVENING Ibid.

51 ELEVEN MILES PER HOUR Huyghe, *Une vie pour l'art*, 113.

51 VIADUCT AT PASSY "Défense du trésor . . . ," n.d., AMN R 30 Généralités.

51 STAFF SUDDENLY HEARD And other related details, Mazauric, *Le Louvre en voyage*, 25.

52 IT WAS "UNTHINKABLE . . ." Huyghe, *Une vie pour l'art*, 115.

53 HE SENT LOUVRE CURATOR Ibid., 45–46.

53 THROUGH THE LOW ENTRY "Etat de situation des Musées Nationaux au 2 septembre 1939 18h30," AMN R 1.1.

53 EVERY ITEM "Etat de la situation au 1er septembre 1939 18 heures," AMN R 1.1.

54 NOT STRONG ENOUGH "Le 5 mai 1940," 10, AMN R 20.2.

55 VAULTED WALL RECESS Ibid., 11.

56 LESSER VALUE "Le 5 mai 1940," 15, AMN R 20.2.

57 RESTORATION SPECIALISTS Huyghe, *Une vie pour l'art*, 114.

58 PAINT TO CRACK Ibid., 113.

58 ALL THE REST Minor shipments, primarily of supplies and works owned by private collectors continued until December 28 (AMN R 1.11).

58 ALSO SUPERVISED "Rapport sur l'évacuation des collections des Musées Nationaux," n.d., AN F21 3976.

## SIX · CHAMBORD

62 "IN A PITIFUL STATE . . ." Clément, *Lettres, Instructions et Mémoires de Colbert*, 405.

62 AN INVITATION Gourcuff and Forget, *Chambord*, 36.

62 BATTLE WITH THE PRUSSIANS Information courtesy of Denis Grandemenge, Régisseur des collections du Domaine national de Chambord, July 1, 2013.

64 PHILIPPE STERN TOLD JAUJARD Philippe Stern to Jacques Jaujard, 12 mars 1937, AMN R 1.1.

64 FIVE-PAGE REPORT Pierre Schommer to "Monsieur le Directeur," 26 août 1938, AMN R 1.1.

64 SIXTEEN-PAGE REPORT Pierre Schommer to "Monsieur le Directeur des Musées Nationaux et l'École du Louvre, Membre de l'Institut," 3 novembre 1938, AMN R 2A.

64 "CHAMBORD IS A BUILDING . . ." Ibid., 9.

65 "INDEED, A GREATER DANGER . . ." Ibid., 9–10.

65 "THIS GLACIER" Ibid., 12.

66 CLOSED TO THE PUBLIC Information courtesy of Denis Grandemenge, Régisseur des collections du Domaine national de Chambord, July 1, 2013.

66 DURING THE COURSE As of January 1940, 2,000 crates of evacuated art and antiquities had been brought to Chambord. By December 1941, they had joined by 400 others, originally stored at Fougères-sur-Bièvre. The collections stored at Chambord included not only items from the Louvre and the other national museums (Arts Décoratifs, Cluny, Versailles, Compiègne and

Saint-Germain-en-Laye), but also certain provincial museums and libraries. Domaine national de Chambord, *Otages de guerre*, 25.

66  BY 1944 COMPRISING  Domaine national de Chambord, *Otages de guerre*, 24.

66  COLLECTION OF DRAWINGS  "Le 5 mai 1940," 19, AMN R 20.2.

66  "IT'S A CIRCUS . . ."  "Les chefs-d'œuvre du Louvre ont pu déménager sans encombre," *Paris-Midi*, 30 novembre 1939.

68  EXPOSED TO LIGHT  Mazauric, *Le Louvre en voyage*, 34.

69  "LET'S SHARE . . ."  Hours, *Une vie au Louvre*, 47.

69  JAUJARD'S ASSISTANT  Polack and Dagen, *Les Carnets de Rose Valland*, 106.

69  MORE THAN THIRTY GUARDS  "Rapport à Monsieur le Directeur Général des Beaux Arts," 18 janvier 1940, AMN R 2A.

69  CANTEEN  Mazauric, *Le Louvre en voyage*, 33.

70  FORMER DINING ROOM  Ibid., 36.

70  ART PRESERVATION  Jacques Jaujard, "Rapport (Résumé) sur l'activité des Musées Nationaux depuis la Mobilisation," 19 janvier 1940, AN F21 3976; Jacques Jaujard, "Rapport à Monsieur le Directeur Général des Beaux-Arts sur les mesures récents prescrites pour assurer la sécurité des Collections des Musées Nationaux dans les Dépots d'évacuation," 18 janvier 1940, AMN R 2A.

71  SCHOMMER WROTE TO JAUJARD  Pierre Schommer to Jacques Jaujard, 16 octobre 1939, AMN R 5.5.

71  HE WROTE URGENTLY  Pierre Schommer to René Huyghe, 20 octobre 1939, AMN R 5.5.

71  AMBULANCE STRETCHER  Report from Schommer to Jaujard, 16 novembre 1939, AMN R 5.5.

72  HE WOULD WRITE  Domaine national de Chambord, *Otages de guerre*, 24, citing letter of 24 février 1944 from Pierre Schommer to Gaston Brière, bibliothèque central des Musées Nationaux, Ms 498 (4.9).

72  TEMPERATURES PLUMMETED  Ibid., 27.

72  FOURTEEN POSTPONEMENTS  Shirer, *Rise and Fall of the Third Reich*, 652.

## SEVEN · CHEVERNY

75  SIXTEENTH-CENTURY  Blancher-Le Bourhis, *Le château de Cheverny*, 7.

75  MEMBER OF THE HURAULT FAMILY  Hurault, "Notice sur Cheverny et sur Ses Mémoires," in Petitot, *Collection complète des mémoires*, 3.

75  WHILE SHE OVERSAW  Martin-Demézil, "Diane de Poitiers à Cheverny," *Bibliothèque d'Humanisme et Renaissance*, 280.

76  WORKERS DAMAGED  "Brigade de Cheverny," 2 novembre 1939, AMN R 30 Cheverny.

77  BABYLONIAN LAW CODE  G. Contenau, "note sur l'évacuation des Antiquités Orientales," n.d., AMN R 2A.

78  LEAST VULNERABLE TO DAMPNESS  Ibid.

78  CLOSE BY EACH CHÂTEAU  Rayssac, *L'exode des musées*, 111.

78  "DOG THAT BARKS . . ."  Ibid.

78  PARTIALLY REOPENED  Marquis de Vibraye to Jacques Jaujard, 18 avril 1940, R 30 Cheverny.

## EIGHT · COURTALAIN

79 THIRTEENTH CENTURY Desvaux, "Les Seigneurs de Courtalain," *Bulletin de la Société Dunoise d'Archéologie, Histoire, Sciences et Arts*, 123.

79 IN 1483 Chapron, Louis-Ferdinand. *Courtalain: châteaux et seigneurs*, 3.

79 IN 1586 Munduteguy, "Courtalain: un château du XVIe siècle restauré au XIXe siècle," *Bulletin de la Société Dunoise d'Archéologie, Histoire, Sciences et Arts*, 5.

79 SEPTEMBER 6 "Note relative à l'organisation et à la vie du dépôt de Courtalain (Eure & Loir), n.d., AMN R 2A.

80 GRAND SALON "Le 5 mai 1940," 52, AMN R 20.2.

80 ONLY ONE-HALF MILE Rayssac, *L'exode des musées*, 104.

## NINE · VALENÇAY

81 FIRST MILLENNIUM Raoul, *Guide historique de Valençay*, 4.

82 "THE SUPREME HAPPINESS . . ." Stendhal and Martineau, *Mélanges de politique et d'histoire*, 114.

82 THEN-STAGGERING SUM Waresquiel, *Talleyrand: le prince immobile*, 318.

83 SAND DESCRIBED Sand, *Lettres d'un voyageur*, Tome II, 89.

83 CONSIDERED NEUTRAL TERRITORY Coulon, "La Vénus de Milo, la Victoire de Samothrace...Des hôtes de marque au Château de Valençay pendant la Seconde guerre mondiale," *Musées et collections publiques de France*, mars 1996, 12.

83 LATER IN THE WAR Vilallonga, *Gold Gotha*, 222.

83 MANY STRONG POINTS Coulon, "La Vénus de Milo, la Victoire de Samothrace...Des hôtes de marque au Château de Valençay pendant la Seconde guerre mondiale," *Musées et collections publiques de France*, mars 1996, 10.

84 FAMILY OF ART COLLECTORS Georges Salles, "Notre Ami Carle," *Collection Carle Dreyfus*, 3.

84 "OLD-TIME PARISIAN . . ." Ferrand, *Gérald Van der Kemp*, 47.

85 GASTRONOMIC SPECIALTIES Mazauric, *Le Louvre en voyage*, 44.

## TEN · EXODUS

89 IN THE BELIEF Shirer, *Collapse of the Third Republic*, 642–643.

90 CROSSED THE RIVER Ibid., 723.

90 BREACH FIFTY MILES WIDE Lottman, *Fall of Paris*, 46.

91 DESIGNED ONLY G. Bazin, "Journal de l'évacuation des depots de la Sarthe, juin 1940–Conclusion," 17 juillet 1940, AMN R 30 Loc-Dieu.

92 MUSEUM OFFICIALS FELT "Dépôt de Loc-Dieu le 17 juin 1940," AMN R 30 Loc-Dieu.

92 WEDNESDAY MAY 29 Germain Bazin, "Journal de l'évacuation des depots de la Sarthe, juin 1940," 17 juillet 1940, AMN R 30 Loc-Dieu.

92 MANY LOUVRE GUARDS Mazauric, *Le Louvre en voyage*, 48.

93 NOT A SINGLE GUARD Bazin, *Souvenirs*, 19.

93 MOST PRECIOUS EGYPTIAN ANTIQUITIES "Inventaire des Caisses du Dépôt de Courtalain (Eure et Loir) ayant constitué le convoy parti le 1er Juin 1940 pour Saint-Blancard (Gers)," AMN R 30 Courtalain.

93 "I'M GIVING YOU..." Desroches Noblecourt, "Un très grand directeur: Jacques Jaujard," *Pillages et Restitutions*, 115.

93 ALMOST HIT "Extrait d'un rapport adressé à M. Cortot, Direction des Beaux-Arts, le 1er juillet 1940," AMN R 30 Saint-Blancard.

93 BETWEEN ENEMY LINES Desroches Noblecourt, *Sous le Regard*, 15.

94 HAVING JUST PASSED Mazauric, *Le Louvre en voyage*, 52.

94 "SINCE THE NOISE..." Desroches Noblecourt, "Un très grand directeur: Jacques Jaujard," *Pillages et Restitutions*, 24.

94 HAVING LEFT LOUVIGNY Germain Bazin, "Journal de l'évacuation des depots de la Sarthe, juin 1940," 17 juillet 1940, AMN R 30 Loc-Dieu.

94 FIRST SCHEDULED STOP André Varagnac to Jacques Jaujard, "Rapport sur le 1er convoi Louvigny–Loc-Dieu," 12 juin 1940, AMN R 30 Loc-Dieu.

95 STEEP SLOPES German Bazin, "Journal de l'évacuation des dépôts de la Sarthe, juin 1940." AMN R 30 Loc-Dieu.

95 CRATES ATOP André Varagnac to Jacques Jaujard, "Rapport sur le 1er convoi Louvigny–Loc-Dieu," AMN R 30 Loc-Dieu.

96 WAS ACCELERATED Germain Bazin, "Journal de l'évacuation des dépôts de la Sarthe, juin 1940," 17 juillet 1940, AMN R 30 Loc-Dieu.

97 DIESEL VEHICLES Bazin, *Souvenirs*, 17.

97 "THE COUR DU CARROUSEL..." Humbert, *Résistance*, 3.

98 CARRIED AWAY Lottman, *Fall of Paris*, 267.

98 JUST RECEIVED WORD Germain Bazin, "Journal de l'évacuation des dépôts de la Sarthe, juin 1940," 17 juillet 1940, AMN R 30 Loc-Dieu.

98 TRAILER CARRYING Bordereaux de chargement 3, 22, and 31, AMN R 30 Loc-Dieu.

98 NO WRAPPING AT ALL Bordereau de chargement 22, AMN R 30 Loc-Dieu; Germain Bazin, "Journal de l'évacuation des dépôts de la Sarthe, juin 1940," 17 juillet 1940, AMN R 30 Loc-Dieu.

98 6 to 10 MILLION Jackson, *France: The Dark Years*, 120.

99 "SLOW MOVING CARS..." Ibid., 120.

99 FROM THE AIR Saint-Exupéry, *Pilote de Guerre*, 111.

99 DUE TO CHAINS Bazin, *Souvenirs*, 18.

99 CAUGHT ON ANOTHER VEHICLE Mazauric, *Le Louvre en voyage*, 58.

99 EQUESTRIAN CENTER Valland, *Le front de l'art*, 13; Jacques Jaujard to Louis Hautecœur, 24 mai 1940, AMN R 30 Valençay.

100 "NOTHING TO FEAR" Charbonneaux, "Le Musée du Louvre pendant la Guerre," discours, Société des Amis du Louvre, 25 juin 1946, 11.

100 NEARBY BOMB Mazauric, *Le Louvre en voyage*, 59.

100 DESTROYED THE BRIDGES Germain Bazin, "Journal de l'évacuation des dépôts de la Sarthe, juin 1940," 17 juillet 1940, AMN R 30 Loc-Dieu.

100 BEHIND THE WHEEL Bazin, *Souvenirs*, 202.

101 AT 3 P.M. Ibid.

101 THREE HUNDRED MILES Itinerary, AMN R 30 Loc-Dieu.

101 "VARIOUS OLD PAINTINGS" Journal des chefs du dépôt, 18 juin 1940, AMN R 30 Courtalain.

101 LOADING AND MOVING Germain Bazin, "Journal de l'évacuation des depots de la Sarthe, juin 1940–Conclusion," 17 juillet 1940, AMN R 30 Loc-Dieu..

## ELEVEN · DEBACLE

103 THAT EVENING Jacques Jaujard to Jérôme Carcopino, 10 juillet 1940, AMN R 2C1.

103 "NOT A SINGLE GUARD ..." Paul Léautaud, Journal littéraire, III (Février 1940 – Février 1956), 79.

103 HAD ALREADY ARRANGED Mazauric, Le Louvre en voyage, 48–49.

104 SHORTLY AFTER 3 A.M. Langeron, Paris, juin 1940, 42.

104 VEHICLE-MOUNTED LOUDSPEAKERS Lottman, Fall of Paris, 350 .

105 LEFT THE NEXT MORNING Shirer, Collapse, 845.

106 FULL MILITARY UNIFORM Williams, The Last Great Frenchman, 112.

107 NUMEROUS REPORTS "Exposé du Comte F. Wolff Metternich," Document 35, Cassou, Le pillage par les Allemands, 159.

109 ON JUNE 19 Jacques Jaujard to Jérôme Carcopino, 10 juillet 1940, AMN R 2C1.

109 "YOU ARE ..." Chamson, "In Memoriam Jacques Jaujard," Musées et Collections Publiques en France, No. 100, 151.

109 STATIONED SOLDIERS "Exposé du Comte F. Wolff Metternich," Cassou, Le pillage par les Allemands, Document 35, 159, 167.

109 HAGUE CONVENTION The multilateral agreement regarding the laws of war had been signed by a number of countries, including Germany, in 1907.

109 ORDER FROM HITLER Keitel, "Secret," 30.6.40, AN 40 1366; French translation in Valland, Le front de l'art, Document 2, 235.

## TWELVE · OCCUPIERS WITH AN EYE FOR ART

111 "ALL MY LIFE ..." "Painters' War," Time, September 11, 1939, 30.

112 IMPORTANT RITUAL Petropoulos, Art as Politics in the Third Reich, 186.

112 FINAL VICTORY Speer, Inside the Third Reich, 178.

112 RIBBENTROP HAD BOUGHT Fest, Face of the Third Reich, 179.

112 END OF 1934 Abetz, Das Offene Problem, 51.

113 SALON EVENINGS Vaughn, Sleeping with the Enemy, 135.

113 SUBVERSIVE ACTIVITY Curtis, Verdict on Vichy, 181.

113 ABETZ WAS BACK Lambauer, Otto Abetz et les Français, 135.

113 NEW ORDER "Au commandant militaire de Paris," Valland, Le front de l'art, Document 3, 235–236.

113 ORDER ALSO EXTENDED His order also called for the seizure of all artworks belonging to Jews and the transfer of the "most precious items" to the German embassy in Paris.

113 ABETZ LAUNCHED Lambauer, Otto Abetz et les Français, 153–154.

113 ALREADY INSTRUCTED JAUJARD "Le Recteur de l'Université de Paris Representant le Ministre" to Jaujard, AMN R 20.6.1; Letter from "Préfecture Département de la Seine, Direction des Beaux-Arts," juillet 1940; "Communiqué à la presse," 27 septembre 1940, AMN R 20.6.1.

113 ABETZ'S REPRESENTATIVES "Messieurs Dirksen & Diesel . . . ," 4 juillet 1940, AMN R 20.6.1.

114 LOW-FLYING PLANES Nicholas, *Rape of Europa*, 178–79.

114 AGREED TO A DELAY Jacques Jaujard to Ministre de l'Education Nationale, 10 juillet 1940, AMN R 2C1.

114 AGAIN START PRESSING Jérôme Carcopino to Maxime Weygand (Secretary of Defense)," 21 juillet 1940; "Note," General Huntziger to General von Stülpnagel, 29 juillet 1940, AN AJ 40 1366.

114 ABETZ HAD NOT OBTAINED CDJC, LXXI-22, report by Sowa, Feldpolizei director, July 8, 1940.

114 EFFECTIVE IMMEDIATELY "Ordonnance du 15 juillet 1940 concernant la protection des objets d'art dans le territoire occupé de la France." Cassou, Le pillage par les Allemands, Document 4, 80–81.

115 TOO MUCH POWER Petropoulos, *Art as Politics*, 127–131; Cassou, *Le pillage par les Allemands*, 43–44.

115 SUBJECT TO JAUJARD'S GUARANTEE Dr. Bunjes, "Procès-verbal," 22 août 1940, AMN R 6.

116 BEST PIECES Speer, *Inside the Third Reich*, 178.

116 SECRET MISSION Nicholas, *Rape of Europa*, 121.

116 "WITHOUT GERMAN CONSENT . . ." Kümmel, "Kümmel Report," 1.

116 COMMITTED NAZI Petropoulos, *Faustian Bargain*, 55.

116 NEW SECRET MISSION NA M1944/RG 239/0022, Hentzen interrogation, June 22–23, 1945.

116 STRONGLY-WORDED NARRATIVE Feliciano, *Lost Museum*, 26.

117 HELP OF AN AIDE Letter from Abetz to SS member Dr. Turner, July 17, 1940, AN AJ 40 1673; Bargatzky, *Hotel Majestic*, 65.

117 GAVE AN ORDER CDJC XCII-27; Bargatzky; *Hotel Majestic*, 66.

117 MASTER POLITICIAN King, *Vienna*, 30.

118 LIFELONG FRANCOPHILE "Exposé du Comte F. Wolff Metternich," Document 35, Cassou, *Le pillage par les Allemands*, 154.

118 WOULD HAVE LIKED "Exposé du Comte F. Wolff Metternich," Document 35, Cassou, *Le pillage par les Allemands*, 163.

118 FIRST WEEK OF AUGUST Jacques Jaujard to Louis Hautecœur, 6 août 1940, AMN R 2C1.

118 POSTPONEMENT Ibid. The matter was not officially dropped until November.

118 NEW ORDER FORBIDDING Laub, *After the Fall*, 75; Bargatzky, *Hotel Majestic*, 66.

118 SECRET MEETING Bargatzky, *Hotel Majestic*, 66.

120 IF PRESENTED CDJC, XCII-27; Lambauer, *Otto Abetz et les Français*, 156.

120  INSPECTION AT CHAMBORD  An inspection was also made the same day at Cheverny as well as at Brissac, which sheltered items from Versailles, the Musée Camondo, other institutions and private collections.

120  WOLFF METTERNICH WAS THERE  Handwritten report from Pierre Schommer to Jacques Jaujard, 16 août 1940, AMN R 30 Chambord.

120  KÜNSBERG AND HIS MEN  Lambauer, *Otto Abetz et les Français*, 156.

120  PROVIDED TO THE GERMAN EMBASSY  CDJC XCII-27.

120  FOUR-DAY ROUND  Lambauer, *Otto Abetz et les Français*, 158.

121  ITEMS TO RIBBENTROP  Feliciano, *Lost Museum*, 35.

121  ROTHSCHILD FAMILY APARTMENTS  Lambauer, "Francophile contre vents et marée ? Otto Abetz et les Français, 1930–1958," *Bulletin du Centre de Recherche Français à Jérusalem,* 159.

121  CHAMPAGNE FLOWED  Pourcher, *Pierre Laval vu par sa fille*, 213, 226.

121  HITLER ALSO GAVE  Order from Keitel, Supreme Command of the German Armed Forces to Commandant en Chef de l'Administration militaire en France occupée, September 17, 1940, Document 138-PS, Nuremberg Trials, International Military Tribunal, *Nazi Conspiracy and Aggression* ("Red Series"), Vol. III, 186.

121  OFFERED THE USE  Petropoulos, *Art as Politics*, 133.

## THIRTEEN · LOC-DIEU ABBEY

123  THE LOCALS CALLED THE AREA  Lafon, *Histoire de la fondation de l'abbaye de Loc-Dieu*, 3–17.

123  DRAINED MUCH OF THE REMAINING SWAMP  Ibid., 39.

123  SWAMPY MIST  Hébrard, *La Chambre de Goethe*, 46.

124  1.5 MILLION MEN  Jackson, *France: The Dark Years*, 126.

124  PLAGUE-INFESTED CITY  Mazauric, *Le Louvre en voyage*, 70.

125  EACH FURNISHED  Ibid., 73.

125  HEAD COUNT  Ibid., 66.

125  MORE THAN 3,100  Germain Bazin, "Journal de l'évacuation des depots de la Sarthe, juin 1940–Conclusion," 17 juillet 1940, AMN R 30 Loc-Dieu.

126  EACH INDIVIDUAL PAINTING  Mazauric, *Le Louvre en voyage*, 78.

126  BENEFITTING FROM THE FRESH AIR  Ibid., 89.

126  UNSUCCESSFULLY TRYING  "Memento Mons. Jacques Jaujard," n.d., AMN R 30 Loc-Dieu.

126  UNIVERSITY OF ROME  "Italians Ask France to Give Up 'Mona Lisa,'" *New York Times*, July 16, 1940, 12.

128  JULY 22  Mazauric, *Le Louvre en voyage*, 82.

128  ASKED SOME FRENCHMEN  And additional details, Ibid., 83–85.

129  OPENED MONA LISA'S CASE  "Ouverture de la caisse L.P.0," 21 juillet 1940, AMN R 30 Loc-Dieu.

130  SUBSEQUENT ANALYSIS  "Note concernant la conservation des Peintures du Musée du Louvre entreposées à l'Abbaye de Loc-Dieu (Aveyron), 22 août 1940, AMN R 30 Loc-Dieu.

130   "WE WATCHED . . ." Chamson, "Dans la familiarité des chefs-d'oeuvres," *Jardin des Arts*, 3.

130   HARDLY DARED   Mazauric, *Le Louvre en voyage*, 90.

130   SOGGY NINETY-FIVE PERCENT   "Rapport sur un hivernage eventuel des tableaux du Louvre dans le Midi," n.d., AMN R 30 Loc-Dieu.

130   POSSIBLE SOLUTIONS   "Note concernant la conservation des Peintures du Musée du Louvre entreposées à l'Abbaye de Loc-Dieu (Aveyron)," 22 août 1940, AMN R 30 Loc-Dieu.


## FOURTEEN · VALENÇAY AT WAR

133   DID NOT COME EASILY   Desroches Noblecourt, "Un très grand directeur: Jacques Jaujard," *Pillages et Restitutions*, 24.

134   "WE ARE SCHOLARS . . ."   Ibid., 25.

134   THE CROWN JEWELS   Valland, *Le front de l'art*, 13.

134   "VISIT THE CAPTIVE GODDESS . . ."   Charbonneaux, "Le Musée du Louvre pendant la Guerre," discours prononcé à l'Assemblée Générale annuelle da la Société des Amis du Louvre, 25 juin 1946, 12.

134   BEFORE THE WAR   Cohan, *The Last Tycoons*, 38.

134   GERMAN SOLDIERS ARRIVED   The curators at Valençay to Jacques Jaujard, 24 juin 1940, AMN R 30 Valençay.

134   TOLD IT WAS IMPOSSIBLE   AMN R 30 Valençay, The curators at Valençay to Jacques Jaujard, 27 juin 1940, AMN R 30 Valençay.

135   DREYFUS MOVED   Ferrand, *Gérald Van der Kemp*, 48.

135   HE ESCAPED   Vilallonga, *Gold Gotha*, 22; Ferrand, Ibid., 47.

135   ALLOWED HIM   Rayssac, *L'exode des musées*, 260.

136   HIS ENTIRE LIFE   Ferrand, *Gérald Van der Kemp*, 52.

136   "A MAN OF THE PREVIOUS CENTURY . . ."   Ferrand, *Gérald Van der Kemp*, 47, 52.

136   "IMMENSE SILENT FORESTS . . ."   Vilallonga, *Gold Gotha*, 222.


## FIFTEEN · PARIS

137   NOT WITH HIS GENERALS   Cocteau, *Journal, 1942–1945*, 128.

138   "I WOULD NOT HESITATE . . ."   Breker, *Paris, Hitler et Moi*, 108.

138   ANYWHERE, INCLUDING PARIS   "Convention d'Armistice Franco-Allemande du 22 juin 1940," Article 3, *Documents diplomatiques français: 1940, les armistices de juin 1940*, 124.

138   ONE ADVISOR TO PÉTAIN   "Note," n.d., AN 2AG 458.

139   COULD NOT RETURN   Paxton, *Vichy France*, 99.

139   CHANGING OF THE GERMAN GUARDS   Mitchell, *Nazi Paris*, 14.

139   INSIDE THE GARDENS   Benoit-Guyod, *L'Invasion de Paris*, 43.

139   MILITARY BAND CONCERTS   Mitchell, *Nazi Paris*, 28.

140   UNEMPLOYED ARTISTS   Jacques Jaujard to Louis Hautecœur, 20 novembre 1940, AN F21 4900.

140 TO AVOID DELAYING Direction des Musées Nationaux, Projet de budget de 1941, AN F21 3981.

140 MUSÉE DE L'ORANGERIE Riding, *And the Show Went On*, 63.

140 ATTENDED BY "Une cérémonie a préludé à la réouverture de plusieurs salles du Louvre," *Le Matin*, 30 septembre 1940.

140 DIRECTED Jacques Jaujard to Louis Hautecœur, 4 octobre 1940, carton 205, MAE.

140 IT WAS A CHANCE "Exposé du Comte F. Wolff Metternich," Document 35, Cassou, *Le pillage par les Allemands*, 172.

140 ALL WORE BLACK Mazauric, *Le Louvre en voyage*, 117.

141 OPENED TO THE PUBLIC "Communiqué à la Presse," 27 septembre 1940. AMN R 2C1.

141 NOT A SINGLE PAINTING Jacques Jaujard to Louis Hautecœur, 4 octobre 1940, carton 205, MAE.

142 OPEN FOR FIVE HOURS "Communiqué à la Presse," 27 septembre 1940. AMN R 2C1.

142 FREE FOR GERMANS "Note pour M. le Directeur Général des Beaux-Arts," 6 septembre 1940.

142 EXCEPT STUDENTS "Communiqué à la Presse," 27 septembre 1940. AMN R 2C1.

142 SIGNS WERE POSTED "Note," 4 septembre 1940, AMN R 2B.

142 "GUIDES WITH GUTTURAL ACCENTS ... " Fonkenell and others, *Le Louvre pendant la guerre*, 13.

142 "WHAT MISERY ..." Gaussen-Salmon, *Une prière dans la nuit*, 145–146.

144 GÖRING WAS ACCOMPANIED Joseph Billiet to Jacques Jaujard, 9 novembre 1940, AMN R 15.2.

144 AUBERT LATER REPORTED Rorimer, *Survival*, 207.

144 WOULD LATER SAY Consolidated Interrogation Report (CIR) No. 2: The Goering Collection, 15 September 1945, NA M1946/RG260/0121.

144 FOLLOWING SPRING "Rapport sur un projet d'échange avec les collections allemandes," 9 janvier 1943, AMN R 15.2.

144 APPROACHED THE LOUVRE Letter from Joseph Billiet, 3 octobre 1940, AMN R 2C 1 (1940).

145 AGREED TO CEDE Jacques Jaujard to Franz von Wolff Metternich, 7 octobre 1940, AMN R 2C1 (1940).

145 OBSCURED THE WINDOWS Fonkenell and others, *Le Louvre pendant la guerre*, 146.

145 OCTOBER 6 Jacques Jaujard to Franz von Wolff Metternich, 7 octobre 1940, AMN R 2C1 (1940).

145 INCLUDED ITEMS Jacques Jaujard to Franz von Wolff Metternich, 21 octobre 1940; Le Masne de Chermont and Sigal-Klagsbald, *A qui appartenaient ces tableaux ?*, 9.

145 150 CRATES Fonkenell and others, *Le Louvre pendant la guerre*, 126.

## SIXTEEN · MONTAUBAN, 1941

147   A NEWER CASTLE  Devals, *Histoire de Montauban sous la Domination Anglaise*, 72.

147   IN 1659  Bouisset, *Le Musée Ingres*, 4, 10.

148   RAIN HAD DAMAGED  "Rapport de Monsieur J.G. Goulinat," 2 septembre 1940, AMN R 30 Loc-Dieu.

148   BAD WEATHER  René Huyghe to M. le Général Commandant le Département de l'Aveyron, 6 septembre 1940; Huyghe, *Une vie pour l'art*, 120.

148   NO RAIN  René Huyghe to Jacques Jaujard, 9 octobre 1940, AMN R 30 Montauban.

148   CARRYING ONLY  "Chargement du Camion 11597 V R 15," 5 octobre 1940, AMN R 30 Loc-Dieu.

149   DID NOT EXPECT  And subsequent details. Mazauric, *Le Louvre en voyage*, 92–93.

149   "LIKE A DOCTOR..."  Mazauric, *Le Louvre en voyage*, 104.

152   MIGHT BE POSSIBLE  Gruat and Martínez, *L'Echange*, 22–23.

152   POSITIVE PUBLICITY  Vinen, *The Unfree French*, 54.

152   SO MANY CHILDREN  Mazauric, *Le Louvre en voyage*, 128.

153   BY BOUCHER  Jacques Jaujard to Louis Hautecœur, 30 avril 1941 AMN R 15.2.

153   1938 TRIP  Saint-Paulien, *Histoire de la Collaboration*, 28.

153   LINGERING LONG  Huyghe, *Une vie pour l'art*, 86.

153   PAINTINGS MIGHT SERVE  Jacques Jaujard to Louis Hautecœur, 28 mars 1941, AMN R 15.2.

154   DARLAN TOLD CARCOPINO  Carcopino, *Souvenirs de sept ans*, 454–455.

154   BY WAY OF EXAMPLE  Jacques Jaujard to Louis Hautecœur, 28 mars 1941, AMN R 15.2.

154   TO SUSPECT  Karlsgodt, *Defending National Treasures*, 246.

155   ISSUED AN ORDER  François Darlan to Louis Hautecœur, 24 avril 1941, AMN R 15.2.

155   LESS THAN A WEEK  Valland, *Front de l'Art*, 135.

155   "WHAT DO YOU EXPECT..."  Hautecœur, *Les Beaux-Arts en France*, 296.

155   CHÂTEAU DE SOURCHES  "Tableaux apportés à Sourches les 27 mai & 23 juin 1942," AMN R 30 Sourches.

155   KEEP SEARCHING  "Télégramme pour l'ambassadeur Abetz," Valland, *Le front de l'art*, Doc. 15, 250–251.

156   AMONG THEM  Valland, *Le front de l'art*, 114.

## SEVENTEEN · SOURCHES

159   ORIGINALLY NAMED  Pesche, *Dictionnaire topographique, historique et statistique de la Sarthe*, 225.

159   FELL IN LOVE  Pérusse des Cars and Ledru, *Le Château de Sourches*, 262.

162   PRIVATE COLLECTIONS  For example, "Le Directeur Général des Beaux-Arts à Monsieur le Directeur des Musées Nationaux," 23 mars 1936, AMN R 1.1.

162  530 CRATES  Karlsgodt, *Defending National Treasures*, 75.

163  LOSING HIS POSITION  Feliciano, *Lost Museum*, 89.

163  PRE-WAR STAMPS  Bazin, *Souvenirs*, 93; Valland, *Le front de l'art*, 115.

163  DEMANDING A LIST  Germain Bazin to Jacques Jaujard, 20 janvier 1941, AMN R 30 Sources.

163  BY TELEPHONE  Jérôme Carcopino to Admiral Darlan, 29 mai 1941, AN 3W 121.

163  FOUR DAYS AHEAD  Letter from Jacques Jaujard to Franz von Wolff Metternich, 3 juillet 1941, AMN R 2C3.

163  TEN THOUSAND OBJECTS  Karlsgodt, *Defending National Treasures*, 207.

164  VIOLENT RELIGIOUS WARS  Bridgeford, *1066: The Hidden History*, 28.

164  GOVERNMENT DECLARED  Brown, *Bayeux Tapestry*, 8.

164  AS EARLY AS JULY 1939  Hicks, *Bayeux Tapestry*, 212.

165  CONCRETE SHELTER  Dubosq, *La Tapisserie de Bayeux*, 24–27.

165  DEMANDED ACCESS  Brown, *Bayeux Tapestry*, 17.

165  SS CAMERAMAN  Hicks, *Bayeux Tapestry*, 222.

165  SCIENTIFIC INVESTIGATION  Ibid., 213.

165  SOLVED THE PROBLEM  And other details of the day's events, Dubosq, *La Tapisserie de Bayeux*, 57–60.

166  AROUND 4 P.M.  "Rapport," 12 septembre 1941, AMN R 30 Sources.

167  TIESCHOWITZ RESPONDED  Hicks, *Bayeux Tapestry*, 228.

## EIGHTEEN · MONTAUBAN, 1942

169  IN MAY 1942  And other details of the painting's move, Bazin, *Souvenirs*, 37–38.

170  RELEASE OF GEORGES SALLES  AMN R 20.6.1, "Libération de M. Georges Salles."

171  PROMISE FROM JOSEPH GOEBBELS  Mazauric, *Le Louvre en voyage*, 76.

171  FORCED TO RESIGN  "Exposé du Comte F. Wolff Metternich," Document 35, Cassou, Le pillage par les Allemands, 174.

171  JAUJARD HAD SENT  Mazauric, *Le Louvre en voyage*, 111.

173  ENTIRE ALTARPIECE  Kümmel, Kümmel report, 19. (Lists all eleven original panels; one of the twelve was a copy.)

173  THREE INDIVIDUALS  Jacques Jaujard to Louis Hautecœur, 7 août 1941, AN 3W78, C5.

174  DRAFTED AN AGREEMENT  Jacques Jaujard to Louis Hautecœur, 31 août 1942, 3W78, C9.

174  MUSEUM OPENING  Karlsgodt, *Defending National Treasures*, 240.

174  "WHEN THE HEAD . . ."  Hautecœur, *Les beaux-arts en France*, 307.

175  ONLY SIXTY-NINE PAINTINGS  "Montauban, le 7 septembre 1942," AMN R 30 Montauban.

175  THE ONLY ROOM  Maurice Sérullaz to Jacques Jaujard, 8 septembre 1942, AMN R 30 Montauban.

176  WRAPPED THE MONA LISA  "Montauban, 11 novembre 1942," AMN R 30 Montauban.

176 FROM THE WINDOWS OF THE MUSEUM Mazauric, *Le Louvre en voyage*, 138.

176 "CAMERAS MORE MAGNIFICENT..." Ibid., 138–139.

176 SENT A REQUEST Jacques Jaujard to Louis Hautecœur, 12 novembre 1942, AMN R 2B.

177 THEY WORRIED Journal du bord, Loubéjac–La Treyne, 1, AMN R 30 La Treyne.

177 POLICE SEARCHED Mazauric, *Le Louvre en voyage*, 146.

177 OFFICIAL PROTEST Procès-verbal of 26 Nov. 1942 meeting of comité des conservateurs, AMN *1BB.

177 "MORE NAZI..." Chamson, "In Memoriam Jacques Jaujard," *Musées et Collections Publiques en France*, No. 100, 152.

177 ACTS OF REBELLION "Enlèvement du polyptyque de l'Agneau Mystique à Pau, par les Allemands (dossier joint)," C3, AN 3W 78.

178 GATHERED TOGETHER "Allocution adressée par M. Jaujard," 30 décembre 1942, AMN R 20.4.

## NINETEEN · INSINCERE INTENTIONS

181 NOVEMBER 1942 Nicholas, *Rape of Europa*, 145.

181 GAVE HIS APPROVAL Jacques Jaujard to Louis Hautecœur, 19 décembre 1942, AMN R 15.2; Demandes des Allemandes rélatives à: L'échange d'oeuvres d'art, l'Autel de Bâle, Un voyage à Berlin de conservateurs des Musées Nationaux," C3, AN 3W 78.

182 "SURROUNDED BY SMILES..." Report by Robert Rey, 18 septembre 1944, AMN R 15.

182 NEGOTIATIONS BEGAN "NOTE," 7 janvier 1943, 16 heures 30, AMN R 15.2.

183 UNDER CONSIDERATION "Comité des conservateurs, Séance du 28 janvier 1943," AMN R 15.2.2.

## TWENTY · CHÂTEAU DE MONTAL

185 SCOURED THE COUNTRYSIDE Jacques Jaujard to Louis Hautecœur, 30 janvier 1943, AMN R 30 Montal; Mazauric, *Le Louvre en voyage*, 154.

186 AGREED TO LEND Jacques Jaujard to Louis Hautecœur, 30 janvier 1943, AMN R 30 Montal.

187 FLOOR ABOVE Ibid.

187 NOT LARGE ENOUGH Mazauric, *Le Louvre en voyage*, 153.

187 TO PROVIDE ACCESS Jacques Jaujard to "Monsieur le conseiller d'Etat, secrétaire général des Beaux-Arts (Direction des services d'architecture), 3 février 1943, AMN R 30 Montal.

187 PACKING MATERIAL "Message pour Monsieur Huyghe," 24 février 1943, AMN R 30 Montal.

187 MARCH 3 René Huyghe to Jacques Jaujard, 2 mars 1943, AMN R 30 Montal.

188 CATTLE TRUCK Jacques Jaujard to Louis Hautecœur, 30 janvier 1943, AMN R 30 Montal.

188 STOPPED THEM  Huyghe, *Une vie pour l'art*, 121. Huyghe wrote erroneously in this memoir that the event occurred during the evacuation from Loc-Dieu to Montauban, but he indicated in an interview with Michel Rayssac (*L'exode des musées*, 463) that it occurred during the move from Montauban, which is more likely.

188 IN APRIL  André Chamson to Jacques Jaujard, 20 avril 1943, AMN R 30 La Treyne.

188 SPOTTED THE CRATES  Mazauric, *Le Louvre en voyage*, 180.

188 OVER ONE HUNDRED DEPOTS  "Note relative à la Protection et à l'Evacuation des Musées de Province, N.D., AN F21 3981.

190 PROVINCIAL MUSEUMS  Rayssac, *L'exode des musées*, 578.

190 FULLY FUNDED  Karlsgodt, *Defending National Treasures*, 99.

190 MORE INSPECTION WORK  Ibid., 83.

190 FIRST INSPECTION  Mazauric, *Le Louvre en voyage*, 166–167.

190 BENEDICTINE MONASTERY  Ibid., 167.

191 UNLESS PÉTAIN HIMSELF  Valland, *Le front de l'art*, 141.

191 SENT HIS REPRESENTATIVES  Jacques Jaujard to Louis Hautecœur, 8 juin 1943, AMN R 15.2.

191 ORDERED THE RETURN  Louis Hautecœur to Jacques Jaujard, 2 juillet 1943, AMN R 15.2.

## TWENTY-ONE · A CHÂTEAU LIFE

193 POTENTIAL TARGETS  For example, see Jacques Jaujard to Louis Hautecœur, 22 août 1940, AMN R 2C1; "Interventions auprès des autorités allemands d'occupation pour la non requisition des logements des Membres du Personnel Scientifique retenus en Province en qualité de Chefs des Dépots d'OEuvres d'Art," AMN R 20.1.

193 BY SQUATTERS  Mazauric, *Le Louvre en voyage*, 119.

193 HALF-ARISTOCRAT  Ibid., 13.

193 TOOK OVER  Schnitzler and Meyer, *Hans Haug*, 157.

194 "WE HAD TO ACQUIRE . . ."  Mazauric, *Le Louvre en voyage*, 45.

194 THE MARQUISE  Desroches Noblecourt, *Sous le Regard*, 116–117.

195 WELCOMED HIM  Bazin, *Souvenirs*, 25.

195 DOWNHILL FROM THERE  "Extrait du journal du dépôt de Sourches de 1940 à 1944", AMN R 30 Sourches.

197 THE LAWSUIT  AMN R 30 Sourches.

197 COMFORTABLE CHAIR  German Bazin to Jacques Jaujard, 13 avril 1943, AMN R 30 Sourches.

197 SOMETIMES WORKED  Rayssac, *L'exode des musées*, 494–495.

197 TWO-MEN PATROLS  Zitman, *Souvenirs d'un sapeur-pompier*, 222–223.

198 AT MONTAUBAN  Mazauric, *Le Louvre en voyage*, 124.

198 IN THE AFTERNOON  Hébrard, *La Chambre de Goethe*, 60.

199 OPPORTUNITY TO BUY  Mazauric, *Le Louvre en voyage*, 164–165.

199 DIFFERENT MEANING  Rayssac, *L'exode des musées*, 493.

201 "BY THE HANDS . . ." Germain Bazin to Jacques Jaujard, 17 janvier, 1 mars, 9 avril 1942, AMN R 30 Sources.

201 ALMOST SIXTY Jacques Jaujard to Louis Hautecœur, 26 janvier 1944, C27, AN 3W 78.

## TWENTY-TWO · RESISTANCE

203 LESS THAN 3,000 Crémieux-Brilhac, *La France libre*, 88.

203 ROOSEVELT SAID Powaski, *Toward an Entangling Alliance*, 120.

203 HOPE OF ASSISTANCE Paxton, *Vichy France*, 38.

204 COMMUNIST POSTER Ibid., 38–39.

205 HAD SWELLED Vincent, *Les Forces françaises*, 20.

205 FEW OCCUPATION TROOPS Ehrlich, *French Resistance*, 154.

205 TAKE TO THE MAQUIS Boursier, Jean-Yves. *Résistants et Résistance*, 44.

206 DOUBLE LIFE Mazauric, *Le Louvre en voyage*, 172.

206 CHAMSON SOMETIMES HEADED Hébrard, *Chambre de Goethe*, 176.

206 SECRECY COULD MEAN Mazauric, *Le Louvre en voyage*, 173.

206 OCTOBER 5 Dr. Kuetgens, "Le militärbefehlshaber en France, Section de l'Admin-istration Protection des oeuvres d'art" to Abel Bonnard, 3 janvier 1944, AMN R 1.10.

207 ABBEY'S PRIEST Mazauric, *Le Louvre en voyage*, 168–169.

207 HIGH-PROFILE Huyghe, *Une vie pour l'art* ,134.

207 KIDNAPPED Ibid., 140.

207 FALSE IDENTITY PAPERS Huyghe, *Une vie pour l'art*, 123.

209 "YOU'RE RIGHT . . ." Desroches Noblecourt, *Sous le Regard*, 123.

209 AREA MAQUIS Nicault, "Quand Valençay abritait la Vénus de Milo," *Revue Berry*, 4.

209 APTLY BAPTIZED Leroi-Gourhan, *Racines du Monde*, 113.

209 RELAYING INFORMATION Ferrand, *Gérald Van der Kemp*, 54.

209 SET EUROPE ABLAZE Dalton, *The Fateful Years*, 366.

209 PARACHUTED Cornioley, Larroque and Atwood, *Code Name Pauline*, xxiv.

210 STOCKPILED Nicault, "Quand Valençay abritait la Vénus de Milo," *Revue Berry*, 5.

210 REGULAR PRESS Thibault, *Imprimeurs et éditeurs, conférence-débat*, 16–17.

210 UNDERGROUND BOOK Extracts of the book were published in a 1944 edition of the underground publisher *Éditions de Minuit*, under Chamson's maquis name, Lauter. The complete book was published in 1946.

210 TUCKED THEM Cellier-Gelly, *André Chamson*, 223.

210 LAST PAGES Mazauric, *Le Louvre en voyage*, 174–75.

211 35,000 VICTIMS Curtis, *Verdict on Vichy*, 84.

211 GIVEN NO REASON Humbert, *Résistance*, 19–20.

211 YOUNG MEN "Etat nominative des fonctionnaires et agents du sexe masculine nés entre le 1er janvier 1908 et le 31 décembre 1923, 28 mars 1944, 17, AMN R 20; Jaujard testimony, 4 mai 1959, R28, AN 3W 82.

212 NO SUCH PERSON Aubrun, "L'action de Jacques Jaujard," 44.

212 KEEP THEM IN FRANCE Jacques Jaujard to von Tieschowitz, 26 juillet 1944, AMN R 2C6.

212 TURNED A BLIND EYE For example, see Parrot, *L'intelligence en guerre*, 238.

212 DENOUNCING THE PILLAGE Aubrun, "L'action de Jacques Jaujard," 117, citing Dorléac, *Art, culture et société: l'exemple des Arts plastiques à Paris entre 1940 et 1944.*

212 CLAUDE MORGAN Lottmann, *Left Bank*, 187.

212 PROVIDED KNOWINGLY Parrot, *L'intelligence en guerre*, 201.

212 SHORT SUPPLY Thibault, *Imprimeurs et éditeurs, conférence-débat*, 20.

212 HOSTED MEETINGS Parrot, *L'intelligence en guerre*, 238; Eychart and Aillaud, *Les Lettres françaises et Les Etoiles dans la clandestinité*, 25.

213 EDITIONS DE MINUIT Dorléac, *Histoire de l'art*, 309.

213 INCONSPICUOUS BUNDLES Parrot, *L'intelligence en guerre*, 183.

213 ALSO SERVED Desroches Noblecourt, "Un très grand directeur: Jacques Jaujard," *Pillages et Restitutions*, 26.

213 WHISKED HIM OFF Dalloz, *Verités sur le Drame du Vercors*, 114.

213 SHOWING HIM THE KEY Interview with Jean Cassou, in Dorléac, *Histoire de l'art Paris 1940–1944*, 309.

213 ALSO HOSTED Bazin, *Souvenirs*, 115.

213 SEVERAL WEEKS LATER Jacques Jaujard to Louis Hautecœur, 4 décembre 1942, AMN R 1.10.

214 HAD SCRIBBLED Bizardel, *Sous l'Occupation*, 205.

214 RENEW HIS REQUEST Jacques Jaujard to Louis Hautecœur, 6 avril 1943, 16 avril 1944, AMN R 1.10.

214 "MONA LISA IS SMILING" Report by Robert Rey, 18 septembre 1944, AMN R 15.1.

214 SMILED TOO Hours, *Une vie au Louvre*, 61.

## TWENTY-THREE · THIEVES AND SPIES

215 HEAVILY GUARDED Valland, *Le front de l'art*, 63.

216 PARALLEL LISTS Carcopino to Admiral Darlan, 29 mai 1941, AN 3W 121; Valland, Ibid., 52–53.

216 SINCE 1932 Bouchoux, *Rose Valland*, 20.

217 STACKING PAINTINGS Valland, *Le front de l'art*, 55.

217 SLAPPED CLOSED Ibid., 56–57.

218 HAD INDICATED Memo from Göring, Document 141-PS, November 5, 1940, Nuremberg Trials, International Military Tribunal, *Nazi Conspiracy and Aggression* ("Red Series"), Vol. III, 188–189.

218 "THE WHOLE QUESTION..." Letter from General von Stülpnagel, January 31, 1941, Document 3766-PS, Nuremberg Trials, International Military Tribunal, *Nazi Conspiracy and Aggression* ("Red Series"), Vol. VI, 652.

218 MADE THEM LEAVE Nicholas, *Rape of Europa*, 132.

220 BAGGAGE CARS CDJC XIII-30, "Report to the Fuehrer," March 20, 1941.

220 "ALL THE PAINTINGS..." Cassou, *Le pillage par les Allemands*, 89.

220 PERHAPS THREE-FOURTHS CDJC XII-51, "Exposé du Ministre Public," 22.

220 SUBSEQUENT ACTIVITY Le Masne de Chermont and Sigal-Klagsbald, *A qui appartenaient ces tableaux ?*, 13.

220 ALL TOLD NA M1782/RG239/P24 and 25, Consolidated Interrogation Report No. 1, August 15, 1945.

222 WATCHMAN'S LOGBOOK Rorimer, *Survival*, 111.

222 OTHER SOURCES OF INFORMATION Valland, *Le front de l'art*, 80–83.

222 GUARDS TOLD HER Ibid., 82.

222 INITIALLY TRANSFERRED The Allies had no way of knowing that in February 1944, the contents of major German depots had been ordered evacuated. NA M1782/RG239/P24, Consolidated Interrogation Report No. 1, August 15, 1945.

222 "NOBODY HERE..." Bouchoux, *Rose Valland*, 39.

223 "DEGENERATE" WORKS Petropoulos, *Art as Politics*, 56.

223 FORBIDDEN TO EXHIBIT Nicholas, *Rape of Europa*, 13.

223 INCLUDING WORKS Valland, *Le front de l'art*, 181.

223 SET IT ABLAZE Note by Rose Valland, AMN R 32.1; Polack and Dagen, *Les Carnets de Rose Valland*, 29.

223 DISAPPEARED Valland, *Le front de l'art*, 178.

## TWENTY-FOUR · FROM HEAVEN AND EARTH

225 RUE MOUFFETARD Biélinky, *Journal 1940-1941*, 85.

225 POUND OF BUTTER Hours, *Une vie au Louvre*, 56.

226 CHESTNUTS AND POTATOES Jackson, *France: The Dark Years*, 250.

226 CONFISCATED Mazauric, *Le Louvre en voyage*, 138.

226 OUT AT DAWN Ibid., 163.

226 RUTABAGAS Pryce-Jones, *Paris in the Third Reich*, 94.

227 CITY'S PERIPHERY Perrault and Azéma, *Paris sous l'Occupation*, 235.

227 LONGCHAMPS RACETRACK Fonkenell and others, *Le Louvre pendant la guerre*, 134.

227 A SMALL POST Zitman, *Souvenirs d'un sapeur-pompier*, 220–221.

228 25,000 TRUCKS "Louis Renault: faits et verités," Supplement au bulletin no. 237, 12 janvier 1995, 13.

228 ALSO KILLED Mitchell, *Nazi Paris*, 58.

228 AS SERIOUS Fonkenell and others, *Le Louvre pendant la guerre*, 134.

228 UNEXPLODED PROJECTILES "Rapport du Chef du Personnel de Gardiennage sur une salve de projectiles, de petit calibre, tirée sur le Musée du Louvre par un avion de nationalité inconnue," 13 juin 1942, AMN T 2A.

228 SHELL CRASHED THROUGH Jacquard Jaujard to Louis Hautecœur, 30 juin 1943, AMN T 2A.

229 TWO FIREMEN "Rapport du Chef du personnel de gardiennage sur la chute d'un avion anglais dans le voisinage du Musée du Louvre," 25 septembre 1943, AMN T 2A.

229 CROWDS PEERED OVER Benoit-Guyod, *L'Invasion de Paris*, 248.

230 HONOR GUARD Hours, *Une vie au Louvre*, 58–59.

244  PROVINCIAL DEPOT  Jacques Jaujard to Louis Hautecœur, 13 janvier 1944, AMN R 1.10.

244  SOLDIERS ARMED  Louis Hautecœur to "la Commission de Protection des oeuvres d'art en France," 23 décembre 1943, AMN R 1.10.

244  UPPED THE ANTE  Jacques Jaujard to the depot heads, 11 décembre 1943, AMN R 1.10.

245  POINTED OUT  Jacques Jaujard to Louis Hautecœur, 13 janvier 1944, AMN R 1.10.

245  BONNARD'S REPRESENTATIVE  "Note au sujet des depots d'oeuvres d'art," 5 janvier 1944, AN F17 13368.

246  FAVORABLY CONSIDERED  Jacques Jaujard, "Note pour la Commission de protection des oeuvres d'art en France, 6 janvier 1944, AMN R 1.10.

247  TWO-POINT PROPOSAL  Jacques Jaujard, "Note pour la Commission de protection des oeuvres d'art en France, 6 janvier 1944, AMN R 1.10.

247  TO INFORM HIM  Jacques Jaujard, "Demande allemande de faire rentrer à Paris les principaux chefs-d'oeuvre des collections nationales," C3, AN 3W 78; note from Jacques Jaujard, 12 janvier 1944, C22, 3W 78.

247  HEADED OVER  Jacques Jaujard to Louis Hautecœur, 14 janvier 1944, AMN R 2B.

247  WORK OF BONNARD  Jacques Jaujard, "Demande allemande de faire rentrer à Paris les principaux chefs-d'oeuvre des collections nationales," C3, AN 3W 78.

247  "ADHERED WITHOUT HESITATION . . ."  Huyghe, *Une vie pour l'art*, 131.

247  WHO WANTED  Louis Hautecœur to Jacques Jaujard, 13 janvier 1944, AMN R 1.10.

248  JAUJARD DESCRIBED  Jacques Jaujard to Louis Hautecœur, 13 janvier 1944, AMN R 1.10.

248  AN ANALYSIS  Jean-Jacques Haffner to Jacques Jaujard, 13 janvier 1944, AMN R 1.10.

249  ARTISTS' ATELIERS  Louis Hautecœur to Abel Bonnard, 14 janvier 1944 AN F17 13368.

249  KUNSTSCHUTZ HAD DISMISSED  Jacques Jaujard to Louis Hautecœur, 3 février 1944, AMN R 2B.

250  CONTINGENCY PLAN  Huyghe, *Une Vie pour l'art*, 123.

250  OBJECTIONS  Jacques Jaujard to Louis Hautecœur, 15 février 1944, C32, AN 3W 78.

250  AGAIN PUSHING  Jacques Jaujard to Louis Hautecœur, 15 février 1944, C32, AN 3W 78.

251  BUNJES TRIED  Note signée JJ pour A. Bonnard, 15 mars 1944, 15h 30. AN 3W 78, C 135.

251  QUANTITY OF TRUCKS  "Note pour Monsieur le Ministre," 27 mars 1944, AN F17 13368.

251  FOLLOWED UP  "Réunion exceptionnelle des conservateurs, Chefs du Département et de Musée," 16 juin 1944, AMN *1BB.

251 HELD IN RESERVE Jacques Jaujard, "Demande allemande de faire rentrer à Paris les principaux chefs-d'oeuvre des collections nationales," C3, AN 3W 78.

251 "THE HIGH STANDARDS..." Jacques Jaujard to Georges Hilaire, 10 mai 1944, AMN R 1.10.

## TWENTY-SEVEN · ROUGH ROAD TOWARD FREEDOM

253 OLD ONES Mazauric, *Le Louvre en voyage*, 13.

253 NO LONGER AVAILABLE Germain Bazin to Jacques Jaujard, 8 mars 1944, AMN R 30 Sourches.

254 "IN THE EVENT..." Abel Bonnard, "Instructions sur les devoirs des Administrations et Services Publics dans l'hypothèse d'operations militaires," 31 mars 1944, AMN R 1.10.

254 SHATTERED WINDOWS Pierre Schommer to Jacques Jaujard, 11 avril 1944 AMN R 30 Chambord.

254 AT 2:20 A.M. "Journal, 1er juin 1944–16 mars 1945," 4 juin 1944, R 30 Montal.

256 BOMBS FELL Depot head Strasse to Jacques Jaujard, 27 juin 1944, AMN R 30 Courtalain.

256 CUBIC FEET Domaine national de Chambord, *Otages de guerre*, 25.

256 AREA BOMBINGS CONTINUED Handwritten note, Pierre Schommer to Jacques Jaujard, AMN R 30 Chambord, 12 juin 1944.

256 STAY ABOARD Boissonneau. "Le bombardier abattu avait épargné les trésors," *Nouvelle République du Centre-Ouest*, août 2009, 4.

257 METAL SHOT Domaine national de Chambord, *Otages de guerre*, 54–55.

257 AT THE LAST SECOND "Lessons abound in WWII bombers," *Contra Costa Times*, May 26, 2008.

258 BOMBS WERE LANDING Germain Bazin to Jacques Jaujard, 23 juin 1944, AMN R 30 Sourches.

258 INDIVIDUAL COMPARTMENTS German Bazin to Jacques Jaujard, 26 juin 1944, AMN R 30 Sourches.

258 THE NEXT DAY Jacques Jaujard to Louis Hautecœur, 16 juin 1944, (Following protocol, Jaujard replied to Louis Hautecœur, his immediate superior, knowing that the messages would be passed on to Bonnard), AMN R 1.10.

259 EMERGENCY MEETING "Réunion exceptionnelle des conservateurs, Chefs de Département et de Musée," 16 juin 1944, AMN *1 BB.

259 EXCHANGE NEGOTIATIONS Dorléac, *Art of the Defeat*, 29.

259 SPECIFIC LEGISLATION Karlsgodt, *Defending National Treasures*, 253.

260 ALL WAS WELL Germain Bazin to the mayor of Bayeux, 8 novembre 1943," AMN R 30 Sourches.

260 SS LIEUTENANT Petropoulos, *Faustian Bargain*, 211.

260 GROUP'S INTENT Valland, *Le front de l'art*, 151.

260 ORDERING HIM Telegram from Dr. Tieschowitz, June 18, 1944, AN AJ 473.

260 BYPASSED JAUJARD "Protocol," July 5, 1944; AN AJ 40 573; Response to von Tieschowitz, 23 juin 1944, AN AJ 40 573.

261 BAZIN SAID Germain Bazin to Jacques Jaujard, 23 juin 1944, AMN R 30 Sourches.

262 JUST BEFORE 1 A.M. Germain Bazin to Jacques Jaujard, 27 juin 1944, AMN R 30 Sourches.

262 SS TROOPS Telegram from Dr. Tieschowitz, June 18, 1944, AN AJ 473.

262 FOR FEAR Bazin, *Souvenirs*, 107.

262 UNTIL NOON Dubosq, *La Tapisserie de Bayeux*, 71.

262 SCALDING LETTER Germain Bazin to Jacques Jaujard, 29 juin 1944, AMN R 30 Sourches.

263 SEVEN WITNESSES Dubosq, *La Tapisserie de Bayeux*, 72.

## TWENTY-EIGHT · INSURRECTION

265 UNTIL 10:30 P.M. Dansette, *Histoire de la libération de Paris*, 74.

265 HALF-HOUR Perrault and Azéma, *Paris sous l'Occupation*, 318.

265 HARDLY USABLE Dansette, *Histoire de la libération de Paris*, 74.

265 "WHAT GOOD..." Mitchell, *Nazi Paris*, 64.

265 MALNOURISHED BABIES Ibid., 119–120.

266 "IN A CRISIS..." "The Day Paris was Liberated," Larry Collins and Dominique Lapierre, *New York Times*, August 23, 1964, SM23.

266 EATING PIGEONS Hotchner, *Papa Hemingway*, 45.

266 URBAN WARFARE Neiberg, *Blood of Free Men*, 66.

266 WOULD DIVERT Ibid., 58.

267 EMERGENCY SESSION "Comité des Conservateurs, Séance exceptionelle du 14 juin 1944," AMN *1BB.

267 OBTAINED AN ADVANCE Procès-verbal de la séance du Conseil d'administration de la Société des Amis du Louvre, 30 juin 1944, SAL.

267 100,000 PEOPLE Tartakowsky, *Les manifestations de rue en France*, 490.

268 RAIL REPAIR WORKERS Ibid., 492.

268 IT WAS THE PARIS POLICE Rudolph, *Au coeur de la Préfecture de Police: de la Résistance à la Libération*, 1e partie, 11.

268 NEVER QUESTIONING Collins and Lapierre, *Is Paris Burning?*, 24.

268 STILL TRUST Neiberg, *Blood of Free Men*, 85.

268 A MADMAN Aron, *France Reborn*, 237.

269 RECEIVED ORDERS Collins and Lapierre, *Is Paris Burning?*, 63.

269 BEFORE AUGUST 15 WAS OVER Valland, *Le front de l'art*, 152.

269 GERMAN WORKERS HAD BROUGHT Polack and Dagen, *Les Carnets de Rose Valland*, 99.

269 BOUCHOT-SAUPIQUE Valland, *Le front de l'art*, 209.

270 SO MUCH FOOD Desroches Noblecourt, "Un très grand directeur: Jacques Jaujard," *Pillages et Restitutions*, 28.

270 "WE MAY HAVE..." Desroches Noblecourt, "Le Musée du Louvre pendant la liberation de Paris," Thézy and Gunther, *Images de la Libération de Paris*, 143.

270 WATCHTOWER Ibid., 204.

271 WITNESSED VOLLEYS Ibid., 202.

271 DESROCHES NOBLECOURT ARRIVED    Desroches Noblecourt, "Le Musée du Louvre pendant la liberation de Paris," Thézy and Gunther, *Images de la Libération de Paris*, 143.

271 MOVE ABOUT THE BUILDING    Desroches Noblecourt, "Un très grand directeur: Jacques Jaujard," *Pillages et Restitutions*, 28.

272 "ECHO PHENOMENA..."    Jacques Jaujard, "Note relative aux recherches faites dans le Musée du Louvre au cours des journées allant du samedi 19 août jusqu'au samedi 2 septembre," 4 septembre 1944, AMN T 2A.

272 SNIPERS ON THE ROOF    "Procès-verbal de la Réunion tenue le 13 février 1940 à la Direction des Musées Nationaux," AMN R 1.1.

273 CODED MESSAGE    Hicks, *Bayeux Tapestry*, 322, footnote 8.

273 SENT WORD    Ibid., 239.

273 "WHAT LUCK..."    Choltitz, "Pourquoi, en 1944, je n'ai pas détruit Paris," *Le Figaro*, 12 octobre 1949, 5.

274 HE WOULD RADIO    Collins and Lapierre, *Is Paris Burning?*, 205.

274 WARNING OF A POSSIBLE REPEAT    Smith, *Eisenhower in War and Peace*, 387.

274 ASKED GENERAL PATTON    Blumenson, *Breakout and Pursuit*, 600.

274 "I TOLD HIM..."    Blumenson, *Patton Papers: 1940–1945*, 511.

275 STOPPED REPORTING    Neiberg, *Blood of Free Men*, 100.

275 ACT ON HIS OWN    Even, (Capitaine), "La 2e D.B. de son Débarquement en Normandie a la Libération de Paris," *Revue historique des armées*,114-116; Blumenson, *Breakout and Pursuit*, 601

275 WAS ORDERED TO BRING    Capitaine Even (Capitaine), "la 2e D.B. de son débarquement en Normandie à la Libération de Paris," *Revue historique des armées*, 116.

275 "TWENTY-FOUR..."    Collins and Lapierre, *Is Paris Burning?*, 194.

275 "WELL, WHAT THE HELL..."    Ibid., 200.

275 AT 7:15 P.M.    Ehrlich, *French Resistance*, 244.

275 "GRIBIUS..."    Blumenson, *Breakout and Pursuit*, 605.

## TWENTY-NINE · RETREAT AND RETRIBUTION

278 BRIEF EXCHANGE    Journal du bord, 8 juin 1944, AMN R 30 Montal; René Huyghe to Jacques Jaujard, 17 juillet 1944, AMN R 30 Montal.

279 ONLY DAMAGE    Hans Haug to Jacques Jaujard, septembre 1944, AMN R 30 Cheverny.

279 EXPLOSIVE TENSION    Ferrand, *Gérald Van der Kemp*, 55.

279 REGIMENT ASSEMBLED    Gérald Van der Kemp to Jacques Jaujard, 11 septembre 1944, AMN R 30 Valençay.

280 ANOTHER SKIRMISH    Ibid.

280 SET FIRE    Ibid.

280 KEPT HIDDEN    Ferrand, *Gérald Van der Kemp*, 54.

280 DODGING BULLETS    Ibid., 56.

281 SETTING FIRE    Dallot, *L'Indre sous l'occupation allemande*, 77.

281 WENT IN SEARCH "Tragédie du 16 août 1944: hommage aux religieuses, *Nouvelle République du Centre-Ouest*, 20 août 2012.

281 DUE TO RUMORS Ferrand, *Gérald Van der Kemp*, 56–57.

281 NO PRISON Cornioley and Larroque, *Pauline*, 85.

281 EMPLOYEES CROUCHED Groussin, *La Résistance dans le canton de Valençay* 357, interview with André Beau, January 16, 2001, 357.

281 HABERDASHERY Ferrand, *Gérald Van der Kemp*, 58.

282 FACE DOWN Ferrand, *Gérald Van der Kemp*, 57.

282 OFFICERS ACCUSED Gérald Van der Kemp to Jacques Jaujard, 11 septembre 1944," AMN R 30 Valençay.

282 COWHAND Hervé Larroque interview with Jean Morel, December 2012.

282 "REVEAL TO THE ENTIRE WORLD. . ." Ferrand, *Gérald Van der Kemp*, 58.

282 THERE TO MAKE WAR Vilallonga, *Gold Gotha*, 223.

282 DIE WITH HIM Ferrand, *Gérald Van der Kemp*, 61.

282 FRENCH FLAG Groussin, *La Résistance dans le canton de Valençay*, interview with André Beau, January 16, 2001, 357–358.

282 PARACHUTE FABRIC Ferrand, *Gérald Van der Kemp*, 61.

283 IF THEY BURNED Vilallonga, *Gold Gotha*, 23.

283 GERMANS RELEASED Gérald Van der Kemp to Jacques Jaujard, 11 septembre 1944, AMN R 30 Valençay; Charbonneaux, "Le Musée du Louvre pendant la Guerre," discours prononcé à l'Assemblée Générale annuelle da la Société des Amis du Louvre, 25 juin 1946, 15.

283 FRONT DOOR Charbonneaux, "Le Musée du Louvre pendant la Guerre," discours prononcé à l'Assemblée Générale annuelle da la Société des Amis du Louvre, 25 juin 1946, 15.

283 JUMPED OVER A WALL Leroi-Gourhan, *Racines du Monde*, 113.

283 ARMS AND LEGS Vilallonga, *Gold Gotha*, 223.

283 EVENTS AT CHAMBORD Pierre Schommer to "Monsieur Michaux à la Commission des Crimes de Guerre," 5 septembre 1945, AMN R 30 Chambord; P. Robert-Houdin, "Rapport sur les évenements qui se sont déroulés à Chambord le lundi 21 et le mardi 22 août 1944, 6 septembre 1944, AMN R 30 Chambord; Domaine national de Chambord, *Otages de guerre*, 50–52.

284 GERMAN TROOPS Boitel, *Les Français qui ont fait la France*, 876.

286 GERMAN OFFICER Bazin, *Souvenirs*, 125.

## THIRTY · LIBERATION

287 ARMORED DIVISION Ehrlich, *French Resistance*, 249.

287 HALF HOUR LATER Ibid., 245.

287 BBC BEGAN Neiberg, *Blood of Free Men*, 205.

287 HAD HOISTED Ehrlich, *French Resistance*, 216.

287 FORBADE ITS DISPLAY Ousby, *Occupation*, 114; *Des loges aux Eloges*, 22.

287 CONVINCED THEM Valland, *Le front de l'art*, 202.

289 DREW ENEMY FIRE Zitman, *Souvenirs d'un sapeur-pompier*, 256–257. Zitman's recollection of the date the Préfecture was occupied is incorrect.

289  FAILING RADIO  Desroches Noblecourt, "Le Musée du Louvre pendant la liberation de Paris," in Thézy and Gunther, *Images de la Libération de Paris*, 143.

289  GRAY DAWN  Charbonneaux, "Le Musée du Louvre pendant la Guerre," discours prononcé à l'Assemblée Générale annuelle da la Société des Amis du Louvre, 25 juin 1946, 16.

289  FLAG RISE  Desroches Noblecourt, "Un très grand directeur: Jacques Jaujard," *Pillages et Restitutions*, 28.

289  NEVER FORGET  Charbonneaux, "Le Musée du Louvre pendant la Guerre," discours prononcé à l'Assemblée Générale annuelle da la Société des Amis du Louvre, 25 juin 1946, 16.

289  FAMOUS ORDER  Blumenson, *Breakout and Pursuit*, 598.

289  CROOKED ROADS  Ibid., 613.

290  THAT SAME DAY  Collins and Lapierre, *Is Paris Burning?*, 296.

290  PAUL SCHAEFFER  Dansette, *Histoire de la libération de Paris*, 272.

290  IN CELEBRATION  Dronne, *La libération de Paris*, 286.

290  ILLUMINATED WINDOWS  Ibid., 285.

290  "IT WOULD BE BEST . . ."  Dansette, *Histoire de la libération de Paris*, 274–275.

290  "I HAVE JUST HEARD . . ."  Collins and Lapierre, *Is Paris Burning?*, 259.

291  THROUGH THE ARCHWAYS  Aury, *La Délivrance*, 30.

291  COMMAND CAR  Valland, *Le front de l'art*, 209.

291  FFI MEMBER  Dansette, *Histoire de la libération de Paris*, 331.

291  GERMANS FIRED  Valland, *Le front de l'art*, 206.

291  SHELL EXPLODED  Ibid., 208.

291  "MAINTENANT . . ."  Churchill, *Triumph and Tragedy: The Second World War*, Vol. 6, 35.

292  SMALL POCKETS  Aury, *La Délivrance*, 29.

292  PILED ON TOP  "House-Top Search for Snipers," *Manchester Guardian*, August 28, 1944, 5.

292  SARTRE  Beevor and Cooper, *Paris After the Liberation*, 55.

293  FORCED TO SHOW  Valland, *Le front de l'art*, 207.

293  OVER SIX HUNDRED  Bazin, *Souvenirs*, 115.

294  FRANTIC PRISONER  "Louvre Exhibit Ruined," *New York Times*, August 29, 1944, 3.

294  SEVERAL OTHERS  Desroches Noblecourt, "Le Musée du Louvre pendant la liberation de Paris," in Thézy and Gunther, *Images de la Libération de Paris*, 143; Desroches Noblecourt in *Pillages et Restitutions*, 28.

295  GUN BARREL  Charbonneaux, "Le Musée du Louvre pendant la Guerre," discours prononcé à l'Assemblée Générale annuelle da la Société des Amis du Louvre, 25 juin 1946, 16.

295  HANDED BACK  Report by Robert Rey, 18 septembre 1944, AMN R 15.1; Jacques Jaujard to Georges Hilaire, N.D., AMN Z 2 (1939–1945).

## THIRTY-ONE · LAST ECHOES OF WAR

301  UNSTABLE  André Leroi-Gourhan to Jacques Jaujard, 11 septembre 1944, AMN R 30 Valençay.

301 FINALLY AGREED  Gérard Van der Kemp to Jacques Jaujard, 11 septembre 1944, AMN R 30 Valençay; André Leroi-Gourhan to Jacques Jaujard, 11 septembre 1944, AMN R 30 Valençay.

301 FINANCIAL RECORDS  Courtesy of Hervé Larroque, conversation with G. Ravineau, 2013.

301 RAILWAY LINES  Foot, *SOE in France*, 342.

301 LARGE BOUNTY  Mockers, *Maquis S.S.*, 16; Cornioley, Larroque and Atwood, *Code Name Pauline*, 81, 167–168.

301 BEDROOM SO BIG  Ibid., p. 84.

301 "I'LL SHOW YOU..."  Cornioley, Larroque and Atwood, *Code Name Pauline*, 98.

302 "THIS IS THE LAST TIME..."  Ibid., 61–62.

302 "THE DUKE HIMSELF..."  Ferrand, *Gérald Van der Kemp*, 61.

303 FOLLOWING YEAR  Vilallonga, *Gold Gotha*, 223.

303 "YOU PUT ALL YOUR ARTWORK..."  Bazin, *Souvenirs*, 113.

303 HUMIDITY CONDITIONS  Rorimer, *Survival*, 44.

303 BY SEPTEMBER  "Le Chef du Dépot de Valençay à Monsieur le Chef du Dépot," 23 septembre 1944, AMN R 30 Valençay.

304 LOUVRE REOPENED  "Communiqué, Réouverture du Musée du Louvre," 3 octobre 1944, AMN Z 1 (1944).

304 WINTER HUMIDITY  "Louvre Treasures Will Remain Away," *New York Times*, July 3, 1945, 15.

304 NATIONAL HERO  A number of newspaper articles are archived in AMN O 30 Jaujard.

306 CEREMONY  Aulanier, *Le Nouveau Louvre de Napoléon III*, 31.

306 WANTED TO RETRIEVE  Hicks, *Bayeux Tapestry*, 242.

306 MAYOR AGREED  Dubosq, *La Tapisserie de Bayeux*, 76–77.

306 NOVEMBER 10  Aulanier, *Le Nouveau Louvre de Napoléon III*, 44.

306 EXHIBITION WAS EXTENDED  Letter from Georges Salles to J. Verrier, 14 décembre 1944, AMN AA 1944 (octobre, novembre, décembre); Aulanier, *Le Nouveau Louvre de Napoléon III*, 44.

306 BLAST DAMAGE  "Journal, 26 December to 28 December 1944," Headquarters, Paris Civil Affairs Detachments, NA RG498, File 494E.

## THIRTY-TWO · COMING HOME

309 GIRONDE RIVER  Kyte, "War Damage and Problems of Reconstruction in France, 1940–1945," *Pacific Historical Review*, 420–422.

310 CURATORS COMMITTEE  "Comité des conservateurs, Séance du 7 juin 1945," AMN *1 BB.

311 SEATED SCRIBE  "Bordereau des caisses sorti du dépôt," AMN R 30 La Treyne.

311 IN SEPTEMBER  "Le Conservateur du Département des Antiquités egyptiennes à M. Schommer, Conservateur, adjoint au Directeur des Musées de France," 18 septembre 1945, AMN R 30 La Treyne.

311 CIVIL AND MILITARY AUTHORITIES "Ordre de mission," 11 juin 1945, AMN R 30 Montal.

311 MOTORCYCLE ESCORT Vilallonga, *Gold Gotha*, 223.

311 ENORMOUS TRUCK Bernard-Legentil, "La Victoire de Samothrace' a regagné le Louvre," Musée, n.d., AMN Z 20; Georges Salles to Colonel Mac-Donnell, 18 juin 1945, AMN Z 20.

311 ON JUNE 16 "Reçu de Monsieur Tranchant," 16 juin 1945, AMN R 30 Sourches.

312 WAS WITNESSED Mazauric, *Le Louvre en voyage*, 207–208.

314 TWO HOURS O'Reilly, "Grecian Girl Who Lost Her Head So Long Ago Is Hoisted to Her Pre-War Place After Hiding Out from Germans in Valencay [sic] Castle, *New York Herald Tribune*, June 22, 1945.

314 HEARD NOISE Courtesy of Hervé Larroque interview with Jean Morel, December 2012.

314 SPECIAL EXHIBITION Schmidt, "Louvre Has Exhibit of 83 Old Masters," *New York Times*, July 10, 1945, 13.

314 TEMPORARY EXHIBITION Fonkenell and others, *Le Louvre pendant la guerre*, 139, 149.

314 BY OFFICIAL DECREE "Le Directeur des Musées de France à Monsieur le Directeur générale des Arts et des lettres, Objet I) Reclassement des fonctionnaires réintegrés," n.d., AMN R 20.5.1.

316 TRAVELED TO GERMANY NA M1946/260/0077, "Weekly Monuments, Fine Arts, and Archives Report," December 26, 1945.

316 SPECIAL EXHIBITION "Comité des conservateurs, Séance du 2 octobre 1945," AMN *1BB 50.

316 BRITISH OFFICER Beevor and Cooper, *Paris After the Liberation*, 190.

316 TRUCK LEFT MONTAL "Convoi du 7 février 1946," AMN R 30 Montal.

316 SIX DAYS LATER "Convoi du 13 février 1946," AMN R 30 Montal.

316 RETURNED TO THE LOUVRE Guillot de Suduiraut, *Gregor Erhart: Sainte Marie-Madeleine*, 23 and 54.

317 IN MID-MARCH "Caisse LD 0," AMN R 20.6.1.

317 APRIL 13 Information courtesy of Denis Grandemenge, Régisseur des Collections, château de Chambord, July 1, 2013.

317 EXHIBITION DISPLAYED Aulanier and Chamson, *Chefs-d'oeuvre de la peinture française du Louvre*, 7–8, 41, 90, 103, 155.

318 SHE AND CHAMSON WATCHED Mazauric, *Le Louvre en voyage*, 213.

318 ITINERARY INDICATED "Itineraire," n.d., AMN R 30 Sourches.

318 ONLY EVIDENCE "Reçu de Monsieur Trachet, Chef du Dépôt," 9 juillet 1946," AMN R 30 Sourches.

318 PLACEMENT OF VELVET "Throng at Gallery as Louvre Reopens," *New York Times*, October 8, 1947, 29.

318 JAUJARD "HAD FOUGHT..." Rorimer, *Survival*, 50.

319 "TO SAVE A LITTLE ..." Valland, *Le Front de l'Art*, epigraph.

# SOURCES

## ARCHIVES

Archives des Musées Nationaux, Paris
Archives nationales de France, Pierrefitte-sur-Seine
Centre de documentation juive contemporaine, Paris
Ministère des affaires etrangères, La Corneuve
National Archives, Washington, D.C.

## INTERVIEWS AND CORRESPONDENCE

Yvonne Bell-Gambart
Guillaume Fonkenell
Denis Grandemenge
Frédérique Hébrard
Hervé Larroque
Elisabeth Rey
Catherine Velle

## ARTICLES, SPEECHES, MONOGRAPHS, THESES

Aubrun, Emilie. "L'action de Jacques Jaujard à la Direction des Musées Nationaux de 1939 à 1944." Master's thesis, Université de Versailles-Saint-Quentin-en-Yvelines, 2003.

Boissonneau, Jean-Louis. "Le bombardier abattu avait épargné les trésors," *Nouvelle République du Centre-Ouest*, 23 août 2009.

Charbonneaux, Jean. "Le Musée du Louvre pendant la Guerre," discours prononcé à l'Assemblée Générale annuelle da la Société des Amis du Louvre, 25 juin 1946.

Chamson, André. "Dans la familiarité des chefs-d'œuvres," *Jardín des Arts*, No. 128–129, juillet–août 1965: 3–7.

Chamson, André. "In Memoriam Jacques Jaujard," *Musées et Collections Publiques en France,* No. 100 (1967), 151-153.

Choltitz, Dietrich von. "Pourquoi, en 1944, je n'ai pas détruit Paris," *Le Fígaro*, 12 octobre 1949.

Chennevières, Henry de. "La France méconnue: M. de Tauzia," *Nouvelle Revue*, Tome 60 (1889): 323–343.

Collins, Larry and Dominique Lapierre. "The Day Paris was Liberated," *New York Times*, August 23, 1964.

*Contra Costa Times*. "Lessons abound in WWII bombers," May 26, 2008.

Coulon, Gérard. "La Vénus de Milo, la Victoire de Samothrace ... Des hôtes de marque au Château de Valençay pendant la Seconde guerre mondiale," *Musées et collections publiques de France*, No. 210, (mars 1996), 11–13.

Darcel, Alfred. "Les Musées, les arts et les artistes pendant le siège de Paris." *Gazette des Beaux-Arts*, Vol. 4 (1870): 285–306.

Desvaux, Virgile-Hippolyte. "Les Seigneurs de Courtalain," *Bulletin de la Société Dunoise d'Archéologie, Histoire, Sciences et Arts* , Tome IV (1885), 110–126.

Du Camp, Maxime. "Les Tuileries et le Louvre Pendant la Commune – II," *Revue des Deux Mondes*, Vol. 29 (1878): 127–151.

Even, Capitaine. "la 2e D.B. de son débarquement en Normandie à la Libération de Paris," *Revue historique de l'armée*, No. 1, 1952: 107–132.

Kümmel, Otto. "Bericht auf Erlaß des Herrn Reichsministers und Chefs der Reichskanzlei RK 118 II A vom 19. August 1940 und auf Erlaß des Herrn Reichsministers für Volksaufklärung und Propaganda BK 9900 - 02/13.8.40/89 - 1/6 vom 20. August 1940."

Huyghe, René. "Le Musée du Louvre dans le Lot," *Les Etoíles du Quercy*, No. 3 (1944).

Kyte, George W. "War Damage and Problems of Reconstruction in France, 1940-1945," *Pacific History Review*, Vol. 15, No. 4 (Dec., 1946), pp. 417–426.

Ladreit de Lacharriere, Marc. *Hommage à Gérald Van der Kemp* (1912-2001). Discours prononcé le 25 janvier 2006, Académie des Beaux-Arts. Paris: Palais de l'Institut, 2006.

Lambauer, Barbara. "Francophile contre vents et marée ? Otto Abetz et les Français, 1930–1958," *Bulletin du Centre de Recherche Français à Jérusalem* 18 (2007): 153–160.

*Le Matin*. "Une cérémonie a préludé à la réouverture de plusieurs salles du Louvre," 30 septembre 1940.

*Living Age*. "Reopening the Louvre," Volume 300, No. 3894, February 22, 1919.

"Louis Renault: faits et verities. La nationalisation des usines Renault, Une nécessité de l'Histoire." Supplement au bulletin no. 237, 12 janvier 1995. Conseil National de la F.T.M. C.G.T., 1995.

Martin-Demézil, Jean. "Diane de Poitiers à Cheverny," *Bibliothèque d'Humanisme et Renaissance*, T. 17, No. 2 (1955): 278–283.

Munduteguy, A.-M. "Courtalain: un château du XVIe siècle restauré au XIXe siècle," *Bulletin de la Société Dunoise d'Archéologie, Histoire, Sciences et Arts*, Tome XX (1993), 5–29.

*New York Times*. "Italians Ask France to Give Up 'Mona Lisa,'" July 16, 1940.

————. "Louvre Exhibit Ruined," August 29, 1944.

————. "Louvre Treasures Will Remain Away," July 3, 1945.

————. "'Mona Lisa' Under Glass," October 13, 1907.

————. "'Mona Lisa' in France," December 31, 1913.

————. "Throng at Gallery as Louvre Reopens," October 8, 1947.

*Manchester Guardian*. "House-Top Search for Snipers," August 28, 1944.

Nicault, Maurice. "Quand Valençay abritait la Vénus de Milo," *Revue Berry*, No. 5 (1988): 2–7.

*Nouvelle République du Centre-Ouest*. "Tragédie du 16 août 1944: hommage aux religieuses," 20 août 2012.

O'Reilly, John. "Grecian Girl Who Lost Her Head So Long Ago Is Hoisted to Her Pre-War Place After Hiding Out from Germans in Valencay [sic] Castle, *New York Herald Tribune*, June 22, 1945.

*Paris-Midi*. "Les chefs-d'œuvre du Louvre ont pu déménager sans encombre," 30 novembre 1939.

Pottier, Edmond. *Le Musée du Louvre pendant la guerre 1914–1918. Notice lue a l'assemblée générale annuelle de la Société des Amis du Louvre le 5 février 1919*. Paris: Imprimerie générale Lahure, 1919.

Rudolph, Luc, coord. *Au cœur de la Préfecture de Police: de la Résistance à la Libération*, 1e Partie, Les Proto Résistants du Coq Gaulois/La Direction des Services Techniques/Les Sapeurs-Pompiers de Paris. Paris, 2009.

Spielmann, M.H., "Picture Thefts," *Times* (London), August 30, 1911.

Schmidt, Dana Adams. "Louvre Has Exhibit of 83 Old Masters," *New York Times*, July 10, 1945.

*Time*. "Painters' War," September 11, 1939, Vol. 34, No. 11.

Ussel, Philibert. "Barbet de Jouy, Son journal pendant la Commune," *Revue hebdomadaire*, X (1898).

Varennes, Françoise de. *Un bienfaiteur de la culture: Jacques Jaujard*. Discours le 29 février 1984, Académie des Beaux-Arts. Paris: Institut de France, 1984.

## BOOKS

Abetz, Otto. *Das Offene Problem: ein Rückblick auf zwei Jahrzehnte deutscher Frankreichpolitik.* Cologne: Greven Verlag, 1951.

Aron, Robert. *France Reborn: The History of the Liberation, June 1944–May 1945,* trans. Humphrey Hare. New York: C. Scribner's Sons, 1964.

Aulanier, Christiane. *Le Nouveau Louvre de Napoléon III.* Vol. 4, *Histoire du Palais et du Musée du Louvre.* Paris: Editions des Musées Nationaux, 1953.

Aulanier, Christiane and André Chamson. *Chefs-d'œuvre de la peinture française du Louvre: des primitifs à Manet.* Paris: Editions des Musées Nationaux, 1946.

Aury, Bernard. *La délivrance de Paris, 19–26 août 1944.* Paris: Arthaud, 1945.

Bailly, Nicolas. *Inventaire des tableaux du roy, rédigé en 1709 et 1710,* Ed. Fernand Engerand. Paris: E. Leroux, 1899.

Bargatzky, Walter. *Hotel Majestic: Ein Deutscher im besetzten Frankreich.* Freiburg: Herder, 1987.

Bazin, Germain. *Souvenirs de l'exode du Louvre: 1940–1945.* Paris: Somogny, 1992.

Beevor, Antony and Artemis Cooper. *Paris After the Liberation, 1944–1949,* New York: Penguin Books, 1994.

Benoit-Guyod, Georges. *L'Invasion de Paris: 1940–1944, Choses vues sous l'occupation,* Paris: Editions du Scorpion, 1962.

Biélinky, Jacques. *Journal 1940–1941: Un journaliste juif à Paris sous L'Occupation,* Paris: Les Editions du Cerf, 1992.

Bizardel, Yvon. *Sous l'occupation: Souvenirs d'un conservateur de Musée (1940–1944).* Paris: Calmann-Lévy, 1964.

Blancher-Le Bourhis, Magdeleine. *Le château de Cheverny.* Paris, H. Laurens, 1950.

Blumenson, Martin. *Breakout and Pursuit.* Washington, D.C.: U.S. Army Department of Military History, 1961.

————. *The Patton Papers:* 1940–1945. Boston: Houghton Mifflin, 1974.

Boitel, Philippe. *Les Français qui ont fait la France.* Editions Sud Ouest, 2009.

Bouchoux, Corinne. *Rose Valland, résistance au Musée.* La Créche: Geste, 2006.

Bouisset, F. Felix. *Le Musée Ingres: historique, une visite au Musée, la salle du prince noir.* Montauban: Edition du Musée, 1926.

Boursier, Jean-Yves. *Résistants et Résistance.* Paris: L'Harmattan, 1997.

Bradbury, Jim. *Philip Augustus: King of France 1180–1223.* London: Longman Books, 1998.

Breker, Arno. *Paris, Hitler et Moi.* Paris: Presses de la Cité, 1970.

Bresc-Bautier, Geneviève and Anne Pingeot. *Sculptures des jardins du Louvre, du Carrousel et des Tuileries.* Paris: Editions de la Réunion des Musées Nationaux, 1986.

Bridgeford, Andrew. *1066: The Hidden History of the Bayeux Tapestry*. London: Fourth Estate, 2005.

Brown, Shirley Ann. *The Bayeux Tapestry: History and Bibliography*. Wolfeboro, New Hampshire: Boydell Press, 1988.

Callu, Agnès, *La Réunion des Musées Nationaux 1870–1940: Genèse et Fonctionnement*. Paris: École des Chartes, 1994.

Carcopino, Jérôme. *Souvenirs de sept ans: 1937–1944*. Paris: Flammarion, 1953.

Carmona, Michel. *Le Louvre et les Tuileries: huit siècles d'histoire*. Paris: Editions de La Martinière, 2004.

Cassou, Jean, ed. *Le pillage par les Allemands des œuvres d'art et des bibliothèques appartenant à des Juifs en France: Recueil de documents*. Paris: Editions du Centre, 1947.

Cellier-Gelly, Micheline. *André Chamson (1900–1983)*. Paris: Perrin, 2001.

Chapron, Louis-Ferdinand. *Courtalain: châteaux et seigneurs*. Chartres: Abbé Métais, 1901.

Chennevières, Philippe de. *Souvenirs d'un directeur des beaux-arts*, Première Partie, Paris: Bureaux de l'Artiste, 1883.

Churchill, Winston. *The Gathering Storm: The Second World War*, Vol. 1. Boston: Houghton Mifflin, 1948.

——. *Triumph and Tragedy: The Second World War*, Vol. 6. Boston: Houghton Mifflin, 1953.

Clarac, Charles. *Description historique et graphique du Louvre et des Tuileries*. Paris: Imprimerie Impériale, 1853.

Clément, Pierre. *Lettres, Instructions et Mémoires de Colbert*, Tome V, Paris: Imprimerie Impériale, 1868.

Cocteau, Jean. *Journal, 1942–1945*. Edited by Jean Touzot. Paris: Gallimard, 1989.

Cohan, William D. *The Last Tycoons: The Secret History of Lazard Frères & Co.* New York: Random House, 2007.

*Collection Carle Dreyfus léguée aux Musées Nationaux et au Musée des arts décoratifs: exposition au Cabinet des dessins du Musée du Louvre, avril–mai 1953*. Paris: Editions des Musées Nationaux, 1953.

Collins, Larry and Dominique Lapierre. *Is Paris Burning?* New York: Warner Books, 1965.

Commission de Publication des Documents Diplomatiques Français. *Documents diplomatiques français: 1940, les armistices de juin 1940*. Brussels: P.I.E.-Lang, 2003.

Cornioley, Pearl Witherington, and Hervé Larroque. *Pauline: Parachutée en 1943, la vie d'une agent du SOE*, 4th ed. Clermont-Ferrand: Editions par exemple, 2010.

Cornioley, Pearl Witherington, and Hervé Larroque. *Code Name Pauline: Memoirs of a World War II Special Agent.* Ed. Kathryn J. Atwood. Chicago: Chicago Review Press, 2013.

Crémieux-Brilhac, Jean-Louis. *La France libre: de l'appel du 18 juin à la Libération,* Paris: Gallimard, 1996.

Curtis, Michael. *Verdict on Vichy: Power and Prejudice in the Vichy France Regime.* New York: Arcade Publishing, 2002.

Dallot, Sébastien. *L'Indre sous l'occupation allemande (1940–1944): Les Allemands dans le department de l'Indre.* Clermont-Ferrand: De Borée, 2001.

Dalloz, Pierre. *Verités sur le Drame du Vercors.* Paris: Lanore, 1979.

Dalton, Hugh. *The Fateful Years: Memoirs, 1931–1945.* London: Muller, 1957.

Dansette, Adrien. *Histoire de la libération de Paris.* Paris: Perrin, 1994.

Desroches Noblecourt, Christiane. *Sous le regard des dieux.* Paris: Albin Michel, 2003.

————. "Le Musée du Louvre pendant la libération de Paris," in *Images de la Libération de Paris.* Ed. Marie Thézy and Thomas Gunther. Paris: Paris-Musées, 1994.

————."Un très grand directeur: Jacques Jaujard," in *Pillages et Restitutions, le destin des œuvres d'art sorties de France pendant la Seconde Guerre mondiale,* 23–39. Ed. Françoise Cachin. Paris: Editions Adam Biro, 1997.

Devals, Jean-Ursule. *Histoire de Montauban sous la Domination Anglaise.* Montauban: Forestié, 1843.

Domaine national de Chambord. *Otages de guerre: Chambord 1939-1945.* Versailles: Editions Artlys, 2009.

Dorléac, Laurence Bertrand. *Art of the Defeat: France 1940–1944.* Trans. Jane Marie Todd. Los Angeles: Getty Research Institute, 2008.

———— . *Histoire de l'art: Paris 1940–44.* Paris: Publications de la Sorbonne, 1986.

Dronne, Raymond. *La libération de Paris.* Paris: Presses de la Cité, 1970.

Dubosq, René. *La Tapisserie de Bayeux, dite de la Reine Mathilde: Dix ans tragiques de sa longue histoire.* Caen: Ozanne, 1951.

Ehrlich, Blake. *The French Resistance: 1940–1945.* London: Chapman and Hall, 1996.

Eychart, François and Georges Aillaud, eds. *Les Lettres françaises et Les Etoiles dans la clandestinité, 1942–1944.* Paris: Cherche Midi, 2008.

Feliciano, Hector. *The Lost Museum: The Nazi Conspiracy to Steal the World's Greatest Works of Art.* New York: BasicBooks, 1997.

Ferrand, Franck. *Gérald Van der Kemp: Un Gentilhomme à Versailles.* Paris: Perrin, 2005.

Fest, Joachim. *The Face of the Third Reich: Portraits of the Nazi Leadership*. Trans. Michael Bullock. New York: Pantheon Books, 1970.

Fonkenell, Guillaume, Sarah Gensburger, Catherine Granger, Isabelle Le Masne de Chermont, eds. *Le Louvre pendant la guerre: regards photographiques, 1938–1947*, Paris: Musée du Louvre Editions, 2009.

Fonkenell, Guillaume. *Le Palais des Tuileries*. Arles: Honoré Clair, 2010.

Foot, M.R.D. *SOE in France: An Account of the Work of the British Special Operations Executive in France, 1940–1944*. London: Whitehall, 2004.

Gaussen-Salmon, Jacqueline. *Une prière dans la nuit: journal d'une femme peintre sous l'Occupation*. Paris: Payot, 1992.

Gourcuff, Isabelle de and Francis Forget. *Chambord: Visitor's Guide*. Paris: Editions du Patrimoine, 2002.

Groussin, Gilles. *La Résistance dans le Canton de Valençay (Les Maquis de Gâtine)*. Châteauroux, 2006.

Gruat, Cédric and Lucia Martínez. *L'Échange: les dessous d'une négotiation artistique entre la France et l'Espagne 1940–1941*. Paris: Colin, 2011.

Guillot de Suduiraut, Sophie. *Gregor Erhart: Sainte Marie-Madeleine*. Paris: Editions de la Réunion des Musées Nationaux, 1997.

Hautecœur, Louis. *Histoire du Louvre: Le Château, Le Palais, Le Musée Des Origins à Nos Jours, 1200–1928*. Paris: L'Illustration, 1929.

————. *Les beaux-arts en France: passé et avenir*. Paris: Editions Picard, 1948.

Hébrard, Frédérique. *La Chambre de Goethe*. Paris: Editions J'ai lu, 1981.

Hicks, Carola. *The Bayeux Tapestry: The Life Story of a Masterpiece*. London: Chatto & Windus, 2006.

Hotchner, A.E. *Papa Hemigway: A Personal Memoir*. Cambridge, MA: Da Capo Press, 2005.

Hours, Magdeleine. *Une vie au Louvre*. Paris: Laffont, 1987.

Humbert, Agnès. *Résistance: A Woman's Journal of Struggle and Defiance in Occupied France*. Trans. Barbara Mellor. New York: Bloomsbury, 2008.

Hurault, Philippe. "Notice sur Cheverny et sur ses Mémoires," *Collection complète des mémoires relatifs à l'histoire de France, depuis le règne de Philippe-Auguste, jusqu'au commencement du dix-septième siècle*, Vol. 36. Ed. Claude-Bernard Petitot, 4–398. Paris: Faucault, 1823.

Huyghe, René. *Une Vie pour l'art: de Léonard à Picasso*. Paris: Editions de Fallois, 1994.

Jackson, Julian. *France: The Dark Years, 1940–1944*. Oxford: Oxford University Press, 2001.

Karlsgodt, Elizabeth Campbell. *Defending National Treasures: French Art and Heritage under Vichy*. Stanford, Calif.: Stanford University Press, 2011.

King, David. *Vienna, 1814: How the Conquerors of Napoleon Made Love, War, and Peace at the Congress of Vienna*. New York: Harmony Books, 2008.

Knecht, R.J. *Renaissance Warrior and Patron: The Reign of Francis I*, New York: Cambridge University Press, 1994.

Lafon, Victor. *Histoire de la fondation de l'abbaye de Loc-Dieu*. Rodez: Ratery, 1879.

Lambauer, Barbara. *Otto Abetz et les Français, ou l'envers de la Collaboration*. Paris: Fayard, 2001.

Langeron, Roger. *Paris, juin 1940*. Paris: Flammarion, 1946.

Laub, Thomas J. *After the Fall: German Policy in Occupied France, 1940–1944*. Oxford: Oxford University Press, 2010.

Le Masne de Chermont, Isabelle and Laurence Sigal-Klagsbald, eds. *A qui appartenaient ces tableaux? La politique française de recherché de provenance, de garde et de restitution des œuvres d'art pillées durant la Second Guerre mondiale*. Paris: Editions de la Réunion des Musées Nationaux, 2008.

Léautaud, Paul. *Journal littéraire*, III (Février 1940–Février 1956), Paris: Mercure de France, 1986.

Leroi-Gourhan, André. *Les Racines du Monde*. Paris: Belfond, 1982.

Lottman, Herbert. *The Fall of Paris: June 1940*. New York: HarperCollins, 1992.
———. *The Left Bank: Writers, Artists, and Politics from the Popular Front to the Cold War*. Boston: Houghton Mifflin, 1982.

Mazauric, Lucie. *Le Louvre en voyage, 1939-1945, ou Ma vie de châteaux*. Paris: Plon, 1978.

Mitchell, Allan. *Nazi Paris: The History of an Occupation, 1940–1944*. New York: Berghahn Books, 2008.

Mockers, Michel. *Maquis S.S. 4: Font-Moreau et Gâtine*. Issoudun: Laboureur, 1945.

Neiberg, Michael. *The Blood of Free Men: The Liberation of Paris, 1944*. New York: Basic Books, 2012.

Nicholas, Lynn. *The Rape of Europa: The Fate of Europe's Treasures in the Third Reich and the Second World War*. New York: Vintage Books, 1995.

Nuremberg Trials, International Military Tribunal, *Nazi Conspiracy and Aggression* ("Red Series"), Vols. III and VI. Washington, D.C.: U.S. Government Printing Office, 1946.

Parrot, Louis. *L'intelligence en guerre*. Paris: Castor Astral, 1990.

Paxton, Robert O. *Vichy France: Old Guard and New Order, 1940–1944*. New York: Knopf, 1972.

Payne, Robert, *Leonardo*. New York: Doubleday, 1978.

Perrault, Gilles and Azéma, Jean-Pierre. *Paris sous l'Occupation*. Paris: Belfond, 1987.

Pérusse des Cars, François Joseph and Ledru, Ambroise. *Le Château de Sourches Au Maine Et Ses Seigneurs*, Paris: Lecène et Oudin, 1887.

Pesche, Julien Rémy. *Dictionnaire topographique, historique et statistique de la Sarthe, suivi d'une biographie et d'une bibliographie*, Tome 6. Le Mans: Belon, 1842.

Petropoulos, Jonathan. *Art as Politics in the Third Reich*. Chapel Hill: University of North Carolina Press, 1996.

————. *The Faustian Bargain: The Art World in Nazi Germany*. New York: Oxford University Press, 2000.

Pourcher, Yves. *Pierre Laval vu par sa fille*. Paris: Le cherche midi, 2002.

Polack, Emmanuelle and Dagen, Philippe. *Les Carnets de Rose Valland: le pillage des collections privées d'œuvres d'art en France durant la Seconde Guerre mondiale*. Lyon: Fage, 2011.

Powaski, Ronald E. *Toward an Entangling Alliance: American Isolationism, Internationalism, and Europe, 1901–1950*. New York: Greenwood Press, 1991.

Pryce-Jones, David. *Paris in the Third Reich: a history of the German occupation, 1940–1944*. New York: Holt, Rinehart, and Winston, 1981.

Quoniam, Pierre and Guinamard, Laurent. *Le Palais du Louvre*. Paris: Nathan, 1988.

Ragueneau, Philippe and Florentin, Eddy. *Paris Libéré: Ils étaient là*. Paris: Editions France-Empire, 1994.

Raoul, R.P. *Guide historique de Valençay*, Châteauroux: Laboureur, 1956.

Rayssac, Michel. *L'exode des musées: histoire des œuvres d'art sous l'Occupation*. Paris: Payot, 2007.

Riding, Alan. *And the Show Went On: Cultural Life in Nazi-Occupied Paris*. New York: Knopf, 2010.

Rorimer, James J. *Survival: The Salvage and Protection of Art in War*. New York: Abelard Press, 1950.

Rozet, M.L. *Chronique de Juillet 1830*, Tome Second. Paris: Barrois et Durprat, 1832.

Saint-Exupéry, Antoine de. *Pilote de Guerre*. Paris: Gallimard, 1942.

Saint-Paulien [Maurice-Yvan Sicard]. *Histoire de la Collaboration*. Paris: L'Esprit nouveau, 1964.

Sand, George. *Lettres d'un voyageur*, Tome II. Brussels: Meline, Cans, 1838.

Sassoon, Donald. *Mona Lisa: The History of the World's Most Famous Painting*. London: HarperCollins, 2001.

Schnitzler, Bernadette and Meyer, Anne-Doris, eds. *Hans Haug, homme des Musées: Une passion à l'œuvre*, Strasbourg: Editions des Musées de la ville de Strasbourg, 2009.

Scotti, R.A. *Vanished Smile: The Mysterious Theft of the Mona Lisa*. New York: Random House, 2010.

Sérullaz, Maurice. "L'exode des collections nationales," in *Pillages et Restitutions, le destin des œuvres d'art sorties de France pendant la Seconde Guerre mondiale*, 15–21. Ed. Françoise Cachin. Paris: Editions Adam Biro, 1997.

Shirer, William. *The Collapse of the Third Republic: An Inquiry into the Fall of France in 1940*. New York: De Capo Press, 1994.

——. *The Rise and Fall of the Third Reich: A History of Nazi Germany*. New York: Simon and Schuster, 1960.

Smith, Jean Edward. *Eisenhower in War and Peace*. New York: Random House, 2012.

Speer, Albert. *Inside the Third Reich*: Memoirs. New York: Macmillan, 1970.

Stendhal [Marie Henri Beyle] and Martineau, Henri. *Mélanges de politique et d'histoire*, Vol. I. Paris: Le Divan, 1933.

Taittinger, Pierre. *Et Paris ne fut pas détruit*. Paris: L'Elan, 1948.

Tartakowsky, Danielle. *Les manifestations de rue en France: 1918–1968*. Paris: Publications de la Sorbonne, 1997.

Thibault, Laurence. *Imprimeurs et éditeurs dans la Résistance: Conférence-débat*, Paris: Institut CGT d'histoire sociale du Livre parisien, 2012.

Valland, Rose. *Le Front de l'Art: Défense des collections françaises 1939–1945*, Paris: Plon, 1961.

Vaughn, Hal. *Sleeping with the Enemy: Coco Chanel's Secret War*. New York: Knopf, 2011.

Vilallonga, José Luis de. *Gold Gotha*. Paris: Seuil, 1972.

Vincent, Jean-Noël. *Les Forces françaises dans la lutte contre l'Axe en Afrique*. Vincennes: Service historique de l'armée de terre, 1983.

Vinen, Richard. *The Unfree French: Life Under the Occupation*. New Haven: Yale University Press, 2006.

Waresquiel, Emmanuel de. *Talleyrand: le prince immobile*. Paris: Fayard, 2003.

Williams, Charles. *The Last Great Frenchman: A Life of General de Gaulle*. London: Little, Brown, 1993.

Zitman, Bernard. *Souvenirs d'un sapeur-pompier*. Paris: Editions France-Sélection, 1972.

# INDEX

Numerals in *italics* indicate illustrations

# PHOTO CREDITS

Every possible effort was made to identify the current copyright owner of each image. However, due to possible changes in ownership and the passage of time since the represented events occurred, errors may have occurred.